ONE

PEOPLE,

TWO

WORLDS

AMMIEL HIRSCH

AND

YOSEF REINMAN

ONE
PEOPLE,
TWO
WORLDS

A REFORM RABBI AND AN ORTHODOX RABBI

EXPLORE THE ISSUES THAT DIVIDE THEM

SCHOCKEN BOOKS, NEW YORK

Copyright © 2002 by Ammiel Hirsch and Yaakov Yosef Reinman

All rights reserved under International and Pan-American
Copyright Conventions. Published in the United States by
Schocken Books, a division of Random House, Inc.,
New York, and simultaneously in Canada by Random House
of Canada Limited, Toronto. Distributed by Pantheon Books,
a division of Random House, Inc., New York.

Schocken and colophon are registered trademarks of
Random House, Inc.

A Cataloging-in-Publication record has been established for
One People, Two Worlds by the Library of Congress.
ISBN: 0-8052-4191-4

www.schocken.com

Printed in the United States of America
First Edition
2   4   6   8   9   7   5   3   1

To my parents

"Educate a child in the way he ought to go,
and he will not swerve from it even in old age." (Proverbs 22:6)

—AMMIEL HIRSCH

Dedicated to the memory of my mother,
who taught me the value of knowledge.

—YOSEF REINMAN

Consider this, you who are engaged in investigation,
if you choose to seek truth. Cast aside passion,
accepted thought, and the inclination toward what you used
to esteem, and you shall not be led into error.

—MAIMONIDES, *Guide for the Perplexed* (1:76)

ACKNOWLEDGMENTS

This book is the result of the vision, creativity, and tenacity of my dear friends Richard and Leslie Curtis. Ever since that first day when I walked into their synagogue, Temple Shaaray Tefila in New York City, to become the assistant rabbi, still wet behind the ears, Richard and Leslie have never let up on me. They urged me to write. They pushed me. They cajoled me. Finally, when Richard, a literary agent, called to tell me of another idea he had—this book—I succumbed. Richard and Leslie practice tough love. They tell you when you are okay, and they tell you when you have to improve. I am, and will always be, deeply indebted to them. Thank you, dear friends.

My coauthor, Yosef, is a unique individual. In person, he is not at all as uncompromising as what you are about to read in print. He is big-hearted and friendly. I wish that the readers could meet him personally and not be limited to his acquaintance through this book. I have found him to be of the highest moral caliber. He is a man of principle. He is deeply learned. I am proud to have engaged with him in this way. My prayer for both of us is in the fulfillment of the words of the prophet: "Let those who revere God speak one to the other. And God will listen and take note." (Malachi 3:16)

Our editor, Susan Ralston, is another one of those people who practice tough love. We are fortunate to have had her guidance.

My parents, to whom I dedicate this book, have been granted the good fortune to enjoy the fruits of their labors. They successfully raised four children into adulthood. Nothing went seriously wrong along the way. My siblings, Ora, Raphi, and Emmet, medical doctors all, are also learned in Jewish thought and tradition. Their insistence on the highest intellectual standards is fierce. I was the third of four children all born a year apart, and the only one not scientific-minded. My siblings never allowed me to get away with anything, a pattern they upheld regarding this book. Their criticism was spirited. It is the way it is done in our family. How glorious!

Finally, as we say in Hebrew, last and most beloved, my Alison and Abigail. They bestow upon me life's greatest gift, unconditional love. I am truly blessed.

—AMMIEL HIRSCH

Writers usually have the luxury of reviewing their completed work and making revisions if need be. In this book, by its very nature, Ammi and I did not have that luxury; there was no going back and revising or restating positions. Writing from an Orthodox point of view, I felt this disadvantage acutely. My arguments and positions in this book are completely my own as an independent scholar, based on my studies and research. They are not to be taken in any way as the official views of the Orthodox rabbinate. Nonetheless, since I was put in a position of defending classic Jewish thought, I could not afford mistakes. Therefore, I owe a debt of gratitude to the rabbis who offered comments and critique.

I want to thank my friend Rabbi Sholom Kamenetsky, who read all the postings and showed many of them to his father, Rabbi Shmuel Kamenetsky. Special thanks to Rabbi Noach Weinberg, who answered my questions with his legendary wisdom and gusto. Last but not least, I also want to express my appreciation to Dr. Shalom Srebrenik of Arachim Institute in Israel for his insightful advice, especially the criticism.

As for the book itself, my primary acknowledgment is to my dear friend and literary agent Richard Curtis, who conceived and initiated this project and was its catalyst; he kept us on an even keel when we could easily have run aground. One of his postings is included in the book, but his contribution was invaluable throughout. Gratitude is somehow inadequate. I also want to acknowledge Susan Ralston, our editor at Schocken, for her deft editorial touch. Special thanks to Altie Karper at Schocken for her past, present, and future efforts on behalf of this book. And of course, this book could never have happened without my coauthor and new friend Ammi. I have found him to be a passionate man, an idealist, and a good friend.

My family has given me much encouragement from the sidelines, for which I am truly grateful. I want to thank my brother and close friend Yisrael for sharing the experience with me from the beginning. I also want to thank my children—my daughter Devora and her husband, Tzvi Follman, my son Chaim and his wife, Cindy, my son Berel and his wife, Sora Rochel, and my son Sholom—for their constant and enthusiastic interest. Above all, I am beholden to my wonderful wife, Shami, for her moral support and for her sensitive reading of the postings to make sure I did not overstep the bounds of decorum.

In closing, I humbly thank the Creator of the Universe for giving me the opportunity to bring honor to His Name, His Torah, and His people. I have tried to perform the task faithfully, and I pray that I have done it well.

—YOSEF REINMAN

PART ONE

January 21, 2000

Dear Ammi (if I may take the liberty),

Since this is my first communication directly to you, I suppose it should begin with something clever and profound, but nothing comes to mind.

I understand that our *shadchan* (a seasoned matchmaker named Richard Curtis) has arranged a dinner meeting as an icebreaker. As far as I'm concerned, there is no ice to be broken, just a little unfamiliarity.

I look forward to meeting you for a number of reasons—the book, the project, the contact with a Jewish world that is quite alien to me at this point, as is mine to you, no doubt. But there is also a personal reason. Over the last month, Ammi Hirsch, of whom I had never heard, has materialized for me as an individual, a fellow Jew with a past and a future, someone who is a little apprehensive about meeting me (which is endearing but unnecessary)—just as I have materialized for you as a real person. Doesn't it therefore behoove us, two Jews passing in the night, to stop and say hello to each other? So, no matter what comes of this, I wish you *shalom aleichem,* and I am happy to make your acquaintance. Perhaps some day it will develop into a friendship. I hope so.

Yosef Reinman

January 26, 2000

Yosef:

I just returned from Israel and was delighted to receive your note. February 2 at 6 P.M. is perfect.

See you then.

Ammi

February 9, 2000

Dear Ammi,

It was a pleasure meeting you in person last week. The setting was good, and the two and a half hours flew by quickly. I'm sure we could have continued talking for several hours more had the maître d' not pointed to the long line of people waiting for tables.

I wonder what the staff and the other patrons thought about the two of us sitting there, me with my beard, *peyot,* and long caftan and you beardless and bareheaded. What could two people like us have in common? Perhaps they thought we were discussing a real estate venture. I'm sure it never occurred to them that we were discussing some of the fundamental issues that divide and cause so much dissension among the Jewish people.

But the truth is we do have a lot in common. We are bound together by blood, history, and some shared religious beliefs. We both carry the burdens of the same thousands of years of Jewish experience, although we may choose to shoulder them differently. We share a bond that is sometimes forgotten when we deal with each other in the impersonal abstract, but when we encounter each other in the living, breathing flesh, that bond is instantly manifested. Whatever differences we may have, ideological or political, we are brothers, and we should care about each other. One of the greatest Jewish values is *Ahavat Yisrael,* instinctive love for another Jew. I believe this is an ideal we both embrace passionately, and it certainly would make a good foundation for what we are about to undertake here.

I am sure that, as we go on, the discussion will reach scorching temperatures, and that is a good thing. If we pull our punches, we will be defeating our purpose. But those punches must never be thrown with anger or malice, only to convince and clarify. After all, we are already brothers, and I am confident that, as we continue along this adventure together, we will also become friends.

Over dinner, we touched on numerous thorny issues, and there is nothing that is not open to merciless scrutiny and discussion. It would be premature, however, to address some of these issues, especially the hot political ones, without first exploring who we are, what we believe, and what we stand for. How can we deal with solutions to political differences when we don't even understand each other? Should we try to beat each other into submission regardless of the human cost to the other side?

I admit that we may never find an accommodation that will satisfy both sides. I admit that after all our correspondence we may just agree to disagree. I admit that there may be no choice but to fight it out in the political arena and let the better fighter win. But let us be aware of the fears, hopes, and concerns of the other side. Let us be aware that we may inflict pain on our brothers and do our best to minimize that pain. At the very least, let us be saddened by it.

So let us begin at the beginning. Let us talk about truth. Over dinner, you quoted the philosopher Isaiah Berlin as saying that the greatest danger to the world is when people believe there is only one truth and that they have it, and you applied this concept to Orthodoxy. Berlin made this statement with regard to the proponents of communism and fascism who believed they had discovered a single, overarching truth that justified the sacrifice of individual humans to grand abstractions. He was speaking about the outlook that "you are either with us or against us." Do you believe that applies to the Orthodox view?

Orthodox Judaism is without question about the search for absolute truth. We believe without question that there is an absolute truth, and that it is contained in our holy Torah. Does that make us dangerous? I don't think so. We have never sought to impose our beliefs on other people. We actually discourage conversion. We believe in the election of the Jewish people to live by a higher standard, to be a "light unto the nations," to teach by example. Our daughter religions, Christianity and Islam, are a different story, of course. But that is an entire discussion in itself.

I would, therefore, like to begin our correspondence by discussing the concept of truth. Do you really believe that there is no absolute truth? That there are many truths? In one of the articles you sent me, you wrote that you accept "the authenticity and validity of Orthodoxy." At the same time, you obviously accept the authenticity and validity of Reform. How do you reconcile these views when Orthodoxy by its very nature rejects the authenticity and validity of Reform? You also told me over dinner that "Reform needs the continued existence of Orthodoxy." I find this intriguing, but I don't really know what you mean by it. Let us use these questions as a springboard to our correspondence.

Yosef

February 16, 2000

Dear Yosef:

Thank you for your initial comments. I entirely agree with you regarding your sentiments on *Ahavat Yisrael*. At its core, Judaism is about the covenant in action. This covenant binds the Jewish people to God and to each other. Thus, the notion of love for fellow Jews is at the heart of the Jewish experience. "All Jews are responsible one for the other" is no mere slogan for me. It constitutes the very essence of my understanding of Judaism. (Hence my disappointment with the rhetoric and actions of many Orthodox Jews and their spokesmen, who so often convey not unconditional love, but intolerant antagonism.)

You mention the concept of absolute truth. Great evil has been perpetrated by people who were convinced that they possessed absolute truth. The implication of this belief is that all other beliefs are, by definition, not true. Taken seriously, this leads to terrible consequences.

Sooner or later, the belief that you possess absolute truth and others do not, leaves you essentially alone at the pinnacle of piety.

You skirted the fundamental issue in your letter to me. You write that [Orthodox Jews] "believe without question that there is an absolute truth and that it is contained in our holy Torah." At the same time, you write: "Orthodox Judaism is without question about the search for truth."

What is it? Are you in possession of truth, or are you searching for truth?

If you are searching for truth, then I am with you. It is not Orthodox Judaism alone that is about the search for truth. Many others are so engaged, including all of the Jewish movements. I too believe that the Torah is the fundamental place where Jews begin the search for truth.

It is this search for truth—interpretation and reinterpretation of ancient texts—that constitutes the Jewish way. This effort by successive
generations of Jews to ascertain the meaning and consequences of the
ancient texts has produced what we call today Jewish thought and tradition. Every important Jewish work—Talmud, responsa, commentary,
Midrash, Jewish philosophy, and even liturgy—is essentially an attempt
to answer the question "What does the Torah mean?"

However, if you say that you are in possession of absolute truth, I
find this most troubling—and yes—it makes those who so believe dangerous. Here is where I raised the thinking of Isaiah Berlin. Berlin writes:
"One belief more than any other is responsible for the slaughter of
individuals on the altars of the great historical ideals. . . . This is the
belief that somewhere in the past or in the future, in divine revelation or
in the mind of an individual thinker, in the pronouncements of history
or science, or in the single heart of an uncorrupted good man, there is
a FINAL SOLUTION."

Much of Judaism was more modest than the way contemporary
Orthodox spokesmen present it. If talmudic rabbis, for example, were
primarily interested in presenting one, absolute truth, they would not
have argued and debated every jot and tittle of Torah verses and subse-
quent commentaries. And they would certainly not have left these arguments on every page of Talmud—usually unresolved—for all future
generations to see!

If Judaism was interested in presenting absolute truth, the Talmud
itself would not have cited passages which are entirely inconsistent with
this notion. For example, in the famous passage in the Talmud describing
the debate between Rabbi Eliezer and the sages over the purity of an
oven. (Baba Metzia 59b) Eliezer defended his ruling by turning to the
heavens. "If the law accords with me, let this carob tree prove it," he said.
Whereupon the tree was uprooted from its place. The sages remained
unconvinced. "If the law accords with me, let the water canal prove it,"
Eliezer insisted. Whereupon the water in the canal flowed backward.
"You cannot bring proof from a water canal," the sages insisted. "If the
law accords with me," said Eliezer, "let the study hall prove it." Whereupon the walls of the study hall leaned and were about to fall. The sages
remained unconvinced. Finally, Eliezer said, "If the law accords with me,

let the heavens themselves prove it." Whereupon a heavenly voice went forth and proclaimed, "The law accords with Eliezer!" Upon hearing this Rabbi Yehoshua stood on his feet and declared: "The Torah is not in the heavens!"

The passage concludes by citing Yehoshua's response to the heavenly voice: "According to the majority shall matters be decided." Upon hearing this God is described as having burst out in laughter: "My children have prevailed over Me, my children have prevailed over Me."

The basic point of this passage is that people must make decisions based upon the circumstances of the day. Even the heavenly voice itself proclaiming God's original intention could not alter the earthly practice. What is the truth? God's original intention, as confirmed by the heavenly voice, or the practice that was followed thousands of years later?

We read elsewhere in the Talmud that Moses—he whom tradition regards as having heard the word of God directly—was transported many centuries ahead into the academy of the venerated sage Akiva. During the lesson, one of the students asked Akiva how he knew that his interpretation of a law was the proper one. Akiva answered that it was given to Moses at Sinai. Moses, however, could not understand the reasoning and could not remember ever having received this law from God. Nonetheless, it is regarded as having been given to Moses. (Menachot 29b)

These passages practically plead for theological modesty. We are human beings, created in the image of God and yet fallible. How audacious is the notion that I alone possess divine truth!

It is not the search for truth that worries me. All people who strive to understand things larger than themselves search for truth—whether secular or religious. This is how we develop and progress. But to actually discover religious truth, well, that is a whole other matter.

I think that Jewish tradition was always quite skeptical of those who claimed to possess and pronounced divine truth. There is a traditional passage that asks what should a person do if a messenger runs into a village and announces that the Messiah has come—and you are in the middle of planting your vineyard. "First finish planting," is the advice, "and then go and check out the news of the Messiah."

I mentioned to you that I accept Orthodoxy, even fundamentalist Orthodoxy, as a legitimate endeavor. After all, it is possible—and looking around the world, obviously popular—to conclude that the original texts should be interpreted in a fundamental way. If there are many pathways to truth—as tradition states, seventy faces to the Torah—then it is conceivable that one such pathway is fundamentalism. I know full well that such a fundamentalist worldview—Jewish, Muslim, Christian, or other—has no room for nonfundamentalist interpretations.

There are still things that we in other camps can learn. I am most impressed with the seriousness of Orthodox Jews in seeking to discover the will of God. Their passion for study is admirable. Many treatises have been produced by Orthodox thinkers that contain relevant and important wisdom. It is good for the wider Jewish community that part of us solves moral and other daily dilemmas through engagement with Halakhah—Jewish law. It keeps that important part of Jewish tradition current and vibrant.

That a part of the Jewish community is fundamentalist is neither surprising nor particularly worrisome. It becomes a problem when such forces acquire political power and seek to use it to impose their fundamentalist worldview on others. And since fundamentalists have a tendency to "rectify" the "sinful" behavior of the "sinners," nonfundamentalists must always be vigilant.

Yosef, you are deluding yourself when you write, "We have never sought to impose our beliefs on other people." I spend a considerable part of my professional life struggling against the ultra-Orthodox attempt to impose their beliefs on other people. In Israel, ultra-Orthodox parties use the force of law to impose their beliefs. The primary reason that they do not behave similarly in the United States is their inaccessibility to the legislative process.

After all, if you believe you possess truth, why should you not feel compelled to impose it on others? Why not bring other people the good news? The American Southern Baptists have used this argument recently to justify their efforts to convert Jews.

How do you know that the Torah is the literal word of God? Do you not have any shred of doubt? Moreover, do you really believe that the thousands of pages in the Talmud were literally transcribed by Moses on Sinai? Do you ever harbor any doubts? Is everything always clear to you?

Ammi

February 19, 2000

Dear Ammi,

When I asked if you believed that Isaiah Berlin's condemnation applied to Orthodox views, you responded by quoting him and recommending that we include his works in the curricula of our *yeshivot,* but you never did answer the question. Had you said yes, I could have tried to show why this is not true, but skirting the issue leaves it unresolved.

Over dinner, I asked you if Reform requires a belief in God. You replied with a story about a congregation in Georgia that applied for membership in the Union of American Hebrew Congregations. The congregation presented itself as humanist and did not believe in God. Their application was turned down.

You chose to answer my question anecdotally rather than directly. What did your answer mean? Did it mean that, yes, belief in God is required? Or did it mean that individuals are not necessarily required to believe in God but congregations cannot profess humanism? We need direct answers.

Our correspondence has been launched on the issue of absolute truth, if it exists and if it can be discovered. There couldn't be a better starting point. It gives us the opportunity to examine our issues from the ground up, to leave no stone unturned.

So let us return to my question of the previous communication. I believe it is very pertinent, and I would like a clear answer. Do you believe there is an absolute truth? You write that all "the Jewish movements are engaged in the search for truth," yet "if you say you are in possession of truth, I find this most troubling." What is the point of searching for truth if you cannot find it?

Furthermore, how can you assign validity to conflicting points of view? How can we both be right if we disagree?

You remind me of the rabbi who agreed to mediate a dispute between two congregants. After listening carefully to one of the litigants, he scratched his chin and said, "You know, you're right!"

He then listened to the arguments of the other litigant. Again, he scratched his chin and said, "You're right!"

The rebbetzin, who was standing nearby, objected. "My dear husband, if he is right, then the other is wrong, and if the other is right, then he is wrong. How can they both be right?"

The rabbi thought for a moment, then he said, "You're also right!"

You have to take a stand, Ammi. Everyone cannot be right.

So let us talk about God. Do you accept the existence of God as an absolute truth? A simple and straightforward question.

When we met, you spoke about Reform Jews as secular Jews (it's amazing how widely our discussions ranged during those two hours). Does that mean that Reform Jews are not religious? Is this because you deny the divine origin of the Torah and even doubt the existence of God?

So what exactly goes on in your temples and your observances? How do you build a relationship on doubt? When you sit down to the Passover Seder, do you say, "Hey, God, if you really do exist, and if you really do oversee the conduct of world affairs, and if you really do want us to celebrate Passover, I want you to know that I'm doing this because I love you"? This is religion? Where is commitment? Where is faith?

It seems to me that your search for truth is not a means to discovery but an end in itself. You have made the unfulfillable search for truth your religion, and this allows you to discard old truths and substitute new truths whenever your needs dictate.

Stop me if you've heard this one. A man once saw his friend carefully scrutinizing the ground under a lamppost in the middle of the night.

"What are you doing?" he asked.

"I've lost a diamond, and I'm looking for it."

"Then let me help you."

After a few minutes, the man said, "I can't see anything. Are you sure you lost it here?"

"Well, I actually lost it two blocks away."

"What! Then why are you looking for it here?"

"Because it's dark over there, and there's light here."

Where are you searching for your truth, Ammi? Don't just look for it in the streets of Manhattan. Search where you lost it. Explore the Torah in depth, along with all the traditional commentaries. Become a serious student of the Talmud. That is where others find the truth. That is where I believe you would find it too.

You imply that the sages of the Talmud are more inclined to your relaxed point of view than to the rigid point of view of the Orthodox. Are you laying claim to the sages of the Talmud? Do you believe for a moment that even a single Talmudic sage would choose a Reform temple over an Orthodox synagogue? The idea is preposterous, and you know it. All of them were Pharisees, and the Reform are far to the left of even the Sadducees.

So what does the Talmud (Baba Metzia 59b) mean when it tells us that God laughed and said, "My children have prevailed over me"? Very simple. The Torah was given to the Jewish people, to be observed according to the interpretation of the rabbis. All that is required of a rabbi in order to render a valid judgment is that he make a strong and honest effort to understand the intent of the Torah. "It is not in the heavens." He is not required to climb into the heavens to find the answers to his questions, but he is required to strain the limits of his knowledge and intellect to discover the meaning of the Torah. If he does, then his judgment is embraced by the Torah; it fulfills the will of God. The Torah further states that the majority rules. If a majority of the rabbis express the same opinion, then that is the law. It decidedly does not mean that a majority of Jews can decide to cancel part of the Torah and ignore its undeniable commandments. To draw such a conclusion would be disingenuous.

As to your reference to Menachot 29b that Moses could not understand what Rabbi Akiva was saying, once again you are quoting stock misrepresentations. But before I clarify that passage, let me clear up the meaning of "Torah from Sinai." I don't know where you got the notion that every word of the sprawling Talmud was given on Sinai. If that is what you were told, I cannot blame you for harboring doubts.

The Torah as it is written is concise to the point of being cryptic. The Torah tells us to wear "tefillin between our eyes and on our arms." What exactly does that mean? What are *tefillin?* How are they made? What do they contain? What does "between your eyes" mean? On the bridge of the nose or higher up on the head? There are thousands of basic questions such as these, and it would be unreasonable to think God did not provide answers for them. And indeed, He did, in the Oral Law that was explicated to Moses parallel to the inscription of the Written Law and taught to the elders and all the people. Ever since, the Oral Torah has been ingrained in the Jewish mind and soul; it is the lifeblood of Jewish observance without which we would not know what to do.

During the talmudic period, the Oral Law was written down for the first time. By then, many disagreements had arisen over the details of the Oral Law, and all of these are reflected in the raging debates of the Talmud. (On a different occasion, we can discuss why the Oral Law was not recorded earlier. Interestingly, the issue arises in this week's Torah reading, where God tells Moses, "Write down these things." The Talmud [Gittin 60b] infers that the Oral Law may not be transcribed. Ultimately, however, it was transcribed to prevent its being forgotten.)

Now let us take a good look at the passage in Menachot from which you have deduced that Moses heard Rabbi Akiva expound laws in his name that he did not remember ever having heard from God. And I quote:

> Rabbi Yehudah said in the name of Rav: When Moses went up to Heaven he found the Holy Blessed One sitting and attaching markings to the letters [of the Torah].
>
> He said to Him: "Master of the Universe, why do You have to do this?"
>
> He said to him: "Many generations from now, a person named Akiva ben Yosef will derive mounds upon mounds of laws from every point [of these markings]."
>
> He said to Him: "Master of the Universe, show him to me."
>
> He said to him: "Turn around [and you will be shown the future]."
>
> [Moses] went and sat at the end of the eighth row [of Rabbi Akiva's disciples], but he could not understand what they were saying. He was crestfallen. Then [Rabbi Akiva and his disciples] continued on to another subject.

His disciples asked [Rabbi Akiva]: "How do you know this?"
He said to them: "It is a law given to Moses on Sinai."
[When Moses heard this], he felt reassured.

When does this take place? After he received the Torah? Not at all.
"When Moses went up to Heaven," before he received the Torah. This
is explained in the commentaries (see Rashi) and is perfectly clear in the
text itself, since God was still putting the finishing touches on the Torah
and had not yet given it to Moses. Knowing he would be the conduit of
the transfer of the Torah from Heaven to the Jewish people, Moses was
crestfallen when he was unable to follow the intricate debates and arguments between Rabbi Akiva and his disciples. How, he worried, would
he qualify to deliver the Torah if he could not fathom it? But when he
heard Rabbi Akiva say that the law was given to Moses on Sinai, he
understood that, even though he could not follow the intellectual rationale behind that law, he would still be able to transmit the results successfully. And thus he was reassured.

This beautiful passage states the exact opposite of what you claim to
derive from it. The Torah is divine and valid, regardless of whether or
not you can fathom the rationale behind it.

I feel that I've said enough for one letter. Still, if I ask you for direct
answers to my questions, I cannot pause here without answering yours.
You asked me how Orthodox Jews can be engaged in the search for
truth if we believe we already have it in the Torah.

Absolute truth is certainly revealed in the divine Torah, but we cannot simply open to, let's say, page 134 and check it out. We have to study
and think over and over again until we can discern the transcendent
truths of existence within the pages of the Torah. It is the work of a lifetime, many lifetimes, but it is the quest that gives life meaning and
value. It is the secret of the spiritual fulfillment which you yourself
admitted to me (again, over that dinner) that Orthodoxy does indeed
deliver.

In closing, I want to restate the questions I am posing to you.

Is there absolute truth?

Are we searching for it, and can it be found?

What validity do you give to the Torah? What is its authority? Do you believe in it, and if so, why?

Kol tuv,

Yosef

February 22, 2000

Dear Yosef:

You seem to have been rather stimulated by my response to you. I am pleased.

I thought I answered your questions directly. I will try again.

As I wrote to you in my previous posting, to the extent that you and others in the Orthodox world believe that you are in possession of some kind of truth that all other people—bless them—have not yet, or will never be capable of understanding—yes, you are potentially dangerous. As I wrote, the reason is that there is perhaps no belief that has caused more misery in the world than the notion that I alone have discovered the final solution (Berlin's term) to the human problem; that I have been favored by God; I alone understand what God wants; I am closer to God than you are.

The problem is that if you think you have discovered what you call "absolute truth," everyone else is either in error or blasphemous. There is no room for other opinions. (Remember we are talking about beliefs, which, by definition, cannot be proved.)

As I mentioned to you, I have seen with my own eyes the arrogance this produces. It is the arrogance that says, "Your Judaism is not Jewish." It is the arrogance that allows ultra-Orthodox Jews in Israel to claim sole ownership of religion, to the exclusion of everyone else—85 to 90 percent of world Jewry. It is the arrogance that causes so much pain to people who might be illegitimate, locked in unpleasant marriages, or *agunot*—chained women.

Yosef, even though you strike me as a nice enough guy—pleasant, polite, engaging—you too are infected with this theological arrogance. Reread your letter to me.

You write such things as "Search [for truth] where you lost it. Become a serious student of Talmud. That is where I(!) find absolute truth." In taking issue with my explanation of the talmudic text, you write, "So what does the Talmud mean? Very simple [!]."

There appears to be a resentment that someone else can possess the same texts—especially the halakhic text par excellence—the Talmud—and interpret them in ways different to your own—let alone extract a new understanding.

You seem to have this need to hold on to what you call "absolute truth." I think I understand why. Since your whole ideology—everything you do, everything you practice, everything you stand for—hinges upon the notion of the Torah being the literal word of God, and the Oral Law also being transmitted on Sinai—any defect that penetrates this theological purity would be devastating.

For centuries there have been commentators who have raised questions about the perfection of the Torah. No less a commentator than Ibn Ezra, in explaining Genesis 12:6, which suggests that the Torah passage was written many years after the circumstances described, wrote, "I have a secret, but let the wise person remain silent."

In your own interpretation of the talmudic text (Baba Metzia), you say "all that is required of a rabbi is that he make a strong and honest effort to understand the intent of the Torah. If he does, then his judgment is embraced by the Torah."

Exactly!

That is the whole point. We humans are fallible. We do not possess divine truth. We might have road maps that point us in a direction. But even if we make a mistake—that too is okay! What is important is the direction. What is important is the process. What is important is the way. That is what the word *halakhah* means—to walk; to progress; to move forward. One generation's understanding might be completely incomprehensible to another's. Why, even Moses did not understand Akiva! But that is okay.

Yosef, this is not to say that "anything goes," or that there cannot be standards, even strict standards. It is to say that even you would agree that countless interpretations have been given; countless practices have been adopted; a myriad of different customs and rulings have been established in different ages—and, as you yourself say, they all fulfill the will of God. They all constitute authentic Judaism.

You keep on asking me for simple, straightforward answers to "simple questions"(!) such as, is belief in God required in Reform synagogues, and do I believe in absolute truth.

That's the thing with you guys—you need, crave, and demand certainty. Any uncertainty throws a monkey wrench in that perfectly constructed theological edifice of yours and threatens to bring it crashing down. One loose theological screw, one flawed philosophical nail—and it all collapses. Hey, the world is an uncertain place. Religion is an uncertain endeavor. Life is a journey. The Jewish people's historical trek is a march toward understanding. It has not stopped. Every generation adds its own component. This was stated by the best of Jewish commentators.

Yosef, I believe many of the things you believe.

I believe in the sanctity of the Jewish people. I believe in the holiness of the Land of Israel. I believe in God, and that God selected the Jewish people for a divine task. I believe that all of our texts—beginning with the Torah and unto this very day—seek to define and refine what this means. I believe that engagement with this process showers us with holiness, as stated in our tradition: "When two people are studying Torah, the shekhinah—the presence of God—is among them." I believe that the Jewish task is to perfect the world under the sovereignty of God.

I believe it.

And yet: I have found no satisfactory explanation of human misery and disease. I have found no satisfactory explanation as to why so many good people suffer and so many evil people prosper. I have found no satisfactory explanation for the Jewish people's sufferings throughout our history. I do not understand why God required or allowed the slaughter of 6 million of His people—2 million of them children—during the Holocaust. But I still believe. I think this is the message of the Talmud in that passage we discussed about Moses being transported to Akiva's academy. Moses witnessed the most brutal torture perpetrated upon the righteous Akiva. The Romans cut up his flesh and measured it in the marketplace. "Lord of the Universe," cried Moses, "such Torah and such a reward!" "Be silent," said God, "for such is My decree."

We must try to discern truth. We must try to discover the will of God. We must struggle to understand. Every generation must continue the search. We can never give up. But there are some matters of belief for which we, of limited capacity, will cry out "Lord of the Universe, such Torah and such a reward?" "WHY?" And sometimes the answer will be: "Be silent, for such is the will of God."

You don't always have to have an explanation. Keep trying to find the answer. The process is good for you. It makes you a better person— more sensitive, more compassionate, more discerning. If you don't find the answer, keep going. This is certainly what the Jewish people and the Jewish journey characterizes.

I think that Winston Churchill could have been talking about the Jews when he said, "Success is going from failure to failure without loss of enthusiasm." We have endured so many disappointments and tragedies, and yet we are still here. That alone is evidence of the presence of God.

Yosef, I know this might be frustrating to you. It is possible to believe in a non-Orthodox way. It is possible to be a non-Orthodox believer. It seems to me that the central question for you is not to challenge the beliefs of those who profess to believe. Far more important for you is what are the sources of authority? After all, I think you would agree with that part of our tradition that emphasizes that deeds are critical to religious fulfillment. As long as you do the right thing, even if you are not fully committed to the underlying belief system or are, in fact, ignorant of it, keep doing the deeds, and perhaps one day you will understand.

In discovering the sources of authority I think we would agree that the search begins with the Torah. I have stated earlier that all of Judaism is, in fact, an attempt to explain the Torah. I think that we would further agree that the Torah as written requires additional explanations.

While Orthodoxy places a premium on Jewish law, we believe that there are other sources of authority. There are other places to look. Midrash, philosophy, poetry, commentary, and contemporary scholarship are all important.

You know what, Yosef; even the gentiles have said some important things from time to time.

And we must be able to embrace the notion of change. The Chatam

Sofer's statement that all change is prohibited is simply untrue. Whom are we trying to kid? Change is the lifeblood of any religion. Change is critical because change is what life is about. People change, societies change, sensibilities change. Judaism's genius was understanding that change is necessary and good. We took the best of what we found around us and adapted it to our belief system.

For example, the Passover Seder that you cited in your letter to me did not originate with the Jews at all. It was modeled after the Greeks. We took the basic structure and adapted it—very successfully—to our own needs. Now the whole world knows about the Jewish Seder, and almost nobody thinks about its Greek origins. This is true genius! The reason, of course, is that the Jews are alive. We are still here. We are still doing what we did so long ago—finding the right blend between continuity and change.

See, that is the key—to find the right blend, the proper balance between change and continuity. Too much change can leave us anchorless; too little change can be suffocating. As the Midrash said, Jews should be like a reed in the water—flexible enough to bend with the winds of time, but not so flexible as to be washed away by the tide.

For these reasons, I have no problem, and, in fact, am thankful that Orthodoxy still exists and appears to be prospering. There is obviously a need out there. It is good that part of the Jewish world is more resistant to change, and that other parts of the Jewish world are less resistant. It keeps both parts honest. It is good that part of the Jewish world engages the Talmud in a central way, and that other parts of the Jewish world search for answers in other Jewish texts, ancient and contemporary. I am content to say that, as long as the process is serious and is rooted in the Jewish way, "these and these are both the words of the living God."

Ultimately, Jewish standards will be set through this process of evaluating and reevaluating texts. The community will find the proper equilibrium. The pendulum might swing one way or another in different generations, but ultimately the community will settle on Jewish solutions to contemporary issues, which will reflect Jewish norms and values. You do not require fidelity to the exceedingly difficult notion that the entire Oral Law was revealed to Moses at Sinai (a claim Moses never made) to conclude that murder is wrong, justice is important, charity is noble, theft is immoral, etc. These and other Jewish mores were produced through the engagement with Torah—in the broadest sense. These values were articulated and refined by generation after generation of Jews struggling to come to grips with the question "What does God want of me?"

Therefore, you can see that this is not moral relativism. There is a difference between the view that says it makes no moral difference whether I take out my rage by kicking a pebble or by killing a person, and our mores saying that it is wrong to murder. There is no need to cling to a fundamentalist worldview to establish this norm.

The episode of the Golden Calf and Aaron's role in it highlights one of the points I have been trying to make. It is not possible to articulate one fundamental truth that can be applied to all cases. Values often conflict. Even virtues are impossible to apply uniformly.

Take, for example, Aaron. He was treated kindly by Jewish tradition. Aaron had abundant patience. The tradition describes him as a lover of peace. What could be nobler? What could be more admirable? What could be more worthy of emulation? These qualities were so esteemed that the priesthood was bestowed upon the line of Aaron.

And yet Aaron was responsible for leading the people toward idolatry. The transgression committed under his leadership was so horrendous that the tradition could not even call it by name, preferring to refer to it simply as "the sin."

Aaron had too much patience. If he had a little more resolve—like his brother Moses—the sin might not have been committed. If Aaron had had a little less patience, the sin must not have been committed.

Aaron loved peace. But if Aaron had loved peace a little less, perhaps the sin would never have been committed.

How do we reconcile the virtues of resolve and patience? How do we reconcile the virtues of flexibility and principle?

And look at Moses. Here was a man who was the closest thing in Judaism to a superior man. There never arose again a prophet like Moses. Moses was a man of principle. How could he not be after speaking directly with God? And yet this very virtue—his commitment to principle—prevented him from being as effective as he needed to be in leading the people. His commitment to principle reduced his ability to be flexible. Flexibility is another important virtue.

Moses was inflexible and impatient. In fact, it was this very attribute—impatience—that prevented Moses from entering the Promised Land. How can we reconcile the virtues of commitment to principle and flexibility?

In Victor Hugo's *Les Misérables* there is a classic example of two fundamental social virtues in conflict. Javert was doing his job—to uphold the law. He pursued Jean Valjean, whom he considered a thief, for decades. Javert thought that he was pursuing justice. Justice requires that the laws of society be upheld. In all societies theft is immoral.

But what about the quality of mercy? Valjean's family was starving. All he did was steal a loaf of bread so that his sister's child could eat. He got five years for stealing a loaf of bread! When he tried to escape—he felt his family would die without him—he was sentenced to another fourteen years!

Mercy is also a virtue. How do we balance the virtues of justice and mercy?

It is these conflicts of values; it is this inability to fully reconcile virtues, which is at the heart of society's need for pluralism.

Balance is the key. As Maimonides suggested, we should try to walk the center path, not too extreme in one direction or another. Hugo states this with great profundity when he writes: "To be ultra is to go beyond. It is to attack the scepter in the name of the throne. It is to maltreat the thing that you support. It is to insult by excess of respect; it is to find in the pope too little papistry, in the king too little royalty, and too much light in the night. It is to be dissatisfied with snow, with the swan, and the lily in the name of whiteness; it is to be the partisan of things to the point of becoming their enemy; it is to be so very pro, that you are con."

Yosef, since you seem to have a need for direct answers, let me try to respond very briefly to some of the other questions and comments you raised:

1. The issue of the humanist congregation: The community was not from Georgia. Furthermore, I mentioned it in the context not of belief in God but rather the search for standards. I tried to suggest that even in

more liberal communities there are standards—institutions have to draw red lines.

2. I did not, as you incorrectly stated, speak of Reform Jews as secular Jews. You must have heard what you wanted to hear. When people join Reform synagogues, they are not asked to articulate their theology. Therefore, it is possible to suggest that belief in God is not required in order to become a member of a Reform congregation. As stated above, that is different from the position taken by the congregation itself. By the way, were you to poll confidentially each of your own congregational and community members, you might find a wide divergence on matters of theology. You might even find some doubters—or Heaven forbid—liberals!

3. As stated herein, often the search for truth produces adequate results. Yes, it is a means for discovery, but if it is seen as the end in itself, I am prepared to accept that too. I mentioned to you that if you are in the middle of planting a vineyard and word comes around that the Messiah has arrived, you are bidden to finish your planting first. We have here a very down-to-earth suggestion on how to react to those who claim to have discovered a higher truth. None of this implies that it is sufficient simply to theorize without creating concrete standards for society. I expanded upon this above.

4. I stand by my interpretation of the talmudic texts we have been discussing. The interpretations you gave strike me as inconsistent, and sometimes supported the very points I was trying to make—as expanded above.

5. I have detailed above my view on the authority of the Torah. And one further point on your notion of the absolute authority of the Torah: By clinging to the idea that Torah constitutes "absolute truth," you in fact weaken the authority of the Torah. Since, by your own admission, the Torah needs interpretation, you have given the interpreters the authority of God Himself. You said so yourself in your answer to me— "as long as they make an honest effort it fulfills the will of God." What the rabbis say constitutes the will of God. How do we know? The text they created says so! How convenient!

But the rabbis changed, and at times even reversed what the Torah— your "absolute truth"—said. The Torah, for example, imposes capital punishment. The rabbis, for all intents and purposes, rendered capital punishment obsolete. The Torah calls for the taking of an eye for an eye. The rabbis changed this to money damages. The Torah calls for the execution of a wayward son. The rabbis rendered this, too, obsolete.

How ironic! By insisting on the perfection of the Torah and by giving human beings the authority to interpret it as though they are rendering God's very word, you have, in fact, replaced the Torah as ultimate authority with the interpretations of the all-too-human interpreters. And lo and behold, these human beings have, from time to time, interpreted the Torah contrary to its original intention, and have changed it, sometimes for the good, and at other times—well, they could have done better!

Ammi

February 27, 2000

Dear Ammi,

When we started, I didn't really know what you were all about. I knew you were very much involved in politics, which made you suspect in my eyes. In addition, I had read some of your materials and found them combative and inflammatory with regard to the Orthodox. I thought you were a tank commander in a rabbi's suit. Nonetheless, I agreed to participate in this venture because of the importance I attached to it, but with real trepidation in my heart.

In your last posting, I believe I saw an eloquent and passionate idealist, a man who feels strongly and deeply about his beliefs, a man of honor, sensitivity, and good will who strives for connection with the Almighty. Although we may disagree on just about all basic issues, I now see that you mean well. If we can keep this conversation on an idealistic level, I think we will produce a document of immense value.

Before we begin, I would like to clear up one point. I do not understand how you can represent Ibn Ezra, the illustrious Orthodox commentator, as a closet Reformer. The verse in question, which appears in Genesis 12:6, informs us that "the Canaanites were in the land then" [when Abraham arrived], and you quote Ibn Ezra as saying, "I have a secret, but the wise person remains silent." From this you infer that this account was written many years after the circumstances described and that Ibn Ezra's "secret" is that the Torah is less than perfect. It seems Ibn Ezra did not conceal his secret too well, since you have so easily penetrated to it.

Well, first of all, no one claims this verse was written at that time. It was written hundreds of years later when the Jewish people were in the desert after the Exodus, as was the entire book of Genesis. Now let us read Ibn Ezra: "It is quite possible that the Canaanites captured the land of Canaan from others. If this is not the case, *yesh lo sode,* and the wise person will remain silent." You seem to have confused the words *lo* and *li. Yesh li sode* would indeed have meant "I have a secret." *Yesh lo sode,* however, means "there is a secret aspect to this matter." This phrasing usually refers to esoteric mystical or kabbalistic secrets, which would explain the need to remain silent. I personally have no idea of the nature of Ibn Ezra's secret; he has successfully concealed it from me. But be that as it may, how can you ascribe non-Orthodox beliefs to Ibn Ezra? What about all the thousands of pages of solid Orthodox commentary he wrote? Don't they stand for anything? You obviously need to connect to the time-hallowed texts, but you are grasping at the wind.

Ammi, I readily admit I make mistakes from time to time, and I'm sure you would admit that you yourself might also make mistakes, although few and far between. As intelligent people, we should want our mistakes pointed out to us, and we should do our best to correct them, wouldn't you agree? I think that is the essence of our correspondence. We are here to define our positions with the utmost clarity so that we can identify our differences and our points of agreement. If we are in error in our own beliefs or in our perceptions of each other, we should do our best to correct those errors.

Let me point out a simple mistake. You begin by deriding people who claim that "I am closer to God than you are." Yet further on you claim that you believe "God selected the Jewish people for a divine task." Doesn't that, by definition, bring us closer to God? Maybe not better, but certainly closer, correct? Clearly, this is a mistake in your thinking. The mistake, of course, is in thinking that all people are equally close to God. They are not.

Judaism is about getting close to God. But you feel it is presumptuous to make such a claim. So what is your position?

Let us talk for a moment about Christianity, Islam, and Judaism. Christianity believes that Islam and Judaism are heretical. Islam believes that Christians and Jews are infidels. Are they both right? Of course not. They both might be wrong, but they can't both be right. Do you agree?

Now let us turn to Judaism. What does Judaism believe? Orthodoxy believes that both Christianity and Islam are false. What do you believe? Are they false? Would you say that you are right and they are wrong? Or would you say that all who say they are right are mistaken, and the only ones who are right are those who say that no one is right? You have to take a stand. What do you believe? What is true and what is false?

Most people in the world—be they Christian, Muslim, Shinto, Hindu, Buddhist, or whatever—believe they are right and everyone else is wrong. This is a fact. It follows logically that most people in the world are wrong in their religious beliefs. You must admit that even if you are right, even if the truth cannot be discovered, most of the world does not know this. Therefore, you are the only ones in the world who have found this absolutely incredible truth that there is no absolute truth.

You chide me for craving certainty, but it seems to me that you crave uncertainty. The world may be an uncertain place, as you say, but some things should be certain. Your love for your family. Your loyalty to your people. Your relationship with your God.

Religion, by definition, is based on divine revelation. If the knowledge of God is not based on communication between God and mankind, then we have philosophy rather than religion. You cannot really have a relationship with God if He has never communicated with you.

You obviously agree that Judaism is predicated on some form of divine revelation. Otherwise, how do you know that the Jewish people have been "selected for a divine task"? I would like to hear about this divine revelation as you understand it. I would like to know how this belief can coexist with fundamental doubt. I would like to know, when you say, "I believe it," on what you base this belief. Is it based on evidence, on reason, on acceptance of what your father and grandfather told you? I am very interested in hearing specifics.

We keep coming back to the issue of truth and knowledge, because all of life hinges on them. Without understanding fundamental truths, life has no meaning, no transcendent value. If there is no immortality of the soul, if there is no Heaven, if there is no eternal reward, if we are all just momentary blips on the screen of this world, what is the purpose of all the pain and suffering, of all the exertions and striving? If there is no afterlife, then we live in a world without justice where the good suffer and the evil prosper and then it is over. Do you agree?

The Torah, in our belief, is the path by which we can discover and engage God. It guides us through the optimistic search for the fundamental truths of existence. It is about infusing life with meaning.

I recently heard a radio commercial for a New York medical center's cardiology department. A shaky male voice comes on and says (more or less): "I'm ninety-two years old. I remember going to Yankee Stadium and watching Lou Gehrig and Joe DiMaggio play. But now I have heart disease. The hospital in my community didn't want to operate on me, but this medical center took my case. They saved my life." The announcer cuts in to make a pitch for the medical center, then we go back to the old man. "Now that I've had my surgery, I'll be able to see a few more Yankee games in my lifetime."

How pitiful. This is how contemporary society measures the value of longevity. A few more Yankee games. A few more well-earned pleasure buttons pushed. Is this the fulfillment to which we aspire?

Orthodoxy is the antithesis of this point of view. Our life in this world is just "a passing shadow, a fleeting dream." The only enduring reality is our immortal souls, sparks of the divine, and therefore, the focus of our lives is our relationship with God and our preparation for eternity.

That doesn't mean that you have to shave your head and live in Meah Shearim. You can enjoy material pleasures and achievements in this world, as long as you keep things in perspective. This past weekend I attended a family celebration in Long Island. I was the only one there with a *shtreimel* [traditional fur hat], but that has never bothered me. We had a wonderful time with our cousins, all of whom are lawyers, doctors, and bankers, all of whom live in stately homes and are prosperous. What have they sacrificed by being Orthodox? Nothing. What have they gained? Everything.

We all understand that God, in the monotheistic concept, needs nothing from us. Judaism addresses not what we can do for Him, which is nothing, but what He can do for us, which is everything. The Torah was given to us for our benefit, even if we don't always understand it. It is good for us to keep the Sabbath, even if we would rather go to the ball game. And the truth is, once we experience the spiritual rewards of a Sabbath properly observed, we wouldn't dream of exchanging them for a day in Yankee Stadium.

But how can you conduct a meaningful relationship with God if you doubt His existence? You say that people have doubts, even Orthodox people. It's true. But you can use doubt as a springboard to knowledge. The Torah instructs us to believe in God, a belief based on logic and rationality, and the Torah also instructs us to continue on to "know God." You can find God if you seek Him. Doubt leaves you nowhere.

But that is what you are doing, Ammi, by saying everything is in doubt, that we are doomed to go "from failure to failure" and call it success, that absolute truth is unattainable. That is untrue. It is attainable if you find it reasonable and if you want it. You can love God passionately only if you believe in Him passionately.

I do not claim to have the answers to all questions. I also have questions. But I do not question the existence of God, nor do I question the validity of the Torah as transmitted on Sinai. I do, however, often question my own abilities to understand the deeper passages, and I have frequent questions about the ramifications and applications of what I have learned. I also know that gravity exists, but I question why sap rises in trees, although I have no doubt that it does.

Incidentally, Ammi, I am curious about what goes on in Reform rabbinical school. What is the program? What is the nature of the knowledge that you are taught? What level of Jewish scholarship is a prerequisite to becoming a Reform rabbi? Are you required to be able to decipher an unfamiliar, unpunctuated, unvowelized page of the Talmud in its original Aramaic form? Are you required to understand Scripture in the original Hebrew or Aramaic? How learned does a Reform rabbi have to be?

Before closing, I would like to go back to our discussion about the Oral Law. You deny that Moses received the Oral Law on Sinai. But don't you agree that some kind of oral law must have come along with the Written Law? When the Torah tells us to put on *tefillin,* what was that supposed to mean to us? Were we supposed to guess? Or was each of us to decide what would be meaningful as *tefillin* for him? Clearly, this commandment must have come with instructions. Do you claim that there was another set of instructions that has since been lost? I have never heard of such a thing, have you? The only set of instructions I've ever come across is the Oral Law, and I think it is safe to assume that there is no other.

I would like to hear your comments on this. I suspect that you question the Written Law as well, and therefore, you have no need to contend with the Oral Law. Is that true?

AN EYE FOR AN EYE

You write, "The Torah calls for the taking of an eye for an eye. The rabbis changed this to money damages."

You assume that the Torah originally took the barbaric position of demanding an eye for an eye literally. As time went on, however, and Jewish society progressed and became more civilized and humane, it was no longer considered appropriate to put out someone's eye or chop off his hand. Therefore, the law was reinterpreted to mean monetary payment.

Don't be such a literalist, Ammi. There is no evidence anywhere, literary or archaeological, that a literal eye for an eye was Jewish practice at any time. Nor is there the slightest hint anywhere in the Talmud that this law was ever taken literally. It is just an assumption based on the language.

But consider for a moment if this is really logical. If, as you think, a change came about because Jewish society was becoming more humane and civilized, why was the law requiring extermination of the Canaanite peoples allowed to remain unmodified and unreinterpreted? Why was capital punishment for carrying a bottle of milk onto the street on Shabbat left in place? Why was the law requiring the annihilation of an *ir hanidachat,* a city that turned to idol worship, left in place? Wouldn't you consider these harsher and more barbaric than an eye for an eye? Think about it. Isn't it more reasonable to assume that the law was always understood as a reference to monetary payment?

The Talmud (Baba Kama 83b) devotes much space to this verse. The discussion begins, "An eye for an eye. Does this mean a literal eye? Don't even consider that possibility. . . ." And then the Talmud proves on the basis of clear textual evidence as well as compelling logic that the verse is not to be taken in the literal sense.

Maimonides (Yad, Damages 1:5) cites the verses (Exodus 21:18–19), "Should a man strike his fellow with a stone or a fist and [the victim] does not die but is confined to bed, if he [eventually] recovers and is able to walk in the street as he did before, then the assailant shall be exonerated and only pay for [the victim's] loss of time and full healing." Here we see the Torah tell us explicitly that an assailant who is not subject to a capital charge pays money. Yet a few verses later (21:25), we are told, "A wound for a wound." Obviously, concludes Maimonides, this phrasing is meant to be taken in the figurative sense.

Ibn Ezra, in the name of Rabbeinu Saadiah Gaon, the head of the rabbinical academy in Iraq during the tenth century, brings additional proof: "We cannot interpret this verse according to its literal meaning. What if a person injures the eye of another person and reduces his vision by one third? How would we make sure that the vision of the aggressor is also reduced by that exact same amount, no more, no less? It would be even more difficult to replicate a wound exactly, especially if it is near a vital organ. It is illogical. . . . As a general rule, it is impossible to reach an accurate interpretation of the laws of the Torah unless we rely on the words of our Sages of blessed memory. Just as we have received the Torah from our ancestors, so have we received the Oral Law. There is no differentiation between the two."

Listen to Ibn Ezra, Ammi. No mysterious secrets. Clear, explicit. You have to admit that he doesn't sound like a Reform rabbi.

One question remains. If the Torah did not intend for the aggressor's eye to be removed, why was this phrasing used? Why didn't the Torah state simply that the aggressor should pay damages?

The Maharal, Chief Rabbi of Prague in the sixteenth century, answers it beautifully. Had the Torah simply ordered the aggressor to pay damages, he might have thought he could just mail in a check or report it to his liability insurance carrier and thereby put the whole matter behind him. Not so, says the Torah. Causing grievous bodily injury is a terrible thing, and you cannot wipe the slate clean just by paying damages. You must beg forgiveness from the injured person. You must repent and beg forgiveness from God. You must redeem yourself by effecting changes in your life. You really should have had your own eye put out in retribution, so terrible was your act. If the Torah allows you to pay damages instead, you are nonetheless obligated to make personal and spiritual amends.

A GREEK CUSTOM?

By the way, what's this with the Passover Seder being a Greek custom? I have never heard such a thing. I did some basic research in the secular sources and found nothing. Are you referring to the custom of reclining on couches, a practice very common in the ancient world? Or are you referring to the entire ritual? Before I take issue with you on this matter, I would like to know exactly what you mean and your source.

I look forward to hearing from you.
Yosef

February 28, 2000

Dear Yosef:
I hope all is well with you.
Ammi

March 7, 2000

Dear Yosef:
It seems to me that we are in agreement on some important principles. Let me try to summarize them:

1. We agree that, as you wrote, "Judaism is about getting close to

God." I might add that Judaism is also about a lot of other things but I certainly agree that it includes getting close to God.

2. If you are implying that people, faiths, and societies should have standards, then I agree with your characterization that "some things should be certain." I already wrote that I am not a moral relativist. I am not sure that we intend the same thing when we use the word "certainty."

3. I agree, as you write, that the Torah is the path by which we can discover and engage God. As you write, it guides us through the optimistic search for the fundamental truths of existence. (There you go again, using that word "search," in almost a liberal way!) It is about infusing life with meaning. As I wrote to you previously, I believe that all of Judaism is really about interpreting and commenting upon the Torah. I might add that there are also other paths one might take to discover and engage God. I think you would agree. Some people, for example, can feel a real closeness to God through nature. Others, when they look at their newborn child, sense the Divine.

4. I agree that life is about more than going to a few more Yankees games. I should add, however, that there are also worse things that people can do than go to baseball games. If baseball gives people pleasure, why not? If an athlete decides to dedicate his life to sport; if an actress decides to dedicate her life to drama; if scientists dedicate their lives to the lab—why not? I think the ancient Greeks were right when they defined happiness as "the full use of your powers along the lines of excellence." Focusing on a particular field of endeavor inevitably leaves you less time for other pursuits.

5. I agree that, as you write, it is good to keep the Sabbath.

6. I agree with your statement that "people have doubts, even Orthodox people."

7. I agree that doubt can be used as a springboard to knowledge.

CERTAINTY

Regarding the concept of certainty, it is one thing to speak about the need for certain standards. All societies have standards that are certain.

For example, all of the societies I am aware of believe murder and theft to be wrong. It is quite another thing to suggest that I know what God wants, since He already revealed it to me (or my ancestors). Again, Yosef, do not confuse the need for creating standards, norms, and mores with the assertion that I know what God has in mind because He revealed it to me.

In creating societal norms—under which people of different persuasions, different religions, and no religions have to live together—it is not enough to say that theft is immoral because God revealed it in the Torah. You must also use your faculties of reason and persuasion. It is not enough to say that capital punishment is moral because God wrote it in the Torah. It is not enough to say that it is moral to slaughter every last breathing vestige of the Canaanites because it is written in the Bible.

For the Jews, we might believe that through engagement with Torah (again not in the narrow sense of the Pentateuch, but in the broader religious process of engaging our tradition) we have determined standards that are clear and unambiguous. In this regard I have been trying to emphasize two points:

First, even these standards change through time and are reinterpreted to mean different things—even to the point of obliterating the original intention. Second, modern societies must be pluralistic because reality is plural. This is as true in the Jewish state as in the United States. To say that society must impose a certain standard in law exclusively because Judaism says so (whether biblical, talmudic, or other) is to violate the fundamental principles upon which modern societies are based.

Even in Israel, whose Judaism would you uphold as the model for contemporary jurisprudence? Which interpreter would you nominate as the decider laureate? Are we going to give more weight to a modern Orthodox opinion, or an ultra-Orthodox opinion; a Chabad opinion or a Satmar opinion; how about a Reform or Conservative opinion?

Moreover, what makes something a Jewish norm is not that it is written in the Torah. It becomes Jewish only after having been interpreted and reinterpreted by generation after generation of Jews, and ultimately accepted by the contemporary generation. (It must be accepted by a critical mass of contemporary Jews; otherwise, by definition, it is not a contemporary norm.) The norm becomes Jewish only after having undergone generation after generation of analysis in a variety of disciplines—law, lore, commentary, philosophy, liturgy, etc.

To illustrate the point, in addition to some of the changes that I mentioned in previous postings, let me remind you that the Bible embraces the concept of patrilineality. Joseph's children were Jewish. Moses' son was Jewish. Solomon's children were Jewish. All three men had non-Jewish wives who did not convert. At some point in Jewish history—responding to the needs of the day—Judaism determined status through the mother. But matrilineality was not the biblical standard. So too polygamy was the norm in biblical times. It is now contrary to Jewish custom and tradition. Slavery and servitude were common in biblical society.

Once you have appreciated that laws, values, and mores change—even according to the strictest Orthodox standards—you should get off that high horse of certainty. The fundamental certainty in the world is that things will change!

Yosef, I do not crave uncertainty. As much as the next person, I would like to have it all laid out for me. As you know, it is hard to go through life without having all the answers. Still, this is the world in which we live. There are many mysteries. The best I can do is keep trying. But I will do so embracing, not repelling, society and modernity.

Many in your community are so fearful of what they might find out there that they have chosen to deal with uncertainty by shutting out any outside stimulus that might lead them down the path of knowledge, inquiry, and information that is not fed to them by their teachers. Of course, in the process they might find out bad things. There are many bad things out there. But they might also discover useful information.

Ultraorthodox religious communities—Jewish and non-Jewish—cling to the notion of certainty because of their deep fear of change. Their fear is understandable. It is a scary world out there. Better, they say, to close off the world. Keep televisions, computers, modern literature, and newspapers far away from our vulnerable children and adults. It is for this reason, I believe, that some ultra-Orthodox rabbis ruled recently to forbid use of the Internet. Yes, they might have been concerned about easy access to pornography, but I think their primary fear was that the Internet is the highway to knowledge. Unfiltered knowledge is dangerous to the fundamentalist mind-set.

CLOSENESS TO GOD

I wrote to you that I believe that God selected the Jewish people for a divine task. How do I know? I suppose that I do not know it in the conventional sense. But I feel it. I intuit it. This is the difference between religious knowledge and scientific knowledge. The thrust of our faith is that Jews are different. Already in the Bible, Balaam gazed upon the Israelites and pronounced "a nation that dwells apart." My texts, my tradition, my culture, have acted as if this proposition were true. The Jewish things we did, wrote, and created were produced in the belief that the Jews are separate and special. So even if I cannot prove it empirically, I feel it. It overwhelms me. That is enough for me. I have no need to assert that I, like Moses, heard it directly from God. The fact that the Torah also says that the Jews are unique is, for me, not proof of the proposition, but rather proof that my people have been engaged in this endeavor for thousands of years and have asserted this proposition.

An individual too should act as if he is special. Well, he is, isn't he? Our tradition proclaims that God created every person as if printing a coin, and yet every coin is different. My people have spent the last three thousand years producing values, acting at all times as if this process was connected to holiness and knowledge of God. I too enthusiastically embrace this idea and have thrown myself into the process. That is what Jews do. That is Judaism—a relentless and never-ending engagement in the process—the Jewish way. Yes, the process produces standards and values that become normative. No, the process never ends. When the process ends, Judaism ends.

When ultra-Orthodox or fundamentalist people say they believe, it is hard for me to fathom what they really mean. How is your belief different from what I have articulated above? Why, for example, do so many people of all faiths proclaim with pious fervor that theft is wrong because God Himself said so, and then go out and steal? It is ridiculously common to easily proclaim "God wrote the Law" and then go out and cavalierly break the law. What kind of belief is that?

Are you willing to easily accept a person's claim that he communicated with God—that God told him to do or say something—as the basis for imposing standards upon society? Today in America there are millions of people—clergy included—who justify everything from slavery to segregation by invoking the name of God. Why does it always seem that God speaks so clearly to the most intolerant people? Why does God make it so clear to a fundamentalist what He wants, while leaving the rest of us so much in the dark?

You write, "You cannot really have a relationship with God if He has never communicated with you." As I already indicated, many people feel they are communicating with God, irrespective of any particular text. For example, I, like many others, felt the presence of God when I looked at my daughter for the first time.

To give you another example, I have rarely had a more powerful religious experience than when I led a delegation of eighty rabbis to Jordan some months before Israel and Jordan established formal peace. As you might imagine, the entire international media stationed in Amman was following our every move. Many Jordanians were very disturbed at our presence. During the trip we received death threats. I, as the leader of the trip, felt under so much pressure that I simply could not wait to get to Israel.

On our last day in Jordan we ascended Mount Nebo. It was a relief to look at the Promised Land and to know that we would cross into it the next day. In all of Jewish history there had probably never been so many rabbis standing on Mount Nebo! From Gilead to Dan, from the Valley of Jericho, the city of palms, to the Negev; from the majestic hills of Judea to the barrenness of the Dead Sea—you could see it all, just as Moses did the day he died. On a clear day you could even see Jerusalem!

I recited the biblical verses in my mind: "And God showed Moses the entire land that he would not enter." Rashi understood this passage to mean that Moses looked down upon the entire future of the land. He saw all of Jewish history before him. "And Moses, the servant of God, died through the kiss of God. He was one hundred and twenty years old, but his eyes were undimmed, his vigor unabated."

From the top of the mountain we too saw the Promised Land and could sense the cycle of Jewish history. We too could sense the glories and tragedies of our past. From the cool pristine air of Mount Nebo we could see it all. And tomorrow we would cross!

Standing atop that mountain in the presence of eighty rabbis, spiritual leaders and descendants of a people who should have died one hundred times over, I felt the wind of God blow across my face. After all these centuries, after all the tragedies, we were still here, looking at the Promised Land from the very spot where Moses breathed his last. And we were about to enter the sovereign Jewish state! The centuries had not dimmed our vision; our vigor was unabated.

For the Jew it is this that gives religious meaning to our existence. We are members of a people that will not die. We were meant to live on. Jewish existence is evidence of the existence of God.

I do not think that to assert the uniqueness of the Jewish people necessarily implies that we are closer to God than others. Maybe we are. Maybe we are not. Perhaps some of us are closer than others. When you say "closer," despite your apparent protestation, I think you mean better. After all, if the religious task is to come closer to God, aren't those who are closer, better?

In any case, I think that it is possible to be special and unique without being better. I have gone through life believing myself, my family, and my people to be special and unique. I have never assumed therefrom that we are inherently superior.

This is not to say that I do not think that we have produced some superior values. We have. We taught the world ethical monotheism. We gave the world the basis of its contemporary jurisprudence. There are also times that we have failed. Some values we produced are not superior at all.

I further believe that some societies are better than others. I think that American democracy is infinitely superior to Taliban rule in Afghanistan, imposed by supposedly pious people claiming to follow the will of God. I think that Western jurisprudence, in general, is far superior to religious law imposed by certain countries around the world, like Iran. I am convinced that Israel is far better off now, with its secular legal system, than were it to be governed by those Orthodox Jews who say they would impose rabbinic law on society.

A few additional comments:

1. You write, "I also have questions." If I understand your argument, it is that your questions relate to the application of the principle but not to the principle itself. You believe in the literal transmission of the Torah; you just have some questions regarding its ramifications and applications. I do not fully understand this. If you question the ramifications of what you learned, why stop there? Doesn't an honest search require you to continue your inquiry into the core principle itself? If a scientist has a hypothesis, and experimentation points to unexpected consequences, isn't he obligated to reevaluate the hypothesis?

2. You do not have to suspect that I question the Written Law. I state it unabashedly. I do not question that it is the starting point for all Jewish discussion. I do not question that at the time it was written it was our people's best effort to engage God, and is the reference for all future discourse. I do not question the Torah's centrality. However, I do not accept the Torah as the literal word of God.

3. This does not mean that I do not have to contend with the Oral Law. I do. It too plays a critical role in Jewish tradition. But I do not need to go through all kinds of theological contortions to assert its relevance. All legal systems with a founding constitutional document develop bodies of work that explain and interpret the founding document. Whether we agree or not on the divine origin of the Torah—the founding document—both of us will be able to change the law to suit the times.

4. The passage about Ibn Ezra was intended to make the simple point that for centuries commentators have raised questions about the divine origin of the Torah. It was not to suggest that Ibn Ezra was a Reform Jew. (Although I think that many great Jewish thinkers of past centuries were more open and flexible in their thought than some Orthodox Jews today.) The explanation you gave—that the verse was written hundreds of years later during the desert wanderings—is unsatisfactory. By stating "the Canaanites were then in the land," the text implies that they are not now in the land. Even under your explanation, while the Israelites were in the desert, the Canaanites were residing in the land. It was only after many years that the Canaanites were finally conquered. So how could the text say that they were then (but not now) in the land?

5. The Passover Seder was influenced by the Greco-Roman practice of the symposium. Read, for example, Lawrence Hoffman in *Passover and Easter: Origin and History to Modern Times,* edited by Bradshaw and Hoffman, pages 8–26.

Ammi

————————

March 11, 2000

Dear Ammi,

When we met last Monday, I told you my son was about to get engaged, and Wednesday night it happened. We are very pleased, and as you can well imagine, very busy. We are also preparing for the *bar mitzvah* of our youngest son in three weeks. In addition, I have to be in Israel next week for a few days. There is so little time, and yet your postings are sitting right here on my desk and staring at me accusingly. I am doing my best to send off a posting to you before I leave for Israel.

As usual, your posting was very provocative, and I have volumes to say about many of your points. But I will restrict myself to a few general comments and reserve my specific comments for future postings.

I want to begin by making four observations about your beliefs or lack thereof. This is what I understand from what you have written. Please correct me if I am mistaken.

Point number one. You have no idea about what God wants or thinks, for you write, "All societies I am aware of believe murder and theft to be wrong; it is quite another thing to suggest I know what God wants since He already revealed it to me (or my ancestors)." It is not quite clear to me, however, if you believe in any kind of revelation. You claim to believe in God; you feel Him in the wind blowing across Mount Nebo and when you look at your newborn daughter. Other than that, do you believe humans have ever encountered Him? Has God ever spoken to our ancestors in any form whatsoever?

Point number two. You do not believe in the constancy of values but in constant change, for you write, "[W]e might believe that through engagement with Torah (again not in the narrow sense of the Pentateuch, but in the broader religious process of engaging our tradition) we have determined standards that are clear and unambiguous. . . . [E]ven these standards change through time and are reinterpreted to mean different things—even to the point of obliterating the original intention." Even when you have "clear and unambiguous standards," they may be gone tomorrow in this process of perpetual change. "[L]aws, values, and mores change. . . . The fundamental certainty in the world is that things will change!" Nothing is constant; everything changes. There are no absolutes.

Point number three. You have clearly demonstrated in all your postings that you believe Judaism must change to adapt to the requirements of a modern, pluralistic society, for you write, "The best I can do is keep trying, but I will do so embracing, not repelling, society and modernity." Your most current definition of Judaism must be adapted to "society and modernity."

Point number four. You reinterpret the Torah all the time to fit your new perceptions, for you write, "[W]hat makes something a Jewish norm is not that it is written in the Torah. It becomes Jewish only after having been interpreted and reinterpreted by generation after generation of Jews and ultimately accepted by the contemporary generation." Even generations of reinterpretations can go right out the window if the contemporary generation doesn't accept them!

I believe I have not misstated your position. In a nutshell, there are no rules. Or rather, the rules are what you say they are, as you see fit according to your contemporary perceptions.

This, to me, is not a description of Judaism but of a well-meaning, secular liberalism. The fountainhead of your values is not the Torah but "society and modernity." You look to society for guidance in establishing your values, and then you reinterpret the Torah to give a semblance of spirituality and tradition to what you have accepted as the currently operative norms and values.

Your Judaism does not guide you. It is a rubber stamp to endorse your latest liberal opinion.

God is not your Master. He is your slave. You drag Him along behind you and use His Name to sanctify the flavor of the month that you choose to embrace. Is this religion? Is this Judaism?

HOMOSEXUALITY

Let me focus on one extreme example. Homosexuality. The Torah explicitly prohibits homosexuality. This view did not mirror the mores of contemporary society; it was not accepted by the licentious societies of the time, especially by the Greeks, who favored homosexual love. For the last thousand years, however, the Torah view was accepted throughout the Western world—until the second half of the twentieth century. Why has homosexuality suddenly become acceptable? Why has the stigma disappeared? This is a subject for a long discussion that touches on the general permissiveness of society, the powerful influence of the media, the early exposure of our youth to alternative lifestyles, but I would rather leave this for a later time. It will get us sidetracked.

But facts are facts. One hundred years ago homosexuality was considered a sin. Now it is accepted by contemporary society. Just yesterday I heard a news report that for the first time a slight majority of Americans no longer consider homosexuality a sin. A triumph of reinterpretation.

One hundred years ago a Reform rabbi would have been scandalized if a gay couple had come to him to be married. He would have pointed indignantly in the Torah to the prohibition, right next to murder, theft, and "love your neighbor." But times have changed. The inevitable change, right? Society no longer considers homosexuality a sin. So therefore, a Reform rabbi today will officiate at the marriage of a gay couple without a second thought. (Have you ever had occasion to do this?)

But wait a minute. What about the Torah? What about the prohibition? No problem. You will interpret and reinterpret the Torah until you have "obliterated the original intention."

Is the "original intention" relevant to you? In your opinion, is the Torah anything more than a "founding document" created by our ancestors to define their concept of a monotheistic deity? If this is indeed what you believe, then I understand why you do not consider the Torah binding. Why should you feel obligated to live by the values and mores of these primitive ancient people who peppered their laws with strange myths and legends about encounters with God that never took place?

Therefore, you do not condemn murder or theft because it is written in the Torah. You write, "[I]t is not enough to say theft is immoral because God revealed it in the Torah. You must also use your faculties of reason and persuasion." In other words, where your faculties don't kick in, the Torah's prohibition in itself is inadequate.

So what if societal norms change? What if murder is condoned? You will condone it too! And you will reinterpret the Torah to back you up.

Don't laugh. What if euthanasia becomes popular in the future? What if society decides that ninety years is long enough for any person to live and then it is time to move over? What if liberal secular society constructs philosophical edifices in support of euthanasia and it becomes widely accepted, with or without the consent of the old folks themselves? Will you stand up against the whole world and protest? Of course not.

How about infanticide? Would you have condoned infanticide if you had lived in ancient Greece where infanticide was popular among the intelligentsia and the aristocracy?

What about abortion? One hundred years ago every self-respecting Reform rabbi would have condemned abortion. He would have been outraged. Would you condemn abortion, Ammi? Are you outraged?

Let's get back to alternative lifestyles. I assume that you accept homosexuality, and I understand you. I really do. From your point of view, why shouldn't you? But let us follow that line of reasoning and see where it leads us. What about bestiality? Do you find that acceptable? Perhaps you do. But what about incest? Do you condone incest? I don't think so. (Pardon me for speaking for you.)

But you certainly know that it was the custom in the Egyptian royal family for brothers and sisters to marry. Well, isn't it possible that society will turn in that direction? After all, what is inherently wrong with brothers and sisters living together? What if they are in love? Doesn't that justify everything? So, it could very well be that society will accept incest at some time in the future. Even if you don't believe it, let us at least deal with this hypothetically. What would you do, Ammi? Would you officiate at the marriage of a brother and sister, of a father and his daughter? I would like a direct answer to that question. Would you—yes or no?

But if you believed in the Torah, you would never do any of these things. If you believed in the Torah, you would have a very clear definition of right and wrong, not this fluid reinterpretive perpetual change. Abraham, the Sages tell us, was called Ivri, because the Hebrew word implies that all the world stood on one side and he stood on the other. He was not afraid to stand up for the truth, even if it contradicted society and modernity.

The Torah forbids homosexuality, period. That is a fact. Does that mean we should be insensitive to the feelings of gay people? Certainly not. But sensitivity does not necessarily mandate approval.

Homosexuality results from a combination of internal and external factors. Both may often be subject to change and modification. Contemporary society, however, conspires to prevent any adjustment in sexual orientation. Positive messages about alternative lifestyles saturate modern literature and the visual arts. At the same time, science has been forced to abandon research into psychological techniques that might be effective in returning the homosexual to the heterosexual fold. In effect, by refusing to acknowledge homosexuality as a problem, society is forcing homosexuals to remain as they are, without the benefit of psychological or spiritual counseling. According to the Torah, this is wrong.

Understand me, Ammi. I do not advocate laws against homosexuals. I do not believe secular governments should regulate sexual morality. But the clergy should speak out on all moral issues, and their positions should be based on religious truth, not on the changing attitudes of secular society. Indeed, if enough of them would do so, perhaps society would allow science to do serious research on the issue of sexual deviation.

What would I say about homosexuality if the Torah did not speak about it? I really don't know. But I do accept the Torah as God's truth, and the Torah states clearly that homosexuality is forbidden.

You will undoubtedly call me a fundamentalist once again, as if to imply that my position is based on ignorance and befuddlement. But you know full well that there are innumerable Orthodox doctors, lawyers, academics, scientists, mathematicians, and intellectuals of every sort, and none of them have a problem accepting the Torah's prohibition against homosexuality. Why? Because it is the revealed word of God. But you don't believe it.

I suspect that at the bottom of all this adaptiveness and reinterpretation is a desire to blend into secular society. You are afraid to be different. Wasn't that the impetus for the creation of Reform, the desire to blend into German society, to be a German in public and a Jew at home? Why are you so afraid to be different? We are different. We are Jews, the chosen people of God, entrusted with the mission of illuminating the world with His message. You yourself claim to believe this. So why make believe we are the same? Why try to blend into the woodwork? We should be proud to be different. You keep saying that "we are not better than anyone else." Not better? Perhaps. Different? Certainly.

I am reminded of the Stockholm syndrome in which captives identify with their captors, à la Patty Hearst. We Jews have been captives of gentile society for so long. We have absorbed their anti-Semitic messages, their aspersions against the holy Torah for which our ancestors gladly gave their lives, and now, many of us accept the mind-set of our captors and try to blend in. I do not accuse you of being another Patty Hearst, but there seems to be some slight element of this syndrome in your ideological position.

IN DEFENSE OF AARON

I refer you back to your posting of February 28. (I cannot resist a slight tangent in defense of a holy man.) You are troubled by Aaron's noble patience, which you claim caused him to lead the people into idolatry. You are also puzzled by his kind treatment by Jewish tradition. Without getting into this at great length, let me point out that the Midrash and the biblical commentaries are in agreement: Martyrdom is fine, but Aaron had to stay alive to try and stall the people until Moses returned. Unfortunately, he was not successful. But he tried.

PLAYING BY THE RULES

You write at length about reconciling values, such as resolve and patience, flexibility and principle. And then you write very revealingly,

"It is these conflicts of values; it is this inability to fully reconcile virtues, which is at the heart of society's need for pluralism." Here, I suspect, lies the crux of the matter. You view Orthodox life as rigid, constrained. You see it as being without freedom, that every Orthodox Jew must fit into the same mold, with no room for creativity and freedom of thought. In contrast, you see yourself enjoying all the benefits of pluralism—in other words, the right to do as you please. I want to take issue with your view of Orthodoxy, both in its interpretation of the Law and in its lifestyle.

You know at least a little about chess, Ammi. We spoke about it last time we met. Chess has rules. But let us say someone knows the rules very well and always follows them—does that make him a good player? Not at all. He can follow all the rules and still lose every time. But within those rules there is the opportunity for extraordinary creativity and brilliance. An inspired player can use those rules to do incredible, dazzling things. Now let us say someone comes along and decides he is not obligated by the rules. He wants his knights to scamper from end to end in a single leap and his pawns to move in all directions rather than just straight ahead. He is, of course, free to do so if he wishes, but the game he will be playing is not chess. It is something else. In order to play chess, you must follow the rules. Moreover, it is those very rules that give the game its richness and texture. Take away the rules, and you are left with nothing.

The same applies to mathematics. If you follow the laws and rules, you can solve problems, be creative, even brilliant. But if you violate the basic rules of mathematics, your work has no value.

This is what Torah is all about. There are basic rules, which are inviolate and incontrovertible, but within the parameters of those rules there is tremendous range for creativity and growth, each individual according to his talents and proclivities. And that is what makes Torah study and Torah living such profoundly rewarding experiences.

You are indeed right about Moses and Aaron. Both loved the Jewish people very deeply, but they were distinctly different individuals. Nonetheless, they were in agreement about the basic rules. We do not find Aaron raising objections to the execution of the wood gatherer for his desecration of Shabbat, do we? Those are the rules. But what do you do when you have a pagan uprising on your hands in the absence of the leader? His nephew Chur stood fast and died. Aaron attempted to manipulate developments and failed. What would Moses have done in that situation? Probably something else. Would he have been successful? No one knows.

Finding flexibility and creativity does not mean abandoning the rules in favor of pluralism. There is plenty of flexibility within the system. The greater you are, the greater your ability to create within the rules. The rules don't negate your freedom of choice. They enhance it. In fact, the power of the rules themselves are the source of creativity.

The study of Torah is the oldest and most magnificent field of intellectual endeavor in history. The sheer energy and genius of the debates that spring from every page of the Talmud and all the countless volumes of biblical and talmudic commentary and analysis are extremely exciting. What motivates so many young people to attend *yeshivot* and *kollelim* is not only piety and devoutness but also the intellectual adventure of Torah study.

I think you would be pleasantly surprised if you would experience this adventure. You admit you are not a Talmudist or an academic, but you must realize that this excludes you from the experience enjoyed by Hillel, Rabbeinu Saadiah Gaon, Rashi, Maimonides, the Vilna Gaon, and the many thousands of gifted Torah scholars throughout the ages. They were playing chess, so to speak, while you are not even playing checkers.

A TIGER IS A ROPE

I have to stop here, but I will answer your points more specifically in later postings. With regard to Ibn Ezra's "the Canaanites were in the land then," he himself (as quoted in my February 27 posting) offers the explanation that it refers to Canaanite conquest. Rashi also explains that the Canaanites, a Hamitic people, were in the process of taking the land from the indigenous Semitic people. There may be other explanations as well. Your interpretation, however, is weak; it assumes a gross editorial oversight. Could Ibn Ezra have meant this? Hardly. Good scholarship takes the entire picture into consideration. You cannot take one element out of context and offer theories to explain it. If those theories do not hold up when you look at the entire picture, they are worthless. That's just bad science and bad scholarship.

You could not possibly read all of Ibn Ezra's work and tell me this man was not the staunchest of Orthodox scholars. Neither of us knows the nature of his secret, but one thing is certain. It does not undermine the authenticity of the Written Law or Oral Law.

There is an old proverb about a blind man who grabbed the tail of a tiger and declared, "A tiger is a rope!" Had he seen the whole tiger, he would have known that what he held in his hands was not a rope but a tail. You cannot grab these little pieces of Torah and declare that they are ropes. If you saw the whole picture, you would realize you had a tiger by the tail.

As for the business about the Passover Seder being derived from the Roman symposium, give me a break. With all due respect to Lawrence Hoffman, whoever he might be, the Passover Seder was ancient long before the Greeks and Romans came along. Not every idle thought that finds its way into print should be accepted as fact. If you have some proofs, tell them to me and we can analyze them.

I know that you strongly doubt that either of us will change the other's mind on the fundamental points. I would like to take issue with you here as well. I hope you are approaching this exchange with an open mind. Here, I would suggest you hang on to some of your beloved uncertainty. As I mentioned before, I think you would gain much from a serious effort to become a talmudic scholar. Not only would it broaden your intellectual scope, it would also give you valuable insight into the fidelity and integrity of the Talmud, the dynamics of the Orthodox community and Jewish history in general. You don't have to join the Lakewood Kollel to study Talmud. If you wish, I could help you arrange it right there in the Upper East Side of Manhattan.

We in the Orthodox world do not fear your ideas as much as you would like to think we do. The only attraction you hold out to our children is the license to indulge in forbidden pleasures. The problems our rabbis have with the Internet are pornography and online relationships with strangers; the easy accessibility of almost limitless information is only a plus. I told you this when we met the first time, but you found it hard to accept. Nonetheless, it is true.

Be well.

Yosef

P.S. I did not say that people shouldn't go see the Yankees. I was simply saying that for a ninety-two-year-old man to define the value of a few more years of life as an opportunity to "see a few more Yankee games" is awfully pathetic. Wouldn't spending some time with his grandchildren be more meaningful?

[The following is a "posting" from Richard Curtis, the friend who introduced Rabbi Reinman and Rabbi Hirsch to one another and suggested that they embark on an e-mail correspondence. —Ed.]

March 13, 2000

Dear Friends:

I've been absorbing the wonderful, thought-provoking, and inspiring interchanges between you, and I've begun to get some measure of the issues—and a glimpse into the minds behind them.

In this first round of correspondence, you have sounded stirring fanfares declaring the classic philosophical positions of Orthodox and Reform Judaism. But I wonder if I could invite you down from your mountains to deal with some practical consequences of your respective approaches. I'm talking not about principles, but about behavior and lifestyles.

I can think of a thousand paths that will lead to provocative discussion, but I've been pondering two in particular that I would like to see addressed candidly, and I am certain I speak for many of us occupying the middle ground, what you might call the Desert of the Perplexed, as we gaze one way and then the other and wonder if both of you are not a little meshuggeh.

The first issue is the role of women in the modern Jewish world. It is impossible for American Reform Jews to imagine ritual and services, temple administration, and clergy without the participation of women. More and more, our rabbis and cantors come from our female population. Then we look across the gulf at the world of the Orthodox and see an institutionalized attitude toward women that speaks more of an alien religion than a sect of our own.

In short, one of the most disturbing consequences of rigid Orthodoxy is a denigration of women that is totally at odds with modern, enlightened American society. This often includes acts of cruelty toward women.

As if that weren't troubling enough, this rigid attitude has excluded women from fulfilling the sweetest and most important of our responsibilities, the study of Torah.

I have been reading a most interesting book, *Words on Fire* by Vanessa L. Ochs. It's about an American woman's journey of discovery as she visits Jerusalem to explore the sacred books of Judaism under the tutelage of women mentors (and at one point with a male learning partner).

I could quote many fascinating passages from her book, but let me quote one and ask you, Yosef, to comment on it.

"Why was the attitude toward women's learning so restrictive in almost all the classical sources? Why was the scope of what women were permitted to learn so limited? Three hypotheses come to mind: Men have believed women had inferior brains; they may have believed women's menstrual blood would contaminate the holy sphere of Torah study; and they may have feared Torah knowledge would give women too much desire for a life of the mind, luring them away from making babies, keeping house, and running businesses."

But now I look the other way, at the natural outcome of a Reform movement that has no limits, an unbridled do-your-own-thing approach that can lead to excesses that most reasonable liberal Jews find dismaying. Perhaps the most extreme of these is approval of homosexuality and even rabbinical performance of homosexual marriages.

The Mosaic commandment against practitioners of homosexuality could not be plainer: They are to be put to death. Modern Reform Jews have joined other moderns in recognizing and expressing compassion for gay men and women. In doing so, however, they have crossed a line that to our Orthodox brothers and sisters must seem like the depths of depravity and a perfect example of what happens when the fundamental rules on which our religion was founded are thrown to the wind.

So, Ammi, let me address this question to you: If there are no limits whatever to our behavior, if we can bend or break the Mosaic precepts at will, simply because it suits us to do so, or because a pressure group lobbies for change, where can we look for a bedrock on which to stand?

I look forward to hearing from both of you.

RC

March 26, 2000

Dear Yosef:

I seem to have stimulated you. I am pleased!

I am torn, because if I felt that I was needlessly antagonizing you by being provocative, I could tone it down. But honestly, Yosef, what I have been writing you is not at all outside the mainstream of discourse for most of the world's Jews.

Now listen, Yosef: You have to address the points I make, not the points you would want me to make.

You continuously take what I write and recharacterize what I say. Then you argue against this mischaracterization. Come on. You can do better.

First: I wrote, "All of the societies I am aware of believe murder and theft to be wrong; it is quite another thing to suggest I know what God wants since He already revealed it to me."

I wrote that in the context of making the case for pluralism in a society where people who live side by side believe different things. I wrote, "In creating social norms it is not enough to say that theft is immoral because God revealed it in the Torah. You must also use your faculties of reason and persuasion."

Since there are many people who believe in revelation, but this belief draws them to different conclusions, and since there are many people who have no religious belief whatsoever, it is not enough to say simply that my truth should be enforced because I really, really believe it.

To give you a few examples:

During the nineteenth century there were millions of southerners who fervently believed that Christianity condoned slavery. Christian preachers and teachers cited the Bible for their justification. These religious proponents of slavery claimed to hear the word of God as clearly as if He were the auctioneer at the slave market. Other Christians argued that slavery is un-Christian. Judaism does not condone slavery.

Whose beliefs should be imposed upon society? Those who claim to hear God the clearest? Those who say that they really, really believe?

There are a billion Catholics in the world, many of whom believe that life begins at conception. They really believe it. They believe that this represents God's will, and that they hear the word of God as clearly as if He were sitting in the obstetrician's office. Judaism does not believe that life begins at conception.

Whose beliefs should be imposed upon society? Those who claim to hear God the clearest? Those who say that they really, really believe?

There are millions of religious Americans who believe that capital punishment is ordained by God. They quote religious teaching, starting with the biblical injunction "an eye for an eye." These people claim to hear the word of God as clearly as if He were operating the electric chair. Judaism has done away with capital punishment—at least de facto.

Whose beliefs should be imposed upon society? Those who claim to hear God the clearest? Those who say that they really, really believe?

Astonishingly high numbers of Americans say they believe in God. Most of them are Christians. They come to God through Jesus. Many of them say that America should be governed by Christian law, not by some secular concept of separation of church and state. These people claim to hear the word of God as clearly as if He were speaking in the well of the Senate. Judaism rejects the notion that any man could be human and divine at the same time.

Whose beliefs should be imposed upon society? Those who claim to hear God the clearest? Those who say that they really, really believe?

For this reason I wrote: "It is one thing to speak about certain standards. It is quite another thing to suggest that I know what God wants since He already revealed it to me." As I wrote, you must also use your faculties of reason and persuasion. These are the rules of the game in

the best societies. Democracy, pluralism, tolerance, theological humility—these are the building blocks of free societies. Remove any of these
building blocks and the long shadow of the totalitarian wrecking crew
appears at our door. You only have to look around the world to see how
many people suffer because arrogant men have usurped the divine gift
of freedom for their narrow and ungodly designs.

And this freedom is good for religion. The United States, the freest
country in the world, is, by all measures, among the most religious
countries in the world. More Americans say they believe in God than do
citizens of many other countries, and more than in all other Western
countries.

With regard to my own beliefs, I indicated that belief is a matter of
feeling and inspiration. It cannot be empirically proven. I gave you
examples in my previous postings. I am happy to expand upon them if
you would like. There are many ways that human beings encounter
God, including through engagement with Torah and sacred texts,
through prayer, poetry, nature, events that occur in our lives, love.

But I believe these moments—at least for me—are rare. Even for religious people most of life is lived in the valleys between pinnacles of
inspiration. But while in the valleys we plug along, trying to make sense
out of a complicated world, learning and gleaning inspiration from our
predecessors. We have accumulated now thousands of years of teachings that should be incorporated into what we say and do. For Jews the
effort becomes authentically Jewish when we stand on the shoulders of
our predecessors and engage in the process handed down to us.

Hence our tradition emphasizes more what we do than what we say.
In fact, Judaism is wary of those who proclaim with great fervor that
they have encountered God in ways superior to the rest of humanity.
Only Moses spoke with God face to face, and there never again arose a
prophet like Moses.

This notion of absolute truth you keep on coming back to is really
not where Judaism placed its emphasis. We focused more on actions.
When your days are done, states the Talmud, you will be asked by the
heavenly court: Did you conduct your business affairs honestly? Did you
set aside time for Torah study? Did you [try] hav[ing] children? Did you
look forward to the world's redemption? (Shabbat 31a)

God will not ask if you believe in "absolute truth." (You raised this notion of "absolute truth" again in your latest posting. You seem to have a powerful need for absolutes.) God will want to know whether you were an ethical person. "If one is honest in his business dealings and people esteem him, it is accounted to him as though he had fulfilled the whole Torah." (Mekhilta)

Yosef, what do you make of so many Orthodox Jews who are not ethical in their business practices, but are so self-righteously observant that they presume to admonish others about what constitutes religiosity or Judaism? What is more important—ethical behavior or observing the laws of *shatnez* (which prohibit the wearing of garments that contain both linen and wool)? Who is a more religious person—he who claims to believe in "absolute truth" or he who considers his "fellow man's property as dear to him as his own?" (Pirke Avot 2:17) Who is more righteous in your eyes, he who attacks fellow Jews for not being religious enough—even going so far as to pronounce that they are not practicing Judaism—or he who loves his neighbor as himself? ("Love your neighbor as yourself, this is the major principle of the Torah"—P.T. Nedarim 9:4)

You are quite revealing when you write about my beliefs or lack thereof(!) Anything that does not conform with your neatly arranged theological filing cabinet receives a "lack thereof" put-down from you.

As important as the individual's relationship with God is, Judaism places more emphasis on the relationship between God and the Jewish people. We are a people. Judaism is the faith of the Jewish people. A person becomes a Jew primarily by being born into the Jewish people, whatever his beliefs may be. When you were born to a Jewish mother, you became a Jew. You do not have to be born again. Once part of the Jewish people, you cannot leave.

Even converts become Jewish not primarily by accepting the full gamut of religious beliefs. The Talmud explains that it is not necessary to expand upon religious teaching when preparing a convert for conversion (B.T. Yevamot 47a). A gentile becomes Jewish by embracing the notion of "your people shall be my people." (Ruth said this before she said "your God shall be my God.")

Now Yosef, since "God speaks to each and every person differently, according to his particular capacity" (Pesikta d'Rav Kahana 12:25), I would like to know how God speaks with you. I have asked you repeatedly what God says to you. Since you have either rejected or deemed inadequate my belief in God, Torah, and Israel, I would appreciate specifics from you: What does God tell you to do? When you get up in the morning, do you speak with God? Has He told you to study at the *kollel*? Has God ever told you to do something that you have not done? How does God inform your daily activities?

Second: You accurately quoted back what I wrote about change, but you have exaggerated the conclusions I drew. You write "you do not believe in the constancy of values but in constant change." This is a mischaracterization. I wrote that "we have determined standards that are clear and unambiguous." I do not believe in change for the sake of change. I believe in adapting our faith in accordance with the times, taking into account new information, developing and deepening philosophies, and new realities of life. We must discover the right blend between constancy and change. I believe that we should be, as the Midrash states, as flexible as the reed in the water, so as to bend with the winds of time, but not so flexible as to be washed down the river.

Yosef, don't just give me rhetoric. Tell me precisely what value that originated in the Torah you believe has not changed. If you were to list a few, I could answer you specifically.

Third: You quote my statement "the best I can do is keep trying, but I will do so embracing, not repelling, society and modernity." You then write, "your most current definition of Judaism must be adapted to society and modernity."

Well, this might be just semantics, but if you are implying that I believe that contemporary society sets the norm on all matters, and we must contort Judaism to fit these norms, then you have mischaracterized or misunderstood my point. I believe that Judaism must (and always has been) informed by contemporary society. That is different from implying that contemporary thought has a veto over classic Jewish thought. When the whole world was worshiping idols, we Jews brought to the world the concept of a monotheistic God. When the whole world was practicing slavery, we Jews brought to the world the idea of freedom. The standard is not what contemporary society thinks. But we should not ignore the sensibilities and pleasures of modernity. And we should certainly not reject or repel modernity.

So many ultra-Orthodox Jews simply reject society. They do not even want to know what is going on: no television, radio, newspapers, art, opera, fiction, science. This, I put to you, is a distortion of centuries-old Jewish practice, and a corruption of Jewish genius. How could Maimonides, for example, have written *The Guide to the Perplexed,* an exercise in Greek and then-contemporary philosophy, if he had not studied ancient and contemporary philosophy?

Yosef, your fear of modernity goes so far as to dictate how you dress. Why do you insist on wearing the clothes of the seventeenth-century Polish nobility—the then-contemporary norm—today? Was that mandated in the Torah, or was that a change introduced sometime along the way? Describe for me the Torah value that has not changed that obligates you to dress as you do.

Fourth: You write that [I] "reinterpret the Torah all the time to fit [my] new perceptions." Are you trying to tell me that you do not reinterpret Torah all the time?! All of us reinterpret Torah all the time. Wasn't Jewish tradition emphatic that it is important to leave room for the next generation to add its own interpretation?

If you agree that Jews reinterpret Torah all the time, then can you not understand that the very act of reinterpretation introduces change? It is not, as you (mis)characterize my thoughts, "there are no rules," but that we must stand on the shoulders of our predecessors and add our own interpretations. By definition, if such reinterpretations are accepted by contemporary Jews, they become normative—at the expense of previous interpretations.

Now having refused to deal with what I actually said, but rather what you want me to say, you conclude: "This is not Judaism, but well-meaning secular liberalism. The fountainhead of your values is not the Torah, but society and modernity. . . . Your Judaism is a rubber stamp to endorse your latest liberal opinion."

Please. I wrote to you previously that all of Judaism is, in my opinion, an interpretation and reinterpretation of the Torah. Everything starts with the Torah. The Jewish way is to engage the centuries of interpretations and then apply them to contemporary issues. How is this "well-meaning secular liberalism?" I think that well-meaning secular liberals would be offended by suggesting that the religious process I have been describing is what they believe.

You have gone into something of a tirade about homosexuality, incest, bestiality, and the like. Despite the rather hysterical tone, I think that within all the excitement you actually raise an excellent point.

If you read texts in a nonfundamentalist way, where are the limits? Despite your rhetorical flourishes about bestiality, incest, etc., it is important to explore the limits to reform. Are there any limits to autonomy?

The answer to the limits of autonomy, I think, is in the common sense of the people. (The Talmud also speaks about going out to the people so as to assess whether our expectations are out of touch with where they are.) When one group of Jews interprets the will of God as being too far outside the mainstream, the people will tell us. Remember, even by your own standards, while the Word might have been given by God, interpretation is a human endeavor.

The pendulum of opinion swings from one side to the other. Solutions that are rejected in one era are applied in another. Solutions that are relevant for one community are rejected by others. Here again, the key from a Jewish perspective is to engage in the Jewish way. If the way selected by a group of Jews is off the chart, the people will tell us. They will tell us verbally, and more importantly, they will vote with their feet.

Regarding homosexuality, let me suggest to you that it is not as simple as your simplistic tirade assumes. I have been convinced that many homosexuals are born with that proclivity. If this is, in fact, the case, then God created them that way. Homosexuality is a serious human issue that causes great pain. On the societal level, it is not the place of the law to go into people's bedrooms and inquire what type of sex they practice. (You might find all kinds of things you prefer not to know about heterosexual behavior too.) Discrimination against people on the basis of sex should not be tolerated.

On a religious level, Jewish homosexuals are our brothers and sisters. They must be treated with sensitivity and compassion. They are not fodder for some kind of intellectual screed in yeshivas and cheders.

Having said all of that, my reading of our tradition is that Judaism has long upheld the concept of heterosexual marriage as the ideal. A marriage in Judaism is a union between a Jewish man and a Jewish woman. As a rabbi, I would not officiate in any other ceremony.

On one level, I am proud of Reform rabbis who perceive this immense area of human and Jewish suffering and are compelled to want to do something about it. Nobody else in the Jewish world is dealing with these difficult human issues in a serious way. But those who are prepared to officiate at homosexual marriages do not represent the majority of rabbis and Jews. I think, by the way, they know that.

There are strengths and weaknesses in all philosophies. There is not one final solution (Berlin's phrase) to all human problems. For this reason, I have suggested to you that despite my rejection of much of your thinking, prima facie, I am not perturbed by the existence of orthodoxies or ultraorthodoxies. (The problem is that religious fundamentalists often do not accept the rules of the democratic game. Then I become very concerned for the reasons I have raised.)

In a nonfundamentalist reading of sacred texts, it is possible to go too far. That is always a risk. I acknowledge this forthrightly. It is possible to lose touch with the people and its core values. My own Reform movement committed this transgression in the late nineteenth and early twentieth centuries when it proclaimed that it considered Jews no longer a nation but a religious community. In its zeal for reform it committed a sin of historic proportions. Never before in the history of Judaism had there been such a pronouncement. Here was a case where we had not reformed Judaism, but had redefined it into some new creation that was far removed from mainstream Judaism.

Had the Reform movement continued down this path, I think that it might have led even to our breaking off from the Jewish mainstream. But the sensibilities of the people restored the Jewish soul that seemed to have abandoned part of the Reform movement.

(Lest you think that we are the only ones in Jewish life who from time to time go too far, there are plenty of examples in Orthodoxy as well. Neturei Karta, for example, is so far off the spectrum as to be truly bizarre. Even Chabad, despite some nice things, has come uncomfortably close to Christianity recently, in its belief that the rebbe was the messiah.)

Looking forward to hearing from you shortly.

Ammi

———————

April 13, 2000

Dear Ammi,

I know it's been a while since your last posting, but we have been busy with my son's *bar mitzvah* and other family celebrations. In any case, a belated welcome back from Zurich. I hope you and yours had an enjoyable Purim.

I have to tell you, Ammi, that I am a little disappointed in you. I have tried very hard in my postings to treat you with respect even as I vigorously attacked your ideologies. I believe I have successfully differentiated between you as a person, whom I value, and your positions, which I do not. I have never deliberately insulted or patronized you.

In this last posting, however, you have attacked me personally by using words like "simplistic tirade" and "silliness." Let me assure you that my self-esteem was unaffected. But I was aggrieved that you should find it necessary to use such tactics. Maybe it is because you sense the weakness of your position, that you have no bedrock under your feet.

You claim that your positions are "not at all outside the mainstream of discourse for most of the world's Jews." This is a theme that keeps cropping up in your postings. You claim legitimacy for your position because the majority of the world's Jews are not religious. Somehow you imagine that this makes you "mainstream."

Later on, you play the same tune again. You establish the limits of your autonomy as "the common sense of the people. The Talmud also speaks about going out to the people so as to assess whether our expectations are out of touch with where they are. When one group of Jews interprets the will of God as being too far outside the mainstream, the people will tell us."

Ammi, this is pure distortion. Do you understand the Talmud as saying that if a majority of the Jewish people would stop eating kosher we should lower our expectations to where they are? This is nonsense. The Talmud is referring to a rabbinic decree designed to "build a protective fence around the Torah." If it is a *gezeirah she'ein hatzibbur yecholin la'amod bah,* a decree that the community finds unbearable, it is canceled. But in no way are we allowed to cancel even one iota of the Torah itself, nor any rabbinic decree that has already taken hold. Do you think the Sages of the Talmud would condone the lack of religious observance among secular Jews because "a majority of Jews will tell them so"?

You do this again and again. You bring quotations from the Talmud out of context and you distort them to support your abandonment of the Torah. (You call it reinterpretation.) But where is your intellectual integrity? How can you ignore the entire scope of the Talmud, the supreme expression of Orthodoxy, and claim to find support in its pages for your euphemistic reinterpretations?

We will come back to this later. But I do understand where you're coming from. You have a serious problem. You need to find a precedent for your own innovations, a peg on which to hang your hat, but you have none. The Jewish sources until the last century or two are all Orthodox, leaving you no choice but to misrepresent and distort them. Why don't you just stand on your own two feet and take responsibility for your positions? Why do you insist on "standing on the shoulders" of the Talmud while you pull the rug out from under its feet? Quote from Isaiah Berlin. Quote from Victor Hugo. Quote from anyone you like. But give the Talmud a break. Please.

MAINSTREAM AND MAJORITY

Now let us talk about this idea called mainstream Judaism. You seem to feel that mainstream and majority are identical. Therefore, since the majority of today's Jews are unfortunately secular, it is mainstream to adapt Judaism to accommodate a secular lifestyle. In this scenario, Reform becomes the mainstream and Orthodox becomes a fringe group.

So let us examine the logic. What determines mainstream Judaism? Let us say that a majority of our people, Heaven forbid, decided to become Jews for Jesus. Would you consider that mainstream? I hope not. So here we have a majority on one side and the mainstream on the other. Because the majority has stepped away from Judaism, it can no longer be considered mainstream. Perhaps you could say that the mainstream of the ethnic group has turned to Jesus, but not the mainstream of Judaism.

Therefore, when we discuss issues pertaining to Judaism, let us not define mainstream by majorities but by adherence to the essence of Judaism.

Now take this a step further. Whose opinions do the Sages have to consider when formulating a decree to "build a protective fence around the Torah"? Which people can tell them when a decree is "unbearable"?

Suppose the Sages wanted to decree a certain stringency with regard to the preparation of food on Shabbat. Let us also suppose that a majority of Jews do not observe Shabbat. Do these people have a right to tell the Sages that their decree is "unbearable"? Not at all. Any decree would, of course, be unbearable to people who find the whole concept of Shabbat unbearable. Clearly then, these people have no say in the matter. Only those people who do observe Shabbat faithfully can make a judgment if a certain additional rabbinic restriction is feasible.

Moreover, listen to your own words. You claim that when a "way selected by a group of Jews is off the chart, the people will tell us. They will tell us verbally, and more importantly, with their feet." They will run away from you if you are off the chart.

Well, haven't your people been voting with their feet? Haven't millions of secular Jews been fleeing into assimilation and conversions to other religions? Reform leads to assimilation, and even well-meaning leaders such as you can only stick their fingers in the dike. These people are telling you something with their feet. Are you listening?

You very generously admitted that the Reform movement made a grievous error in the nineteenth century when "it proclaimed that the Jews were no longer a nation but a religious community." One day you may also admit that you made a grievous error by abandoning the commandments of the Torah and causing a tide of intermarriage and assimilation. So what will you do? Will you say, "We are sorry"? How will that bring back the many millions of people who are forever lost to the Jewish nation? They are voting with their feet, Ammi. Listen!

Let us explore a little further down this path you have charted out for yourself. You have no absolute truth, no absolute values. You do not believe God gave the Torah to humankind, and therefore you claim the right to change (reinterpret) it as you see fit, constantly adapting it to a changing society.

So let me ask you, if you live by the norms of society, how are you different from any liberal secular American? What makes you Jewish? We've been over this ground, and you wrote that you intuit a special mission for the Jewish people to lead the world toward the light. In other words, you are guided by the norms of the Jewish people rather than the norms of general society; the prevailing mind-set and will of the Jewish people instructs you in what is right and wrong. Correct me if I am misrepresenting your position.

Why would you think the Jewish people are better equipped to know right from wrong? Are we better than other people, more intelligent? Maybe we're worse! Isn't this somewhat racist, pardon the expression? For thousands of years the Jewish people knew right from wrong because God showed them the distinction. But if God does not show it to you, who gives you the right to preach to the world about right and wrong?

Follow this even further. You say that you are guided not by the norms of society, but by the norms of what you call the mainstream of the Jewish people. All right, let's see where this puts you.

You wrote that you are against homosexual marriage, that "a marriage in Judaism is a union between a Jewish man and a Jewish woman. As a rabbi, I would not officiate at any other ceremony. . . ." Bravo. Ironically, as fate would have it, one day after you sent me this posting, the Central Conference of American [Reform] Rabbis endorsed homosexual marriages. You must have felt the tide sucking the sand out from under your feet.

So what do you do now? Have you already changed your position to conform to the new norms of Reform society, or will you stand firm in your convictions for a while? And if so, what gives you the right to take a position that differs from the norms of what you consider the Jewish mainstream?

Now backtrack just a bit. I asked you why Reform considers Jewish norms preferable to the norms of society. You will probably answer that it is because you are standing on the shoulders of your predecessors and building on an ancient value system. Well, tell me, on whose shoulders does Reform stand when it endorses homosexual marriage? Certainly not Jewish shoulders.

You claim that your way is "to engage the centuries of interpretation and then apply them to contemporary issues." That is an excellent description of the Orthodox way, but what have you got to do with the centuries and millennia of interpretation? Who ever interpreted the Torah to mean that you do not have to keep Shabbat? Who ever interpreted the Torah to mean that you do not have to eat kosher? Who ever interpreted the Torah to mean that you do not have to wear *tefillin?* You do not apply them. You discard them.

On my recent trip to Israel, a friend told me about his neighbor, a secular Israeli, who came to America for a family *bar mitzvah.* The affair was held in a Reform temple, and the buffet featured all sorts of cheeses and meats—including pork! The man was scandalized.

"How can you allow such things?' he asked the rabbi.

"Well, we don't keep kosher," the rabbi replied.

"Neither do I," said the Israeli. "But this is a *shul!*"

"True," said the rabbi, "but we interpret kosher in the spiritual sense." The man was disgusted. This is Torah?

Ammi, give up your transparent reinterpretations. Admit that you are not guided by the Torah but by the trends in society. As you say, "time will tell whether the Jewish people agree," right? And on what will "the Jewish people" base their judgment? On contemporary values, nothing else. And what about the "sacred texts"? Your rabbinate will know what to do.

I know you keep stating that you are not a moral relativist, but methinks thou doth protest too much. Reform is moral relativism; your morality is what society says it is. Today homosexual marriage, tomorrow who knows what. You've taken a wrong turn somewhere, my friend, and you have no idea where this road will lead you.

You are, of course, free to believe whatever you wish. You don't have to believe in the divine origin of the Torah. You don't have to believe in absolute truth. You are free to create any value system that suits you. But please! Don't claim that you are a natural continuation of the original Judaism. Don't force your own bizarre reinterpretations onto the Torah.

Now please don't misconstrue my opposition to homosexual marriage as antagonism to homosexuals. They should be treated with sensitivity and compassion. But I believe this should be done by individual interaction with wise, sensitive, and discreet rabbis who really want to help them.

You say you are convinced that some homosexuals are born with that proclivity. Perhaps it is so. But there are undoubtedly many homosexuals who could live normal heterosexual lives if only help were available to them. Gay writers describe the homosexual life, in the best of circumstances, as hard, lonely, and not particularly gay. Why should homosexuals not be given an opportunity to enjoy the blessings of true parenthood and heterosexual marriage? The Christians are making serious efforts in this direction, and they have had some successes. Why shouldn't your Reform colleagues do the same? For that matter, why doesn't psychology pursue serious research in this direction? Because the gay lobby does not want any stigma attached to alternative lifestyles. That is why untold thousands of homosexuals are not being offered a true choice in life. Is this moral? Your councils should deal with the problems of homosexuals rather than pronounce a blessing over them and declare the issue resolved.

I am speaking, of course, only about the moral leadership expected of the clergy. I absolutely agree with you that no secular government has the right to legislate against homosexuals or any other kind of private sexual activity. I agree that society should not discriminate based on orientation. But I would differ from you with regard to schoolteachers and pastors. I believe heterosexual families should not be forced to expose their children to alternative lifestyles. *Heather Has Two Mommies* should be taught in public schools only if all the parents ask for it.

THREE MORE DISTORTIONS

Before I go on, let me just point out three more distortions of Talmudic sources that appear in your posting.

You quote from Nedarim (9:4) that "love your neighbor as yourself, this is the major principle of the Torah." The Hebrew is *zeh klal gadol b'Torah,* precisely translated as "this is *a* major principle of the Torah." By substituting the definite article "the" for the indefinite article "a" you have skewed the entire meaning of the quotation. According to your distortion, loving your neighbor is the preeminent principle of the Torah. That is false. It is only one of many great principles of the Torah.

You then quote from the Mekhilta that "if a person is honest in his business dealings and people esteem him, it is accounted to him as though he had fulfilled the whole Torah." Another distortion. Do you mean to say that if a person is ethical and deals honestly in business he need not fulfill all the other commandments of the Torah? Is this what you are reading into the Mekhilta? You must know that a number of other commandments are also characterized as being compared to the whole Torah—Sabbath observance, Torah study, wearing *tzitzit.* Do you mean to say that a person who wears *tzitzit* is exempt from all the commandments of the Torah? You can't be serious. All it means is that these commandments are of primary importance, not that fulfilling them exempts you from all the rest.

Next distortion. You quote from Pesikta d'Rav Kahana that "God speaks to every person differently, according to his particular capacity." I am impressed by your erudition. It took me a while to find this quotation. But again you have skewed the meaning to fit your purposes. You imply that the Midrash is suggesting many paths to God—a wind blowing on your face on Mount Nebo, looking at your infant daughter, sitting at the opera, reading poetry—and thus you ask how God speaks to me. This really is the core of your belief, that every person can choose his own way and is not bound by the Torah.

Well, believe it if you wish, but don't cram it down the throat of the Midrash. The Midrash is discussing the stand at Mount Sinai when every Jew was endowed with the gift of prophecy to enable him to hear the voice of God directly. Therefore, every Jew received it differently, depending on his capacity for prophecy. But in day-to-day life, God speaks to us through the Torah. True, if you open your eyes, you can sense God's presence in the wind, in every blade of grass, in the sound of children playing. But only through the Torah can you know what He wants from you.

THREE PRINCIPLES

You ask me to tell you some values that originated in the Torah that have not changed. Fine. I will give you three. One, there is a God who created the universe. Two, He chose the Jewish people for a special mission and promised them the Land of Israel. Three, we all have free will to choose between good, for which we will be rewarded, and evil, for which we will be punished; the Torah tells us what is good and what is evil.

MEASURING ETHICAL BEHAVIOR

You say, "What is more important, ethical behavior or observing the laws of *shatnez*?" I don't understand why you feel you must choose between the two. Can't you be ethical without wearing *shatnez*? You are really saying that *shatnez* is unimportant, even though it is written in the Torah, because it doesn't fit into your value system. Your question really mocks the Torah.

You ask me what I make of "so many Orthodox Jews who are unethical in their business practices." First of all, I don't know what you mean by "so many." Have you taken a survey? Do you know what percentage this represents? My answer is that all violations of the Torah are unacceptable, whether they are in the realm of the individual's relationship with God *(bein adam la'Makom)* or in his relationship with other people *(bein adam lachaveiro)*.

Your implication, however, is an insidious put-down of Orthodox Jews. Well, allow me to respond at some length.

Let us say we are scientists conducting an experiment to determine if a certain exercise is beneficial. We take two groups of people. One group does the exercise daily for a year. The control group does not. After a year, we evaluate the results. Do you think all exercisers are now healthier than all nonexercisers? Not necessarily, since many other factors come into play. Instead, each group produces a bell curve, which we hypothetically divide into three segments. Then we compare each segment with its counterpart on the other curve. If the exercise was indeed efficacious, we would find the top segment of exercisers healthier than the top segment of the nonexercisers, and so forth, for the middle and lower segments.

Now let us apply this method to the bell curves for Orthodox and secular Jews. The top segment represents our *tzaddikim,* our holy rabbis, *roshei yeshivah,* and spiritual leaders, people like the Chafetz Chaim, the Chazon Ish, Rabbi Moshe Feinstein, and many hundreds of others. If only 10 percent of the stories we hear about them are true (and the percentage of verifiable stories is probably much higher), there are no other people in the world that can even compare with these incredible people.

So let us compare the middle segments, the average people. Once again, there is no comparison. When they are not working, your average Orthodox people are extremely busy learning Torah, doing *mitzvot,* raising money for the poor, visiting the sick in hospitals, performing endless acts of kindness for their neighbors and strangers alike. (An Israeli survey found that hospital patients were four times more likely to be visited by an Orthodox stranger than by a secular stranger.) Again, there is no comparison.

Which brings us to the bottom segment. All right, there are some Orthodox people in the bottom segment who are unethical in their business practices, but what do we find in the bottom segment of the secular Jews? Rampant drug use. Adultery. Violence. And unethical business practices on top of everything else. Absolutely no comparison.

But you, my friend, who are so adept at distortions, have decided to compare the lowest segment of the Orthodox curve to the higher segments of the secular curve. Foul!

DRESS CODES

You write that my "fear of modernity goes so far as to dictate how you dress. Why do you insist on wearing the clothes of the seventeenth-century Polish nobility?"

How do you define modernity? If you mean being open-minded, informed, and aware of changes and developments in society, I believe I am as modern as you are. If you mean choosing to adapt your lifestyle to the latest mores, values, and fashions of society, then I grant you the honor of being modern. I do not care for it.

Last week, my son, a seventh-grader, celebrated his *bar mitzvah*. In honor of the occasion, he made a *siyyum* (completion) on Sanhedrin, one of the largest tractates in the Talmud. He understands Hebrew, Yiddish, Aramaic, and a few words in Spanish and Russian. He is a voracious reader, a computer whiz, tests out in math and science on a twelfth-grade level and in reading on a first-year college level. He can draw a map of the world from memory and tell you population figures for most of the major cities, and he has a very good grasp of world, American, and Jewish history. But, he does not watch television, and is thereby deprived of seeing people get their brains blown out every evening and an endless stream of sexually suggestive scenes and images. He loves Jewish music and listens to it constantly on his CD player, but he never listens to rock, hip-hop, gangsta rap, heavy metal, or any of the other genres that appeal to the baser side of human nature. He listens to the Yankees on the radio. He also listens to the news and reads Jewish newspapers.

Would you call this boy modern? I think he is modern in everything except for the culture, and that part of modernity we can do without. I prefer that he be sheltered from it during his formative years; it will not make him a better person.

My son once asked me why millions of young people today have spiky hair and rings in their eyebrows. I told him that they do this because they want to be different. He thought this was hilarious. But he actually touched on a very important point. Where does this need to be different come from? It comes from a spiritual sense that we are formed in the *tzelem Elokim,* the image of God, and therefore we each have a unique role in the world. But those who do not know how to be unique settle for being different.

The Torah way of life helps people find their unique role. You yourself admitted to me that our way is spiritually fulfilling. Our young people do not spike their hair and pierce their bodies. They respect the ways of their elders, even if they may not always admire their elders as individuals. There are, of course, some that drift away because of the seductions of secular life and the rigorous demands of an observant lifestyle. It is a small number by comparison, and the community works hard to bring them back. Many eventually return. Some do not.

So why do I wear my long caftan? I do not believe my religion requires it. You've met one of my brothers. He wears a business suit. So do my other brothers. I wear the long caftan for the same reason those young kids pierce their bodies, for the same reason you dress like a Yuppie. I want to make a statement. I want to say that I am different, that I reject the prurient messages of contemporary culture even as I welcome and applaud the advances in science, medicine, and technology. I want to say that I am different, that I want my life to be intensely Jewish, filled with Torah and spirituality, not violence and vulgarity. I want to say that even though I speak six languages, read the three major newsweeklies and several scholarly publications, have read thousands of books and authored over twenty of my own, I am happy to be ignorant about what goes on in the movies and on television. I think I am the richer for it. I dress as I do because I want to be identified with my own people, and I bless the United States, which gives me the freedom to do so. I have no desire to be melted into any pot, and I am delighted to see Indians in turbans and African-Americans in dashikis expressing the same lack of desire.

You ask me to "describe for me the Torah value that has not changed that mandates you to dress as you do." In fact, this is one of our oldest values. The Midrash tells us that the Jewish people were redeemed from Egypt "because they did not change their names, their garb and their language." This goes to the very heart of what the Jewish people are. Our historical role is to be different and to be proud of it. We bear the responsibility of setting an example for other people, to make a *kiddush*

Hashem by what we do and, Heaven forbid, a *chillul Hashem* if we act improperly. You, on the other hand, are unwilling to be different. You want to dress like everyone else and look like everyone else, so that you can blend in and be one of the crowd.

You want to know if I speak to God when I get up in the morning. Yes, I do. Every morning I say the daily blessings, thanking God for giving me another day of life, for the wonders of my bodily functions, for the privilege of learning Torah and performing the *mitzvot*. I say the Shema, expressing my love for God and my devotion to Him. I put on my *tefillin,* and I pray Shacharit. I pray for myself, for my family, for all the Jewish people. That is what I say to God in the morning.

You also ask me what God tells me to do. Unfortunately, I have never enjoyed the gift of prophecy, but He speaks to me quite clearly in the Torah. I know what He wants from me, and I try to do it.

You ask if God has ever told me to do something that I have not done. The answer is yes, but I am not proud of it.

I believe I have answered your questions. If I omitted something, please bring it to my attention, and I will respond in a later posting.

Now it is my turn.

SAFEGUARDING THE SUPPLY

We know what Judaism represented for thousands of years. It accepted the historicity of the Written Torah. It accepted the Oral Law as divinely inspired. It accepted the Halakhah as supreme. The parameters of Jewish life were defined by the 613 *mitzvot*. Our ancestors gave their lives for the Torah.

Now we have this new phenomenon called Reform, which came along to fix something that ain't broke. For all the centuries during which the Jews were confined to the ghettos, they never really felt drawn to the outside. The overcrowded conditions were, of course, difficult to endure, but they never felt drawn to become part of the dominant culture. What was out there to attract them? Christianity? They knew that what they had in the ghetto was far better. During the

Enlightenment, however, the tremendous new idealism in the gentile world exerted a strong attraction for many Jews coming out of the ghettos during the Emancipation. But there was a vast chasm between enlightened gentile society and traditional Jewish society, and therefore a new way had to be found. Presto chango. Reform was born. You could now have your cake and eat it too.

But this enlightened gentile world turned out to be not so enlightened after all, and the idealism has dissipated like the morning mist. All the grand ideas are gone, discredited by history.

And what was the result of this desertion of staunch Orthodoxy? Two hundred and fifty thousand Jews were baptized of their own free will in the nineteenth century alone, more than all the forced conversions of the entire Middle Ages, and today, secularized Jews have an appalling rate of intermarriage and assimilation. And the irony of it all is that Orthodoxy in our times is full of prosperous entrepreneurs, academics, scientists, and other professionals who are enjoying all the intellectual and economic fruits of progress without sacrificing their rich spiritual heritage.

So where is Reform today? Somewhat lost, I think. Aspirations for a homeland are abandoned and then revived. The *bar mitzvah* is canceled and then reinstated. *Mitzvah* observance is dropped and then again recognized as a good idea, but not mandatory, Heaven forbid. It is a movement constantly defining and redefining itself, constantly interpreting and reinterpreting according to the dictates and demands of the people.

By the way, Ammi, isn't it interesting that the law of supply and demand is reintroducing elements of the Torah into your movement? You should thank the Orthodox. We're safeguarding the supply so that it will be there for you when you ask for it.

You write, "With regard to my beliefs, I indicated that belief is a matter of feeling and inspiration. It cannot be empirically proven." This is very dangerous. You have no solid ground to stand on, just your intuitions and feelings, and yet you dare speak in the name of God. What gives you the right?

Why do you think the Torah condemns idol worship so strongly and so often? Who cares what someone does in the privacy of his backyard?

Why does the Torah condemn a false prophet? Doesn't he speak from feelings and inspiration? Is that so terrible?

Because if you can talk in the name of a divine power, you have claimed for yourself more than just the right to have your own opinion. You have appropriated for yourself the moral authority of a divine messenger, and you have the power to do whatever you want. Expressing your thoughts and feelings in the name of God is such a dangerous thing, because we know how unreliable this is. We know that we make mistakes.

You have no right to speak in God's name because of some feelings that you have. Judaism has always fought against this approach. Judaism says you are not allowed to speak in God's name because of something you intuit. You have to know what God wants.

We do not follow the Torah because we intuit it is true. What do beliefs matter if they're based on wind blowing on a mountain? We follow the Torah because we know it is true. I always try to avoid using the word "believe" when I write to you, because I don't want you to compare my belief with yours. My belief is based on knowledge. Yours is based on intuition.

I would like to define very clearly where each of us stands by making a list of principles which I believe (know) to be true.

1. I believe (know) that God created the world *yesh m'ayin (ex nihilo)* with a specific purpose in mind. Do you agree or disagree?

2. I believe He revealed this purpose to the Jewish people and gave us a special mission in this world. Do you agree or disagree?

3. I believe that Abraham, Isaac, Jacob, Joseph, Moses, Aaron, and all the other people mentioned in the Torah existed as described in the Torah. Do you agree or disagree?

4. I believe there was an Exodus and that the Jewish people received the Torah at Mount Sinai. Do you agree or disagree?

5. I believe each of us has a soul, an indestructible divine spark that lives on forever even after the body dies. Do you agree or disagree?

6. I believe God always rewards goodness and punishes evil in one way or another. Do you agree or disagree?

I would like you to give me clear and direct answers to these questions so that we will know where we stand. What are your positions? What is taught in Hebrew Union College? What do you tell your people? What do you tell the children?

You write, "Even for religious people, most of life is lived in the valleys between the pinnacles of inspiration. But while in the valleys we plug along, trying to make sense out of a complicated world."

Ammi, my friend, you do not have to plug along in the valleys between rare pinnacles of inspiration. The Torah gives us the opportunity to have a constant flow of inspiration in our lives in between those high pinnacles that come along every once in a while. By living in connection with God, by knowing what He wants and doing our best to make Him proud of us, we can enjoy profound spiritual satisfactions that enrich every day of our lives.

MATRILINEAL DESCENT

I want to make some final remarks before closing. You write that "a person becomes a Jew primarily by being born into the Jewish people, whatever his beliefs may be. When you were born to a Jewish mother you became a Jew." I agree wholeheartedly. I do not believe that you are one whit less of a Jew than I am. I also note that you speak of being "born to a Jewish mother." You probably did this in deference to me, and that was very respectful of you. Thank you. But I would like to say something on the issue of patrilineal descent.

In your posting of March 7, you write that the Bible embraces the concept of patrilineal descent to establish Jewishness but at some point in Jewish history Judaism decided to switch to matrilineal descent. You cite as examples the children of Joseph, Moses, and Solomon, all of whom were considered Jewish even though their mothers "did not convert."

I beg to differ with your scholarship. First of all, what makes you think they did not convert? The Talmud (Yevamot 76a) states clearly that all of Solomon's wives converted; it really defies reason to think the illustrious Jewish king would marry out of the faith or that his wives would refuse to convert. In European history, consorts of kings always converted to their husbands' religions. Why would it be otherwise in Solomon's kingdom? (Unfortunately, these conversions were not always the product of profound conviction, and the results were sometimes quite dreadful.) I would also expect that Joseph and Moses converted their wives, although I am not sure how the process worked prior to the Giving of the Torah.

It is hard to determine how Jewishness was established before the covenant at Sinai, but let us examine the evidence from the point when the Torah was given and onward. Was it patrilineal as you say, or matrilineal as Jewish tradition claims?

There is some confusion in the Reform literature I have read on this topic between the determination of Jewishness and the identification with particular branches of the Jewish people. Jewishness is determined by having a Jewish mother, as you yourself have written. But with which branch of the Jewish people is this young Jew associated? To which tribe does he belong? Does he belong to the priestly caste, the Levites, or the Israelites? These questions are determined by the father's lineage, assuming of course that the father is a Jew.

I present you with three proofs.

First, let us look at what the Bible tells us about an *eved ivri,* an indentured Jewish manservant (Exodus 21:4). "And if his master should give him a wife who will bear him sons or daughters, the woman and her children shall belong to her master, and [the manservant] shall go forth by himself." Here we have a Jewish man sold into temporary bondage who is given a gentile slave girl as a wife. When his period of indenture expires, the man goes free, but his children remain with the master. Obviously, the status of the child follows the mother who is a gentile slave. If the child would be considered Jewish, he would be exempt from permanent ownership by another Jew.

Second, let us take a look at the Amnon and Tamar affair in the Second Book of Samuel. Amnon and Tamar were David's children by different wives. In II Samuel (13:1–14), we read that Amnon was smitten with Tamar, who was the sister of his half-brother Absalom. He feigned sickness and asked the king to let "my sister Tamar come" and take care of him during his illness. When she came, Amnon forced himself on her. She pleaded with him to stop and said, "I beg of you, speak to the king, for he will not withhold me from you." Amnon, however, was too impatient, and the affair ended in tragedy.

The Talmud (Sanhedrin 21a) points out that Tamar was the daughter of a *yefat to'ar,* a beautiful gentile woman whom David captured in one of his wars. The Torah (Deuteronomy 21:10–14) recognizes that a beautiful female captive holds a powerful attraction for her Jewish captor, but the Torah wants to discourage him from making a hasty decision to keep her. Therefore, he is allowed one act of intimacy after which there is a cooling-off period. If he still wants her, he can convert her and marry her. Such a woman is called a *yefat to'ar.*

Tamar, the Talmud explains, must have been the daughter of a *yefat to'ar.* Otherwise, how could she have thought that the king would allow Amnon to marry his sister? Clearly then, she was conceived from that first act of intimacy before her mother converted to Judaism, and therefore, she was Amnon's sister only biologically but not legally. The logic is strong.

What also becomes clear from this episode is that Jewishness is determined by the mother. Since Tamar was born to a gentile woman, she was not Jewish from birth. Instead, she was a convert and therefore she would have been allowed to marry Amnon. Had her Jewishness been determined patrilineally, then she would have been David's daughter and Jewish from birth. How then could she expect to marry David's son Amnon, her own brother?

Third proof. Let us read from Ezra (10:2–3): "And Shechaniah the son of Yechiel, one of the sons of Elam, answered and said to Ezra, 'We have broken faith with our Lord and married foreign women of the peoples of the land, yet now there is hope for Israel concerning this thing. Therefore, let us make a covenant with our Lord to send away all the wives *and all that were born from them. . . .'*" The italics are mine. Need I say more?

Ammi, you yourself have to admit that matrilineal descent has been accepted by the Jewish people as the standard for determining Jewishness for thousands of years. You also have to admit that it will continue to be the exclusive standard for a very significant percentage of the Jewish people. And therefore, you also have to admit that by endorsing patrilineal descent you are doing irreparable damage to the Jewish people.

I know that accepting patrilineal in addition to matrilineal descent will temporarily shore up your hemorrhaging membership. I know that it will help you deal with all the mixed marriages that have resulted from your relaxation of religious observance. But look at the price you are paying. You are erecting a brick wall between yourself and the core of the Jewish people, the fountainhead of our future. You claim to be the movement of inclusion. Well, you are including plenty of gentiles, but excluding plenty of Jews. Is it worth it?

Brotherhood is a two-way street, Ammi. Right now, regardless of what you believe, regardless of what you practice, you and I are full brothers, and I would go to the ends of the earth for you. As would any other Jew. But if your mother would not be Jewish, there would be nothing between us. You would be a gentile to me, and although there is nothing wrong with gentiles, I would have no interest in reaching out to you as a Jewish brother.

Maybe you do not consider brotherhood with me such a great prize, but what about all the other millions of Jews who recognize only matrilineal descent? Are you ready to write them all off?

As for me, Ammi, I do consider my brotherhood with you and with all the other Reform Jews of matrilineal descent a great prize. I consider it priceless.

Yosef

April 28, 2000

Dear Yosef:

I think that we have sufficiently explored various strands of belief to allow me to summarize where we stand. When we met, you told me that your motivation for writing this book was, in part, to reach "my audience"—those who might not pick up a book that you wrote on your own, but who through me might be tempted to explore your thoughts. I found that to be a reasonable motivation. I am motivated in part by similar interests. I do not delude myself that anyone in your community will be swayed in any way by my thoughts. I am not even particularly interested that they would be. I am content that there are Orthodox Jews who believe with perfect faith in the ideas that you have articulated.

However, overwhelmingly, most Jews are not and will not be Orthodox. To the extent that there are people who unnecessarily idealize Orthodoxy, to the extent that there are those who feel in some way that they are on a lower rung of the religious ladder, I wish to dispel these myths. While, as I mentioned to you, there are many things I admire about Orthodoxy, there are also many flaws in Orthodoxy and the Orthodox community. How could it be otherwise with human beings, imperfect and mortal? For you to lay out your beliefs, and to have them refuted, questioned, and expanded by me and then for me to offer counterbeliefs is, I hope, useful to many good Jews who cannot accept some of the more audacious claims of Orthodoxy. I hope that it will strengthen their faith. There is nothing particularly original in our arguments. Oceans of ink have been spilt analyzing the very ideas with which we have been engaged. But I think it is useful, and I hope helpful, to lay out the ideas side by side in this manner.

To clarify: Modern thought has demonstrated for me conclusively that the Torah was written by human beings. It is not productive for us to review all of the evidence in this book. A day in any decent library will allow our readers to see scores of sources documenting the evidence. I have produced for you some of the early sources—premodern—that question the purity of the claim that every word in the Torah was written by God and transmitted by Him to Moses. I did this not to rehash the evidence of the documentary hypothesis, but to remind you that even what you call "Orthodox" sources were already pointing out that the belief that God dictated every word of the Torah to Moses, and that Moses wrote down every word, was far more complicated than appeared. (You misuse the term "Orthodox" when referring to premodern sources. There really was no Orthodoxy before the advent of Reform. The term "Orthodox" arose in response to Reform.)

In this context, I mentioned Ibn Ezra. In addition to Genesis 12, which we have discussed, Ibn Ezra is also concerned with Deuteronomy 1:1, which states: "These are the words which Moses spoke unto all Israel beyond the Jordan." The verse implies that someone else wrote this, because why would Moses have to identify the place where he spoke to the Israelites? If the Israelites had not yet crossed the Jordan, why would Moses use the term "beyond the Jordan?" Ibn Ezra goes on to cite five other troublesome verses (including Genesis 12) in saying, "If you know the secret of [these verses], you will discover the truth."

You indicated to me in one of your earlier letters that you do not understand Ibn Ezra's secret and that neither do I. Fair enough. But it is at least possible, if not plausible, that Ibn Ezra was alluding to the very secrets I am articulating but that he could not reveal in his day. At the very least, Yosef, it makes you think, no?

The Talmud also asserts that parts of the Torah were not written by Moses. How could Moses have written verses describing his death and its aftermath?

Thus there is a passage which claims that Joshua wrote the last eight verses of Deuteronomy describing Moses' death. (Baba Batra 15a) Ibn Ezra suggests that Moses did not write the last twelve verses of Deuteronomy. The Torah itself makes no claim that God wrote every single word. When the word *torah* is used in the Torah, it means "teaching," not one unedited integral work.

All the more reason to reject the claim of the Oral Law. There is much wisdom in the Talmud. Tremendous values and institutions were developed by our people through talmudic, midrashic, and other halakhic discourse. The Talmud has intrinsic worth. However, it is not reasonable to suggest that the Talmud constitutes the literal word of God as transmitted by God to Moses on Sinai. To accept such a claim is to suggest that talmudic rabbis were infallible. I believe that the Talmud, like everything else, was influenced by, and responded to, the circumstances of the day. It is the secret of its genius. The value of the Talmud is not diminished by asserting its human construct. Quite the contrary; its value is enhanced.

When I use "Torah," (as opposed to "the Torah"), I refer not only to the five books of Moses, or to the Bible, or to the Talmud or the Midrash, but to the totality of Jewish thought. Torah is the Jewish people's reaching out to God. What a glorious testament to the Jewish search for God! I also believe that in many ways God has responded to the Jewish people. I believe it because I feel it strongly. I intuit it. I deduce it. I reason it. Barring direct communication, this is the only way.

I believe that God and human beings are in partnership one with the other, and that human beings are given freedom to choose. I have cited passages from the Talmud itself to illustrate this point. "The Torah is not in the heavens!" "According to the majority shall matters be decided!" "Upon hearing this God burst out in laughter: My children have prevailed over Me." The Talmud provides ample evidence for modern interpreters to feel authentic in their interpretations. That the Talmud would suggest that the Laws of Moses were unrecognizable to Moses is encouraging to contemporary Jews.

I believe in the sanctity of the Jewish people. I believe that the existence of the Jewish people, defying all odds and historical norms, testifies to the existence of God. I believe that Torah was created by the Jewish people in partnership with God. It is our living faith. It is our testament. It is our legacy to the world.

I do not look at the Torah as a history book. I think that many of the events described in the Torah have historical origins; however, I do not consider every word to be literally true. The fundamentalist viewpoint that the world is less than six thousand years old because that is what Genesis implies is irrational to me. I have no interest in disfiguring reason and twisting myself into theological contortions every time a dinosaur bone is discovered.

(I use the term "fundamentalist" not in a derogatory manner. I mean by this the belief that one interprets sacred texts in a fundamental way. That the term now implies fanaticism hints at the dangers of a fundamentalist approach to the world, but there are many fundamentalists who are good, decent, and peace-loving people.)

That the Torah asserts the existence of God, and that humanity is the pinnacle of creation, created in the divine image—this is the fundamental point of Genesis to me.

I concede that I would be fascinated if archaeological evidence were to emerge "proving" the existence of Abraham. However, theologically, I am less concerned about whether Abraham really existed. That the Torah asserts the uniqueness of the Jewish people, and that through the Jews humanity will be blessed, is for me the fundamental point of the passage about Abraham's selection.

I concede that I would be fascinated if archaeological evidence were to emerge "proving" that the Israelites crossed the parted sea. Theologically, I am less concerned about whether the exodus from Egypt and the revelation at Sinai occurred as described. That the Torah asserts the divine imperative to be free and that the Jews believe that we covenanted with God for all time—this is the fundamental point of the Exodus to me.

I am less concerned about whether the conquest of the Land of Israel occurred as described in the Book of Joshua than that for the Jews Eretz Yisrael is the Promised Land, that we have claimed this land for as long as there were Jews; that we have cultivated and loved this land, that we have treated it as a divine gift and as the centerpiece of the covenant with God—this to me is the essential point.

I and most Jews celebrate Purim not because we believe in the literal biblical rendition, but because it is an opportunity to celebrate Jewish survival in the face of anti-Semitism. I celebrate Chanukah despite the fact that it was wholly created after the Bible, because it is another opportunity to celebrate the indestructible yearning to be free.

I go to synagogue not because it was mentioned in the Torah—it was not—but because it is where Jews meet God. I think that we can encounter God elsewhere as well, but the Jewish community, qua community, convenes in holy gatherings in synagogues. The synagogue is the central Jewish institution.

I recite the prayer "who has chosen us from amongst all the nations" before reading the Torah because it affirms my belief that the Jews are special and we should strive toward the highest standards. I recite the Shema because it is the watchword of our faith, asserting and affirming the belief in God.

And more: I do all these things because my father did them; his father did them; Jews throughout history have done them.

I am not discomforted by adding new traditions and practices. Jewish tradition did this all the time. The prayer book was not set until many centuries after the Bible. The first true prayer book emerged only in the ninth century. Some prayer books are different than others simply because of the preferences of a particular community. The *bar mitzvah* ceremony is a very late development.

I do not feel that I can make changes willy-nilly. The needs of the Jewish people outweigh for me the needs of any particular community or movement. However, I do feel that I can make changes and I also feel fully authentic in being selective. How can we not be selective? If you are Orthodox, there are 613 traditional commands you feel are inherent in Jewish observance. Six hundred and thirteen! How can anyone observe these commands all the time every day? You are forced to choose and prioritize what you consider to be more important.

The Talmud also does this. "R. Simlai said 613 precepts were communicated to Moses. David came and reduced them to eleven. Isaiah came and reduced them to six. Micah came and reduced them to three. Isaiah came and reduced them to two. Amos came and reduced them to one." (B. Makkot 23b–24a)

"The Sabbath is equal to all the other precepts of the Torah." (Exodus Rabbah 25:12)

In the well-known debate between Rabbi Akiva and Simeon ben Azzai, Akiva said that "Love your neighbor as yourself" is a great principle of the Torah, whereas ben Azzai said an even greater principle is Genesis 5:1: "This is the record of Adam's line. When God created Man He made him in the likeness of God." (In response to one of your earlier postings criticizing my translation of this passage, I have seen it understood in both manners—i.e., this is a great principle, and this is the greatest principle. Both understandings are fine for the point I am trying to make here, so I have translated in the manner preferred by you.)

I am not saying that the Talmud is suggesting that to observe one precept is enough. However, the Talmud is highlighting the idea that behavior, even admirable behavior, requires prioritization. Perhaps in the passages cited here the Talmud is suggesting that all expectations flow from one overarching principle. But even for discussion purposes the Talmud must prioritize. The human mind cannot grasp so many precepts. Human behavior requires prioritization.

You too are selective. You wrote to me in your last posting that you have refrained from doing things that God told you to do (as you understand such commands), albeit you are not proud of this. While you did not detail these shortcomings, presumably the transgressions you committed were deemed by you to be minor—or at least not as major as some other potential transgressions you did not commit, such as murder or adultery.

And more: If something is morally offensive, I consider the community capable of discarding, altering, or ignoring it. Jewish theologians, teachers, and leaders have been doing this since the beginning. As I wrote before, in this way the rabbis rendered capital punishment, slavery, and polygamy obsolete. Moral awareness is God-given. It distinguishes us from animals. God would not have given us moral awareness if we were not able to use such awareness for perfecting society. God could not have condoned the stoning of a wayward child to death. Even the rabbis understood this, which is why they explained it out of existence.

The question is not whether things change. Of course they do. The Mishnah states: "The laws of the Sabbath are like mountains hanging by a hair, for there is very little in the Torah and there are many laws." (Haggigah 1:8) The question is how to change and the degrees of change.

Since I do not feel that all wisdom resides in me, I am happy to have Orthodoxy do its thing. It is valuable to have part of the community continue to develop Halakhah. If you think, as you wrote, that you are "safeguarding the supply so that it will be there for you when you ask for it," that too is okay with me. I would not want all the Jews of the world to be Reform. I have learned much from Orthodox Jews, and I am sure that the Jewish community will continue to benefit from its serious approach to Jewish life. To continue to replenish the halakhic supply is important. The Orthodox world comprises part of the fine balance necessary to sustain a vibrant, exciting people facing ever-changing challenges. If you think that one day millions will come and join Lakewood and other ultra-Orthodox communities—hey, there could be worse motivations.

I believe in the sensibilities of the Jewish people. I think you are mistaken when you write that "the majority of the world's Jews are not religious." Do not confuse "religious" with "Orthodox." They are not one in the same. And do not confuse "observant" with belief in God. Most Jews say they believe in God.

Let me now briefly relate to a number of comments you raise.

THE REFORM MOVEMENT

You have rather harsh things to say about the Reform movement.

You write, "Reform leads to assimilation." This is the standard canard

I hear all the time from ultra-Orthodox propagandists. It is precisely the opposite.

Do you honestly think that were it not for the Reform movement all these people would be in Orthodox synagogues? You write, "These people are telling you something with their feet. Are you listening?"

The Reform movement is now the largest Jewish stream in the United States. It dwarfs Orthodoxy. What, Yosef, are the people telling us? What do you think they are telling you? Only 6 percent of American Jews identify themselves as Orthodox! Are *you* listening?

Were it not for the Reform movement, assimilation would be unbearable. All these millions came to us for a reason. And the reason was that what you were offering was perceived by them to be no longer relevant, fulfilling, reasonable, tolerant, moderate, pious, or uplifting. What we are offering strikes them as more relevant to their lives and sensibilities. Having said that, I acknowledge that there is a very serious problem of assimilation in America and that all of us are part of the solution.

The Reform movement has made huge contributions to Jewish life, which can already be appreciated, but in the future I believe will be considered historic. Here are a few: First, we have played a major role in preventing assimilation. Given the choice between Orthodoxy and nothing, like most Jews in Israel, American Jews would have chosen nothing. Unlike in Israel, however, where Jews live in a Jewish state, choosing nothing for American Jews would have led to the disappearance of many more millions of Jews.

Second, we have made it normative in Jewish life to be part of contemporary society. With the exception of fairly marginal numbers in ultra-Orthodox communities, most of the world's Jews now consider part of their Jewish value system to interact with, and even lead, modern societies. Most of the world's Jews now incorporate contemporary norms into their worldview. Even Yeshiva University, ostensibly the bastion of mainstream Orthodoxy, calls itself a university and requires higher secular education of its rabbinical students. "Torah and Science" is how they define their philosophy.

Third, we have restored the role of ethics to a primary position in Jewish communal life. Of course, the ethics of the prophets were always present in Jewish discourse and awareness. But it was the Reform movement, with its insistence that the Jewish community act in accordance with the highest ethical communal standards, that was primarily responsible for the renewed emphasis on the ethics of the prophets as the standard for the Jewish community.

Fourth, we have permanently changed the role of women in Jewish life. Women are now leading major pulpits across America. Women are religious role models—teachers, preachers, cantors, and rabbis. The equality of women, which Reform recognized first, now is the norm in the Conservative movement. And we have begun to influence the Orthodox world as well. This is not the place to detail this fascinating development. I will limit myself to stating that much of the Orthodox world will be ever more accommodating to the public role of women as the years go by.

Fifth, we have made it acceptable to be creative and innovative. There has been an explosion of new alternative worship experiences. More and more people are accessing Judaism through different portals, which are now available to them in their communities.

Sixth, we are beginning to change the discussion in Israel. There is now a much greater appreciation of the breadth and depth of Jewish experiences. There is a much greater understanding of the dangers of one stream of Judaism monopolizing Jewish life. It is still early in the process, but I believe that one day the Reform movement will be perceived as having played a major role in changing the character of Israeli society permanently and for the better.

(For a more thorough analysis of some of these points, read *Reform Judaism Today* by Rabbi Eugene Borowitz.)

Perhaps from time to time the Reform movement goes too far. When that happens, the people will tell us. The pendulum is constantly swinging.

I agree with the thrust of your disappointment about the synagogue that served pork. Whatever the individual does in private, the community should be as embracing as possible, and should not so publicly and provocatively make it difficult for kosher-observing Jews to participate. It is offensive. I can only add that I have traveled to many Reform synagogues and have not once had a similar experience.

THE SOURCES

I have mentioned to you before that you seem acutely offended when I quote from Jewish sources, particularly the Talmud. I think it is because you folks apparently abrogate to yourselves the sole right to fully understand and correctly interpret Jewish sources.

I want to set the record straight. You do not have exclusive ownership of Jewish sources. They are not—as you write—"the supreme expression of Orthodoxy." They are the creation, property, and legacy of the Jewish people. They are subject to interpretation and reinterpretation. The more learned one is, the better, but they are also open for anyone to study and understand. Madonna is studying Kabbalah, for Heaven's sake!

I have said that I do not look at the Talmud primarily as a source of law. I read it as a source of Jewish values. For example, I am interested in the thirty-nine prohibited categories of work on Shabbat, not in order to strictly adhere to halakhic prohibitions. I am much more interested in the values the sources are trying to convey about the nature of the Sabbath and the sacredness of time and space.

As I have said many times, I am perfectly happy for you to study and understand the same texts differently. It is mostly good for the Jews (except when it leads to extreme acts). To stay with this example, I think that it is important for present and future generations that there are various models of Shabbat observance. Just because I have allowed myself to change various observances does not mean that I want your form of observance to disappear.

MAINSTREAM AND MAJORITY

I did not fully understand your discussion about mainstream and majority. According to the Oxford dictionary, "mainstream" means the "prevailing trend of opinion." "Majority" means "greater number" or "the

larger part." They are obviously related, because if the greater number
of people hold a particular opinion, it is the prevailing opinion.

In the talmudic passage I cited earlier, "according to the majority
shall matters be decided," the majority decision on such matters makes
them "mainstream," no?

In any case, without getting into too much sophistry, the point I want
to make is that I consider most of the Orthodox world to be within
the mainstream, along with most of the non-Orthodox world. Some
Orthodox movements are fringe. And we can say with complete assur-
ance, the Orthodox in America are in the minority. The non-Orthodox
are the majority.

RIGHT FROM WRONG

You write, "For thousands of years the Jewish people knew right from
wrong because God showed them the distinction. But if God does not
show it to you, who gives you the right to preach to the world about
right and wrong?"

First, as the Mussar movement used to say, when I preach, I talk to
myself, but I have no objection to others hearing what I say. You do not
always have to speak in the name of God to say something to the world.

Second, I do believe in some way that to know the distinction between
right and wrong comes from God. Our moral sensibilities are created and
informed by God. I do believe that Torah encompasses divine inspiration.

Yosef, enough already with the "you have no absolute truth, no
absolute values, what makes you Jewish?" I have answered this already.

What makes a person Jewish is his mother (or his conversion).

What makes a value Jewish is the way it was developed and its level
of acceptance.

CHANGE

I agree with the three principles you cited that originated in the Torah—
belief in God, Jewish chosenness, and free will. (Although all three were

greatly expanded later in Jewish tradition.) This is not really what I meant when I asked you to cite examples of unchanging principles. I meant behavioral principles.

I am much more interested in the behavioral principle of dress that you claim to believe is in the Torah and has not changed. I was fascinated by your response to me about the reasons for your dress. I completely identify with your need to be different. I can relate to that. Jews are different. I was surprised that you wrote that you wear a long caftan for the same reason young kids pierce their bodies. Still, it is good for people to express their own identities and individualism.

But why choose the garb of medieval Polish Christian nobility as the symbol of your distinction? The caftan that you wear is Persian in origin and was worn widely throughout the Turkish empire. Surely this is nowhere in the Torah. I asked you to cite a Torah value, and you cited the Midrash(?!) as your source. The Midrash was written many hundreds of years after the Torah. (You did this again regarding the wives of Joseph, Moses, and Solomon. You cited the Talmud's statement that Solomon's wives converted.)

Also, if you already point to the Midrash in explaining that the Jewish people were redeemed from Egypt "because they did not change their names, garb, and language," why did you change both your garb and language? Whatever the Jews in Egypt wore, it was not a caftan. Whatever the Jewish people spoke, it was not English or Yiddish. (The rabbis of the Talmud spoke Aramaic as their vernacular.)

The eighteen articles of clothing mentioned in the passage of the Talmud (Shabbat 120a) that details dress during talmudic times are very similar to the dress of the Greeks.

MODERNITY

You say that you reject the prurient messages of contemporary culture even as you welcome and applaud the advances in science, medicine, and technology. Fair enough.

But they go hand in hand. You cannot have freedom to create in science and repress the creative spirit in culture. This freedom might lead to cultural phenomena you might not approve of, but if you want to advance in science, medicine, and technology—and, I might add, economics—you must allow for freedom across the board. Hence the need for tolerance in society.

To the best of my knowledge, fundamentalist Afghanistan, fundamentalist Iran, fundamentalist Saudi Arabia, contributed no significant advances in science, medicine, or technology.

Furthermore, I completely reject your implication that except for science, medicine, and technology, nothing good has been created by modern American or Western culture. I do not agree that you are richer for not having seen movies or television. (Might I also add theater, opera, modern art, etc.?) If you haven't seen these, how would you know?

I agree that modernity is not the end of human development. We still have a long way to go. Pre-Nazi Germany was among the most developed and cultured societies in the world.

Still, I believe that society steadily progresses. I consider this to be a Jewish belief. It is connected to the yearning for redemption and the dawning of the messianic era. As long as we never forget the limitations of the human condition, there is nothing wrong, and everything right, in believing that tomorrow will be better than today and today is better than yesterday.

I happen to find this largely true for much of humanity. Never before in the history of mankind have so many people lived so long, so healthily, so prosperously, so educated, and so free.

KNOWLEDGE OF GOD

You write: "Judaism says you are not allowed to speak in God's name because of something you intuit. You have to know what God wants. We follow the Torah because we know it is true. My belief is based on knowledge."

Hmm.

THE SIX PRINCIPLES

You asked me whether I believe in the six principles you articulated. (Do they correspond to the six tractates of the Mishnah?) Regarding the principles dealing with a literal understanding of the Torah, I think that I have adequately addressed this in the current and previous postings. With regard to the others, you and I probably agree, although perhaps not in the way you intend.

Ammi

April 30, 2000

Dear Ammi,

Your long posting dated April 28 was quite interesting, but right now I must work on my response to Richard's question regarding women. We will surely return to these subjects later on, and if I fail to answer any of your questions, please bring them to my attention again.

Nevertheless, I have to take a little time out to defend the honor of Ibn Ezra. The man must be turning over in his grave. Nowhere does he say what you claim he says. He is just being secretive and mystical. Do you have any inkling of what he means by the "secret of the twelve" in Deuteronomy 1:1? I don't. But since he alludes to unspecified secrets, you take the liberty of inserting your own heretical beliefs into his dead mouth. Furthermore, you make him out to be a duplicitous hypocrite who wrote thousands of pages of staunchly Orthodox commentary (such as the one I quoted regarding "an eye for an eye") yet slipped in a few mischievous hints that it was all a sham. Why didn't he just become a doctor or a mathematician if he felt that way? These were accepted career paths for a nice Jewish boy even then. Ammi, you do a great injustice to a holy sage who is not here to defend himself. It is not nice.

Let me just get specific for a moment or two. You quote Ibn Ezra's suggestion that Moses did not write the last twelve verses of the Torah (which follows one opinion in the Talmud), but you fail to quote him in context. Ibn Ezra goes on to say that Joshua wrote these verses "through prophecy"; otherwise, how did he know what God said to Moses in the privacy of the mountaintop? You, however, do not believe in prophecy. According to you, those verses are the product of some unspecified author's vivid imagination. Not exactly eye-to-eye with Ibn Ezra, is it?

One final point. We got into this whole brouhaha about Ibn Ezra because of his cryptic comments on Genesis 12:6, *"Vehakena'ani az ba'aretz*. And the Canaanites were then in the land." You focused on the word *az,* "then," and deduced that the Canaanites were in the land "then but not now," at the time the verse was being written. And so you jumped to the conclusion that Genesis must have been written when the Canaanites were no longer in the land, perhaps a thousand years later. This, you contended (quite unreasonably), was Ibn Ezra's mysterious secret, effectively making him into a closet Reform rabbi.

But let's take a closer look at the word *az.* The word can mean "then," and it can also mean "since then," as a few minutes with the Mandelkern Concordantia will show you. For instance, we read in Judges 13:21, "And the angel of God no longer appeared to Manoah and to his wife, then *[az]* Manoah knew that he was an angel of God." Does this mean that Manoah knew this then but did not know it later? Of course not. It means that from that point on Manoah knew he had been speaking to an angel. Similarly, *vehakena'ani az ba'aretz,* which was written in the desert after the Exodus, means that "the Canaanites were in the land from that time on."

Now let us take a look at Genesis 49:4. "Then *[az]* you desecrated it, my couch departed." What does *az* mean here? Perhaps our own Ibn Ezra can enlighten us. *"Az chilalta,"* writes Ibn Ezra, *"from the day* you desecrated it, my couch departed." I rest my case. Let Ibn Ezra rest in peace.

All the best,
Yosef

May 1, 2000

Dear Ammi,

It's been a while since Richard posed his questions about the role of women in Orthodox society. I have, however, given the matter a lot of thought while driving my car or standing in line at the bank and checkout counters. I knew this question would be coming down the pipe, but it's still hard when you finally come face-to-face with it.

The difficulty is not so much in the response itself as in conveying it in a relevant and meaningful way. We are touching on some of the most fundamental differences between the Orthodox and secular lifestyles and exploring different mind-sets.

Before we begin, I want to emphasize that, as you know, I am not a practicing member of the Orthodox rabbinate nor am I affiliated with any official Orthodox organization. I am primarily a talmudic scholar and author, and I also consider myself an independent thinker. What I am about to say here is my personal opinion. I am not speaking in the name of the Orthodox rabbinate nor in the name of Orthodoxy in any form. But I do believe that other Orthodox rabbis, even if they have different insights on these issues, would not find my response inconsistent with accepted Orthodox doctrine.

From Richard's standpoint as a Reform Jew, he perceives a "denigration of women that . . . includes acts of cruelty." These are harsh value judgments, and I would like to take issue with both of them.

A few months ago, I hired an attorney, a secular Jew, to handle some legal work for me. He remarked to me that he used to consider Orthodox women oppressed and repressed, but somehow every Orthodox woman he has ever met seemed intelligent, poised, confident, and fulfilled. I suspect that Richard would have a similar reaction if he met a random sampling of Orthodox women. The trapped women in anti-Orthodox literature do not commonly populate the real Orthodox world. They are the imaginary projections of secular-oriented writers who would feel oppressed and denigrated in what they mistakenly perceive as the Orthodox woman's role.

As for the acts of cruelty, if and when these things happen, they are the very rare exception to the rule. The overwhelming majority of Orthodox women enjoy the devotion, respect, and fidelity of their husbands. I haven't the slightest doubt that secular women suffer much greater cruelty at the hands of their husbands. After all, what can be more emotionally cruel than faithlessness, the fear of which plagues all secular women (and men), whether or not they care to admit it? Furthermore, in the light of today's AIDS epidemic, faithlessness can actually be deadly. Nonetheless, according to the Kinsey Report, about 85 percent of American men are unfaithful to their wives. Orthodox women (and men) do not worry about faithlessness. If it ever happens, it is a bizarre aberration; concerns about faithlessness are not a significant factor in Orthodox marital relationships.

Contemporary secular thought on women's issues is deeply influenced by feminism, which has done both service and disservice to American society in general and women in particular. Feminists have advocated equal pay and opportunity for women in the workplace, equal opportunity in academia, the prevention of sexual harassment and the protection of women from physical, emotional, and mental abuse—all admirable goals. Feminists have also raised sensitivity levels across the board and somewhat debrutalized American society, and we should be grateful.

For some reason, however, they have also tried to eradicate all differences between men and women, to deny any natural divergence between men and women other than those imposed by cultural bias; boys play with trucks and girls with dolls, they insisted, because that is what they are given in early childhood. They derided "the myth of women as caregivers and nurturers" and promulgated their own myth that men and women are interchangeable.

This is nonsense, of course, as numerous academic studies have demonstrated, not to mention everyday experience and just plain common sense. (In fact, a popular book of recent publication, *Men Are from Mars, Women Are from Venus,* shows how recognizing the inherent differences between men and women will improve a relationship.) Nonetheless, this sort of artificial thinking has insinuated itself into the cultural consciousness and continues to manifest itself in many subtle and damaging ways.

Let us now take a closer look at these differences. All people have both masculine and feminine sides, with men being primarily masculine and women feminine. The masculine tendency is aggressive, driven, focused on achievement and conquest. The feminine tendency is to seek completeness and harmony. If we were to assign symbols to these tendencies, we would choose an arrow for masculinity and a circle for femininity.

Therefore, men can sometimes be less sensitive than women, because their masculine sides instinctively incline them to see other people in the context of their own goals. Women, on the other hand, are more likely to respond to their dominant feminine sides and see the complete person, with all his needs and feelings. The Talmud (Berachot 10b) tells us that a woman is better at evaluating a stranger than a man. The Midrash (Bereishit Rabbah 18:1) credits a woman with *binah yeteirah*, or superior insight. Basically, the desire and ability to see the complete picture endows women with special intuitive skills. It is their dominant feminine side in action.

A friend of mine, a tournament chess player, pointed out to me that there are very few female grand masters, and he asked me why I thought this was so. His own answer was illuminating. He said that someone once asked Bobby Fischer what gives him the strength to make the incredible mental, emotional, and physical effort that championship chess requires. Fischer replied, "All the effort is worthwhile in order to see the ego of my opponent crushed right in front of my eyes." This monomaniacal focus on winning is utterly masculine. A woman, in most cases, will see her opponent as a complete person, with a spouse and children and perhaps an old, sick mother, and she will recoil from crushing him. But a man sees a one-dimensional antagonist standing between him and the achievement of his goals, and he has no compunctions.

We find this same distinction on the collective level. Western society is characteristically masculine—aggressive, self-centered, fast-paced, intensely achievement-oriented. We look to the individual for products, goals, end results. Everything is measured by accomplishments, regardless of the costs. Imagine if someone were to ask you, "What have you accomplished this past year?" Now imagine you were to tell him, "Well, I improved the quality of my family life and deepened my relationship with my wife." This person would think you lost your mind, and he would laugh at you. But tell him you made $2 million, and he will look at you with respect. It wouldn't matter to him if your family and your marriage may have suffered in the process. People are not interested in the whole picture. If a baseball player throws hundred-mile-per-hour fastballs with his right arm and has terrible eczema on his left arm, American society will not see him as incomplete.

Eastern societies, on the other hand, are historically more feminine in that they seek unification of all the aspects of the personality; they will not see the pitcher with ugly lesions on his left arm as complete. They are more serene, inward-looking, and fatalistic (although they are becoming more and more Westernized in recent times).

Which way is better?

Each has pluses and minuses. The Eastern way provides peace of mind but is plagued by poverty and social lethargy. The Western way provides growth and development but leads to much stress and distortion. Obviously, the ideal would be a balance between the two. Perhaps there are countries in the world that have something akin to balance. The United States emphatically does not. We are a masculine society all the way. This has given us a position of preeminence in business, science, technology, and just about everything else, but it has also given us preeminence in numerous social ills. It is the price we pay, not for freedom, but for our macho ways.

So which way is better for individuals, the masculine or the feminine? Here again we need to bring our feminine and masculine sides into balance to attain wholeness. How do we do this?

In Judaism, this is accomplished by marriage. According to the Talmud (Yevamot 63a), a man is incomplete until he marries a woman, and vice versa. When a man and a woman unite in a truly loving marriage, they become a unified, complementary whole with a powerful masculine drive and a powerful feminine anchor. They have a real shot at achieving harmonious balance and finding happiness and fulfillment.

But it is not enough for a man and a woman to be united in body and heart. They also have to be united in their aspirations, in the purpose of their existence, and they have to share equally in the effort to reach that goal and the rewards of its fulfillment. This is where Judaism veers sharply from the secular mode.

Most modern secular men or women emerging from adolescence have a list of priorities. First, they want a career or profession to give them a sense of purpose and identity. Second, they want financial success to give them the wherewithal to enjoy the good things in life. Third, they want a life partner to provide them with love and companionship. Fourth, they want children to bring them pride and all sorts of emotional satisfactions and to care for them in their old age. (Of course, they love their children, but they don't aspire to have children for the sake of their unborn children but for their own sake; it is good to have children.)

Then they will go after these priorities in this exact order. First, they will graduate college and establish themselves in their chosen fields. Second, they will settle into comfortable lifestyles and build up portfolios for the future. Third, they will find mates and marry, somewhere in their late twenties or early thirties. Fourth, they will consider having a child or two, somewhere in their mid-thirties. Without going into the psychological and sociological consequences of postponing parenthood until early middle age, everything sounds responsible and put together. But is it really?

Let us analyze this marriage model. Essentially, everything this husband and wife are doing is self-centered, designed to fulfill personal physical or emotional needs. Each one is focused on his or her own needs and looking to the other to provide them, and in order to accomplish this they have formed a partnership, a negotiated arrangement between two disparate individuals, each of whom has agreed to serve the other's needs in exchange for having his own needs served. Even having children, in this arrangement, is no more than a need that occupies fourth position in the hierarchy of priorities. Many people choose to forgo it altogether; it's just not worth the bother. This is not exactly a formula for success.

So he goes to his law office and she goes to her law office or corporate executive suite or whatever, and they meet at home or in a restaurant for dinner.

Now, no matter how sweet and attractive this woman may be, she has been masculinized; her masculine side has been so strongly reinforced that in outlook she is no longer as dominated by her feminine side. (The current issue of the *Atlantic Monthly* features an excellent article about how the masculinization of the American female has resulted in the emasculation of the American male. The myth that the educational system discriminates against girls has skewed the proportions to the extent that within a few years two-thirds of college students will be female, and boys are developing serious problems in school. Masculinized females have careers to pursue, but where do emasculated males go? Down the tubes.)

So what happens when a modern secular man and woman, both heavily masculinized, decide to marry? They may be physically complementary, but emotionally and spiritually, they run on parallel tracks. Since they are both career-oriented with overriding personal ambitions, they do not share a common goal. Therefore, if one partner is successful in his career, it does not help the other's aspirations. On the contrary, since they are living together, it is only natural that they will measure their own success against the progress of their partners. When one forges ahead, it just underscores the inadequacies and failures of the other. So they automatically fall into a pattern of competition in their career paths, and this conflict, by extrapolation, affects their status within the family. Eventually, it also affects their intimate relationship.

Well, it is no surprise that marriages like these produce a high rate of divorce. And here we find ourselves facing a vicious cycle. Young couples contemplating marriage are fully aware that there is a fifty-fifty chance the venture will fail. So they make prenuptial agreements and postnuptial agreements, and the wife makes sure she has a solid profession in hand so that she will be able to provide for herself and any possible children in the not unlikely event that the husband drops out of the scene. Very prudently, they do whatever they can to minimize the unpleasant consequences of divorce. But of course, this only increases the likelihood of divorce.

The result is what we are witnessing today—the breakdown of the institution of marriage and the traditional two-parent family unit. Everyone is out for himself, pursuing his own personal goals, and the society as a whole is thoroughly masculinized. Even the strong sexuality that pervades the culture is an expression of masculinity. Pornography, powerful sexual media images, predatory men and women in bars, these are all masculine; feminine societies are far more reticent about sexuality. The Talmud tells us (Kiddushin 2b) that it is "the way of the man to pursue the woman." In America, everyone is in pursuit. The society is out of balance, and its structure is antithetical to successful family life.

Now let us compare the secular model with the Torah model. The four priorities are in exactly the reverse order! Priority number one is to have children. This is the first *mitzvah* in the Torah, "Be fruitful and multiply." Jewish men and women are not commanded to have children in order to fulfill their own personal needs. Rather, they are given the responsibility of perpetuating the Jewish people, of bringing honor and glory to God through the sanctified role of parenthood, of raising children and molding them into special human beings who will spread Torah in the world and to future generations. We don't want one or two children. We want many. The more the better. We are not worried about the population explosion. Let the burden of population control be borne by Germans and Poles and Ukrainians and Russians and Hungarians and Slovakians and Spaniards and all our other historical enemies who have so efficiently controlled our population over the centuries. No matter how great a Jewish population explosion we produce, we will never replenish our losses.

Priority number two is to get married in order to have children. Jewish children have to be produced and raised in the context of a Jewish home, and the primary purpose of the marriage is to create that sanctified home where children are born, nurtured, and taught how to live a Jewish life, where they learn to shine the light of Torah into every little corner of their lives, where they experience the constant presence of God. When a man and a woman marry, the Talmud tells us (Sotah 17a), the Divine Presence rests between them. The Jewish home is not a place to park yourself between the office, the theater, and the restaurant, a place to kick off your shoes, watch television, and grab a bite to eat before you go to sleep. The Jewish home is a temple, a school, a library, the place where Judaism lives, blossoms, and flourishes.

The pleasures of marriage are not its primary purpose. They are the inducements. God did not create food to tickle the taste buds. He created taste buds to make sure people eat food and get the nourishment they need. Although people with eating disorders abuse it, food was created to provide nourishment. Despite all the abuses of sexuality prevalent in our society, God created sexuality to induce people to get married, conduct a loving physical relationship, and have children.

Priority number three is to make money. It is expensive to run a Jewish home. The cost of a solid Jewish education for each and every one of the children is high. Then there are the costs of Shabbat and the festivals and all the other observances that make life in a Jewish home such a rich and rewarding experience.

Priority number four is a career. A career provides spiritual fulfillment and personal satisfaction by giving you the opportunity to be productive and contribute to society at large. Furthermore, if the career is lucrative, you will also be able to promote and support worthy causes within the community. But the career always remains in fourth position in the hierarchy of priorities, and if there is a conflict between the family and the career, the career must give way. If a well-paying, prestigious job will take a toll on the family, find a different job.

In Orthodox society, careers are not the primary measure of status. Torah scholars, community activists, and people of high spiritual standards enjoy far more status than careerists. Of course, we instinctively respect any great intellectual accomplishment and the accumulation of great wealth, but we do not believe they automatically make a person more worthy. Worth is measured by Jewish accomplishment, by closeness to God, by nobility of the soul and exaltation of the spirit.

What are the roles of the man and the woman in such a Jewish home?

The woman is the *akeret habayit,* the mistress of the home, the high priestess of this *mikdash me'at,* this minor temple. She has the primary responsibility for the physical, emotional, and psychological well-being of the whole family, including her husband, herself, and the holy Jewish children they bring into the world. It is a daunting task that requires the singular intuitive and nurturing skills of the woman, the one who has superior insight, the one who sees the whole picture. It is the ultimate expression of femininity.

The man is more outward-oriented. In contrast to the woman who is the family's minister of internal affairs, so to speak, the man is its minister of external affairs. He is charged with the responsibility of *vehigita bo yomam valailah,* to make Torah study the focus of his life and to convey what he learns to his children and to the Jewish people at large, to be a solid link in the broad-spectrum transmission of Torah from Sinai into the future. It is also his responsibility to fulfill the obligations of the family in the realm of communal affairs; for instance, the burden of building a synagogue falls on the man as a strong obligation, while the woman's participation is at most voluntary. The man is also required to be the breadwinner, the provider of the financial fuel that keeps this temple running. If he is incapable of doing it completely on his own, the woman should also lend a hand to supplement their income, but she must try to do so in a way that is least distracting from her primary responsibilities.

Today nearly all Orthodox women in the United States and Israel have at least some level of higher education. Many of them have professional careers or run successful businesses, but they are almost invariably not career women. They do not seek social status through their careers, nor will they receive it. Their primary careers are as mothers, wives, high priestesses of their own temples, and everything else they do is secondary. The same should also apply to Orthodox men, although unfortunately this is not always the case. We live in an imperfect world, amid gentiles who are career-oriented and materialistic, and some of us may lose sight of the primacy of Torah in Jewish life.

In addition, both husband and wife are expected to take an active role in philanthropic projects. Almost all Orthodox people are involved in at least several community institutions, whether it be the synagogue, the schools, open-door hospitality, charities, families in distress, catastrophic medical assistance, free loan societies, and an endless array of other philanthropic enterprises. It is not enough to write a few occasional checks, even big ones. You have to get out there and do things, either directly or on the organizational and fund-raising ends. This is such an imperative in Orthodox life that some people of modest means in Israel keep boxes of pacifiers in their homes to distribute to parents whose babies lose their pacifiers in the middle of the night; unable to afford more substantial forms of philanthropy, they have come up with an inexpensive way to make a meaningful difference.

So here we have an entirely different approach to marriage, where both husband and wife seek fulfillment in the home, the children, and the community, where the man is free to be primarily masculine and the woman is free to be primarily feminine. It is no wonder that the Orthodox divorce rate is so low, and I believe most of the divorces that do occur are caused by husband and wife losing sight of the Jewish model and seeking the secular model of lifestyle and marriage. Going back to our symbols, a Jewish marriage combines the masculine arrow and the feminine circle to create an upward-rising spiral.

I know I am painting a very rosy picture here, and one might think I am suggesting that every Orthodox home is a haven of bliss, a place suffused with sweetness and light. I wish. But sadly, it is not so. Orthodox people are also human. We all have complexes, inadequacies, insecurities, and all sorts of other imperfections that take a heavy toll on connubial bliss and happiness in general. But at least we are working with a marriage model built for success and fulfillment. At least we don't begin married life with two strikes against us.

So whose role is more important—the man's or the woman's? The question is a little disingenuous. Judaism introduced individual rights to the world, but it also puts heavy emphasis on the collective. We are individuals, but also members of Klal Yisrael. We are all pulling together (or should be) in one direction for one common goal, to spread the light of Torah and bring honor and glory to God's Name, to make a *kiddush Hashem.* We are a *mamlechet kohanim v'am kadosh,* "a kingdom of priests and a holy nation," and we all work in the same holy temple. We are a team, and each does what he can, to the best of his abilities, to achieve the common goal. Some of us are Kohanim, some are Levites, some Israelites, some men, some women, and we are less concerned with our privileges than with our responsibilities.

Which is the more important part of a car—the wheels or the engine? They are equal because one is worthless without the other.

In the context of the Jewish family, which is more important—the minister of internal affairs or the minister of external affairs? The question is moot, because one would be ineffectual without the other.

In the mutual relationship of a Jewish marriage, the issue is not really equality, but prerogatives. Here again the roles are clearly defined. The man takes precedence in protocols and observances; for instance, it is the man's responsibility to make Kiddush for the family. In needs, however, the wife takes precedence; if husband and wife both need a new garment and there is just enough money for one of them, the money goes to the wife.

All successful institutions and relationships must have good rules for resolving conflicts. In a Jewish marriage, the rules derive from roles that are clearly defined and complementary.

I do admit that this strong emphasis on marriage and children in Orthodox life creates problems for singles who have tried but failed to find spouses and for couples who have tried but failed to have children. Where do they fit into Orthodox society? I do not have a pat answer for you. It is a problem. The prophet Isaiah declares (56:3), "Let not the infertile say, 'Behold, I am a withered tree.' . . . For so said God to the infertile who keep My sabbaths and choose those things that please Me and hold fast to My covenant, 'And I will give to them in My house and My walls a position and prestige better than sons and daughters, an everlasting name that will never be cut off.'" Many people have taken the words of the prophet to heart and gone on to lead spiritually fulfilling Jewish lives. In our own times, we have the examples of the Satmar Rebbe, the Lubavitcher Rebbe and the Chazon Ish, all of whom were childless and all of whom made tremendous contributions to the Jewish people. Whether on a grand scale or on a small scale, thousands of childless people have earned "position and prestige better than sons and daughters" in the House of God.

Now let us talk about women learning Torah. This Vanessa Ochs that Richard mentioned is obviously a woman from a secular background who goes to Israel to check out the Torah, but she examines these sacred, ancient writings through the filter of her own secular biases. She has no understanding of their context or their role in Jewish society. She also has a chip on her shoulder. Listen to her three reasons for women being restricted in the realm of Torah study—inferior brains (!), menstrual blood would contaminate the holy sphere of Torah study (yikes!), and the fear that "Torah knowledge would give women too much desire for a life of the mind, luring them away from making babies, keeping house, and running businesses."

Let's take these one at a time.

Inferior brains? Most Orthodox women are intelligent and well educated. The level of proficiency in Torah studies demanded of them is very high. The average high school girl has a thorough knowledge of classical commentaries, such as Rashi, the Ramban, Ibn Ezra, Sforno, and Rabbeinu Bachya, and is perfectly capable of researching the texts in the original Hebrew or even Aramaic. She is also rigorously trained in philosophy, law, and Jewish history. In addition, she completes a full complement of general academic studies, including higher mathematics, accounting, and computer science. Most Orthodox girls spend eight to nine hours a day in school and another two to three hours doing homework. After high school most girls pursue their religious studies for another year or two in an accredited seminary and then go on to some form of higher education. Talk about intellectual stimulation.

Menstrual blood? Please. There is absolutely no source anywhere in the Bible or the Talmud that connects menstruation with a restriction on Torah study. I do not see how a person can create such an invention out of whole cloth and publish it in a book.

Now let us look at number three. Aha! Doesn't the secular bias jump out at you? Do you hear the condescension in "making babies, keeping house"? This woman has the secular model firmly implanted in her head and finds it difficult to reconcile it with the Torah. She is right. It is irreconcilable. She does not understand Torah life. To her, "making babies and keeping house" are the work of empty-headed housewives who double as breeding cows. To the sophisticated, highly intelligent, highly educated Orthodox woman, however, making babies and molding their personalities is an exalted spiritual calling, and keeping house for them is a high honor and a profound pleasure. Ms. Ochs can pore over the ancient texts from morning to night in her archaeological mode, and she will still not get it unless she readjusts her mind-set and flicks the chip off her shoulder.

So what is the Jewish woman's relationship to Torah study?

There are really two aspects to Torah study. First, we are required to study Torah in order to learn how to live a Jewish life. This level of Torah study applies to men and women equally and extends into numerous areas of the Torah. It mandates a solid knowledge of Halakhah, Chumash, sacred writings, classical commentaries, Jewish thought, and Mussar.

Then there is Torah study for its own sake. Essentially, this means the study of the Talmud, the repository of the Oral Law. If all that were required of us was to know what to do, men would study only those subjects required of women as well. The study of the Talmud, however, is an end in itself. It is the grand process by which the Oral Law is received by each generation from its predecessor and passed on to its successor.

Talmud study is a tremendous undertaking, the work of a lifetime. You can't just study a piece here and there and expect to have any decent perspective on its totality, as I've pointed out again and again during these exchanges. Talmud study is not for part-timers. It requires serious commitment and sharp focus. If a woman is fulfilling her role in the greater scope of the Jewish destiny, if she is creating, building, and guiding one of the minor temples within which Judaism lives and flourishes, it would be extremely difficult for her make a parallel commitment to serious Talmud scholarship, to plunge into the "sea of the Talmud." If she expects to fulfill her own role, it would be extremely difficult for her to get up early in the morning to spend an hour or two studying before she tends to her daily responsibilities and then come back in the evening for another few hours of study. It is almost always a choice—the home or the Talmud, not both.

Women are not forbidden to study the Talmud; they are simply not encouraged to do so. There have been women in Jewish history who have been able to accomplish the feat of achieving a high standard of Talmud scholarship without sacrificing their role as Jewish women. Among these are the prophetess Deborah and the brilliant Beruriah, the wife of Rabbi Meir. But they have been few and far between.

So if most Jewish women cannot make a serious commitment, shouldn't they at least be encouraged to learn a little bit? The answer is no. The Talmud (Sotah 20b) explains that if a father teaches his daughter the Oral Law he is in effect teaching her to be duplicitous. As the old saying goes, "A little knowledge is a dangerous thing." Dabbling, especially in Talmud study, only leads to misconceptions and falsehood. Those who make a commitment to Talmud study know the experience. The Sages describe Talmud study as "bitter at first and sweet only afterwards." It is a real struggle. It takes a good five to ten years of hard work, usually at least seven hours a day beginning in early adolescence, until you even begin to see the bigger picture.

Therefore, in the division of roles, the wife is entrusted with enriching the marriage relationship and the domestic quality of life for the entire family, and the husband is entrusted with the responsibility of Talmud study. In the broader sense of earning merit for Torah study, of course, the wife shares equally with her husband in all the Torah he accumulates.

Before closing I would like to address one more point. Richard wrote that "it is impossible for American Reform Jews to imagine ritual and services, temple administration, and clergy without the participation of women. More and more, our rabbis and cantors come from our female population."

There are two issues here. Since the external obligations of the family are the responsibility of the man, as I have explained, synagogue functions and attendance fall into his purview. The woman's participation in synagogue services is only voluntary, and therefore her role is secondary.

But there is also the deeper issue of *tzniut*—modesty. In Orthodox synagogues, the women sit on the other side of a *mekhitzah,* a partition. Some non-Orthodox people find this offensive. Perhaps this is the "denigration" to which Richard referred in his posting, since Reform Jews are accustomed to men and women sitting together. But our way is expressly mandated in Halakhah and in the Talmud. A man is forbidden to pray within sight of a woman. Why?

As I've explained earlier, Judaism is not concerned with simply making us good. Judaism is designed to make us holy, "a kingdom of priests, a holy nation." Sexuality is holy only in the context of a loving union between husband and wife in the privacy of their chambers. Elsewhere, it is the opposite. Most encounters between men and women have undercurrents of sexuality, at least to some extent. This may be unavoidable to some degree in everyday situations, but in a synagogue, where we are supposed to be striving for holiness, how can we allow undercurrents of sexuality to intrude? The undercurrents may be faint, but they are real. Therefore, we have the *mekhitzah.*

So, you ask, why not put the men behind the *mekhitzah*? The answer is that these undercurrents of sexuality flow mostly in one direction. If you remember, it is "the way of the man to pursue the woman." The man, whose masculine side inclines him to one-dimensional perceptions, is stimulated by the mere physical aspect of a woman. A woman, however, whose feminine side inclines her to seek unity, will need to see the man in the context of a comprehensive relationship in order to be stimulated. The exposure of the woman's body is inflammatory, not the man's. In a casual conversation between an attractive man and an attractive woman, the man's thoughts will easily turn in a libidinous direction, but if the woman is not masculinized, hers will not. Therefore, putting men on the other side of the *mekhitzah* and having women conduct the services accomplishes nothing. But with women behind the *mekhitzah,* men have no problem concentrating on their communication with God without the slightest improper thought or feeling. That is the idea.

As for your female rabbis and cantors, what can I say? If you're striving for holiness, this is not the way.

Be well, my friend.

Yosef

———

May 23, 2000

Dear Yosef:

While I was not overwhelmed by your analysis of the innate characteristics of maleness and femaleness, I was impressed by your description of Orthodox family life. If you were describing your own family, you are fortunate indeed.

I have two general caveats. First, despite your efforts to be careful in generalizing, I think that you paint an idealized picture of Orthodox (or ultra-Orthodox) life, and imply a generalized and thus incomplete (and inaccurate) picture of non-Orthodox life. And despite your care, I suspect that there are many more problems in Orthodox households than is implied in your description.

Many books and studies have, of course, been written about Orthodox domestic life that portray a far different picture. Recently in the

New York *Jewish Week* (May 19, 2000), Rabbi Abraham Twersky, an ultra-Orthodox expert on mental health, is quoted as saying, "Perhaps physical violence is less common [in the Orthodox world than outside it] but emotional abuse is the same or higher. It begins with a man saying 'I will make motzi and kiddush,' but then says, 'I am the only one who can sign checks, you may not have credit cards, I don't like you talking to your mother and friends so often.'" The article asserts that Orthodox women, particularly ultra-Orthodox women, often stay in abusive marriages longer than other women for fear of the damage to their family's reputation.

Second, if the household you are describing is voluntary, I am happy for those who choose to live this way. People should have the right to conduct their affairs as they see fit. If they choose to live the lifestyle you describe, I can only admire those who testify to its benefits, and who appear to be sincere in their testimony. There are many virtues in the family life you describe. Perhaps the most important virtue of all is that this lifestyle creates an encouraging environment to sustain Jewish life into the next generation.

However, no amount of explanation or rationalization by you of the traditional role of women will convince the vast preponderance of modern women (and men) that what you are describing is relevant to them in its broad application. No amount of passion from you will convince the preponderance of modern women (and men) that your description of Jewish tradition is the sole interpretation and the exclusive path to virtue. I am aware of many non-Orthodox families who also live truly virtuous lives and who create a Jewish environment that encourages Jewish continuity.

Again, it is important for me to emphasize that I found your description of the home as a minor temple uplifting. If the women in such households sincerely want this for themselves, and they are happy and fulfilled, that is wonderful. Still, I suggest that it is not at all as simple as you imply.

And furthermore, Jewish tradition has many things to say about women that you did not mention that I think even you would find problematic. You seem to truly respect women ("a man should love his wife as himself and respect her more than himself," Yevamot 62b). Your sug-

gestion that Orthodox husbands and wives play an equal, albeit different, role in the family suggests an inherent virtue in women ("Israel was
redeemed from Egypt by virtue of its righteous women, Mishnah Sotah
11b)." Your acknowledgment that women too can be learned in Torah
implies an admirable respect for women's capacities ("Women have
greater faith than men," Sifre Numbers 133).

Therefore, I think it would make even you wince to read Maimonides'
instructions that if a wife refuses to carry out such wifely duties as wash-
ing her husband's hands and feet, or serving him at the table and making
his bed, she is to be chastised with rods (Yad, Ishut 21:3, 10); or Rabbi
Eliezer's warning that "whoever teaches his daughter Torah teaches her
obscenity" (Mishnah Sotah 3:4); or the Midrash's characterization of
women's qualities—greedy, eavesdroppers, lazy, and jealous (Genesis
Rabbah 45:5); or the suggestion that women are dishonest (Genesis Rabbah 18:2); or the implication that women are foolish or "light-minded"
(Shabbat 33b); or the linkage of women with witchcraft (Pirke Avot 2:8).

It might surprise you to hear that many non-Orthodox families share
a number of traits that you cite as common in Orthodox households.
For example, most of the families I have observed in my rabbinate consider their children to be their primary love and responsibility. If you
have any doubt about their desire to educate their children properly,
walk into any Reform synagogue religious school on Sunday morning
and witness the passion with which parents (mostly mothers) engage
the school's principal and teachers. I know many parents who, even in
the big city of New York, make tremendous financial sacrifices to ensure
their children's proper education.

Furthermore, your suggestion that the moral priorities of Orthodox
families are children, marriage, money, and career, in that order, and
that the priorities of non-Orthodox families are exactly reverse, is taking
undue license in describing both Orthodox and non-Orthodox families.
And in any case, all of these priorities are really interlocking and inter-
woven, making it impossible to neatly isolate them from the general
purposes and reality of family life.

Many ultra-Orthodox parents and grandparents live largely unhappy
lives. In Israel, for example, many are very poor, and worse, they have
transmitted this poverty to their offspring. Many of their children and

grandchildren cannot afford even basic necessities, and live off the largesse of the state, that is, taxes mostly paid by non-Orthodox Jews. Many ultra-Orthodox parents and grandparents in Israel have children and grandchildren who are intolerant, militant, and violate many of the commandments you have cited—especially the obligation to love your fellow Jew.

Now I am being very careful not to generalize. I am not suggesting that all or even the majority of ultra-Orthodox families live this way. But enough do to make it a common phenomenon. I simply suggest to you that the question of who lives the more fulfilling life is really quite irrelevant. If ultra-Orthodox families find satisfaction and they do not do harm to others, that is okay. But their family life, which, as I said, contains many fine virtues, is not a useful model for most people. In fact, it is allowed to exist in Israel precisely because of the alternative lifestyle of the majority of Israeli Jews who sponsor and subsidize it.

This is a distortion of Jewish values. Judaism never saw great romance or virtue in poverty. Poverty is debilitating. It chips away at a person's and a community's self-esteem. It encourages corruption and, in Israel, political extortion. Of course, wealth is not the be-all and end-all of existence. But without money Torah cannot be studied, schools cannot be built, and families and societies cannot maximize their potential. Most of the great Jewish scholars of history worked. They studied and taught to the best of their ability, but they also earned a living. I think that most of our great historical scholars would be dismayed to observe the state of contemporary ultra-Orthodoxy in Israel and many other places, which justifies its way of life by invoking the values of these great scholars.

Jewish family life must allow for the full expression, legitimacy, and equality of women. If the women themselves choose to live the lifestyle you describe, fine (although some later regret this). But do not suggest that your model is the only model. There are numerous non-Orthodox families that live admirable, productive, and authentically Jewish lives.

These families encourage and sustain Jewish continuity. They are the majority, and no matter how many children are born into ultra-Orthodox families, it is these non-Orthodox families that will bear the brunt of responsibility for the future of Judaism. They raise Jewish children. They study Judaism and are observant to the best of their abilities. They join synagogues, often at great expense and financial sacrifice. They are the ones who support their synagogues and keep them alive. They are charitable to Jewish and non-Jewish causes. They practice true *tzedakah*—not merely charity in the secular sense, but when they give money, they see it as fulfilling a central Jewish obligation to bring justice to the world.

Many Orthodox institutions survive through the generosity of these non-Orthodox families!

These families want to be part of, and help shape, society, and they reject the approach you described earlier that seeks to be sheltered from modern culture. They place at the center of their values the Jewish obligation to perfect the world. They take seriously the Jewish challenge to be a light unto the nations. They work hard to provide for their families.

I would like to comment specifically on two additional points you made:

1. Regarding the charitable impulse of Orthodox families, my general impression is that you are correct in describing Orthodox Jews as charitable. Some Orthodox families are exceedingly generous. This is a trait that is worthy of admiration and emulation. However, Orthodox charity tends to be parochial. It mostly goes to Orthodox institutions. Very little goes to non-Jewish causes, and even in the Jewish community, Orthodox, and especially ultra-Orthodox, contributions do not tend to go to the main institutions of Jewish life serving the entire Jewish community. Ultra-Orthodox contributions to the federations, the Jewish National Fund, Israel Bonds, and the various agencies that deal with Klal Yisrael—the community-at-large—are not proportionate.

2. Your views about the differences between men and women are the basis of your justification of women's role in the house. You graciously use the term "minister of internal affairs" to describe her authority over household matters, but I wonder. For all intents and purposes, your view is that a woman's place is in the house. You assert that if she has any time left over she might be free to pursue other interests, including earning additional money for the household. But how many women will have substantial time left over after four, five, six, or more children?

This then becomes the basis for your argument that women should not be encouraged to study. In your view (quoting the Talmud), they should not even be encouraged to study a little bit! "A little knowledge is a dangerous thing," you write. It has nothing to do with their innate capacity, you say. You even cite two women who accomplished great feats. It is just that almost all women do not have the time. You write, "It is almost always a choice—the home or the Talmud, not both." (This is not the view of ben Azzai, who states that "a man is obligated to teach Torah to his daughter," Sotah 20a).

But you make no such time distinction for boys and men. Most boys do not grow up to be talmudic scholars. Most men do not spend nearly as much time as you do studying Talmud. You have no hesitation to teach them. In fact, you urge such men to study a *daf yomi*—a daily page of Talmud—even if they cannot do more than that. Well, why isn't "a little knowledge a dangerous thing" for men?

Further, if, in fact, the reason for discouraging women from studying and assuming communal leadership is their responsibilities at home, then isn't it also the case that study and leadership would be available to women if they did not have such onerous family responsibilities? Many women could fall into this category. Unmarried women, childless women, and women whose children are adults, under your analysis, should be able to study and assert communal leadership.

And if you were to argue that Talmud study must begin early in life in order to master it, then how do you explain men who came to study later in life and became leaders of their communities. The great sage Akiva did not even begin to study until the age of forty!

You will forgive me if I am more than a bit skeptical about your assertions that it is only the different roles that men and women assume that prevent women from public and communal leadership. "It is almost always a choice—the home or the Talmud, not both," you write. Well, if you say it is a choice, then some women will choose Talmud. Am I correct to assume then that you would have no problem if she chooses Talmud? And if she chooses Talmud couldn't she do as well in her studies as men? And if so, why couldn't she become a communal leader? Why not a rabbi or a cantor? (Michal, the daughter of King Saul, would lay *tefillin,* according to the Talmud [Eruvin 96a], and the Sages did not attempt to prevent her.)

I think that the real reason has little to do with a woman's time management or life choices. It is rather connected to ultra-Orthodoxy's sense of where a woman belongs—in the home. You come closer to the truth when you describe the problems of modesty. It is not modest for women to assume equal roles. It overly tempts men, who are unable to control their sexual urges. Any public or self-expression of women is discouraged because of men's inability to control themselves. ("The voice of a woman is indecent," Berachot 24a) Hence separating women behind a barrier in synagogue; hence discouraging or prohibiting their communal roles.

Despite your protestations and my belief that you personally are respectful of women, I suspect that deep within part of the tradition's approach is a disrespect for women's intellect and character; perhaps fear of women or simply "this is their role." Even regarding the two women you mentioned as achieving great "manly" feats, Deborah and Beruriah, part of the tradition just couldn't resist a few digs. Deborah is compared to a wasp (Megillah 14b). Beruriah was described as having been seduced by one of her students and was said to have committed suicide (Rashi).

Yosef, the proper analogy is not, as you suggested, "Which is the more important part of a car, the wheels or the engine? They are equal because one is worthless without the other."

Rather, it is more like the driver and the passenger. Men and women are both necessary for the vehicle called Judaism. But men constructed the traffic laws. The police are men. The judges are men. In the ultra-Orthodox community men are in the driver's seat. You navigate the traffic laws of life and look back from time to time in the rearview mirror asking your women where they want to go, but reminding them that some places—the positions of communal visibility and influence—and thus authority and power—are off-limits.

Again, if women are prepared to accept this role, okay. I know many people who do not like to drive. They prefer to be in the backseat. But if the purpose of a car is to take you from one place to another, the driver of the car determines the direction and speed. The passenger might have influence. She might even become a sort of backseat driver. Still, all the advice in the world will not get you there. The driver gets you to your destination.

In Orthodox law, women are inferior in their inheritance rights. Women are inferior in divorce law. Only a woman can occupy the inferior status of *agunah*—unable to remarry because she is figuratively "chained" to a husband whose whereabouts are unknown.

Women are inferior in positions of communal authority and public responsibility. (Yosef, there is a difference between saying women can become rabbis, cantors, witnesses, judges, only they do not want to, and saying that women are prohibited from so doing, or events so conspire against them as to make it virtually impossible to accomplish such aspirations.)

In the more liberal Jewish movements there is an effort to practice full equality, and I concede that it involves breaking the historical mold. It is much more relevant to the vast numbers of Jews than the model you are proposing. There is ample room in Jewish tradition to comfort us on our search. Even the Almighty is often described as the shekhinah—the feminine manifestation of God.

Yosef, as we conclude the first part of our discussion, I strongly recommend that you take a look at *Beyond Reasonable Doubt* by Rabbi Louis Jacobs (Littman Library of Jewish Civilization). In it is a wonderful discussion of some of the issues we have raised, including an analysis of Ibn Ezra's commentaries, the talmudic passages of Baba Metzia and Menachot, and the role of human beings in the development of Jewish laws and traditions.

Ammi

PART TWO

May 24, 2000

Dear Ammi,

Have you ever visited anti-Semitic sites on the Internet? I did when I first got my Internet service, and I haven't been back there since. Once is far more than enough. Still, I don't regret having done it. I wanted to see what our enemies have to say. I wanted to know what evil lurks in the hearts of hateful men. It is astonishing.

I visited about a half-dozen white-supremacist sites. (I also peeked in on the Nation of Islam and Hamas, a real fun evening.) The things they say about us would make your hair stand on end. Most of the hate propaganda is off the wall, but some of it is slick, sophisticated, and strangely persuasive.

One link led me to another, and soon I found myself in Holocaust denial sites. If you followed the David Irving libel suit in the British courts, you're familiar with much of what I saw there. According to the Holocaust deniers, fewer than 100,000 Jews died in German concentration camps during the War, primarily from disease. There were no gas chambers, no atrocities, no genocide. The statistics are lies. The photographs are fakes. Some of the stones at Auschwitz were tested, they report, and no traces of gas were found, clearly proving that everything was a Jewish hoax, a Zionist plot to gain the sympathy of the Allies and coerce them into giving Palestine to the Jews. The whole Holocaust was nothing more than a ruse by cunning Jews to give the world an undeserved guilt trip.

As the son of Holocaust survivors, of course, I find Holocaust denial to be nonsense. I am practically a Holocaust survivor myself. I was born just a few years after the War here in New York. My father is the sole survivor of a large rabbinic family from Galicia in southeastern Poland. His mother, all his brothers and sisters, and all their children perished in the ghettos and the camps; his father died a year before the War. My father was saved only because he was drafted into a forced-labor battalion by the retreating Soviet Army in 1941. My mother's family in Kiev fared better. They fled to Samarkand in Uzbekistan. But my mother's grandfather remained behind and was shot in Babi Yar. As a child, many of the adults I knew were Holocaust survivors. Years later I had the privilege of editing a series of personal memoirs called the Holocaust Diaries, and I had occasion to interview many survivors at length.

No one can deny the Holocaust to me. It is firmly implanted in my memory, and it will be there forever. No one can deny it to my children either because they too have met and spoken to many survivors. But what about my grandchildren? And what about their children?

Yesterday, our daughter came to visit us with her adorable three-year-old and one-year-old daughters. They are so sweet and innocent, so trusting, and I wondered if they would ever know the extent of the hatred that innumerable people in the world harbor against them just because they are Jewish. They will surely run up against anti-Semitism all too often in their lives, in one form or another. It would be naïve to think otherwise. But would they be aware of the depths of inhumanity to which our enemies can descend? Would they know about the Holocaust? Would they know that 6 million of their people were brutally slaughtered by murderers with a cultured veneer?

Imagine a hypothetical scenario, which is unfortunately becoming increasingly less hypothetical. The time is one century in the future. Holocaust revisionism is growing. The public is unsure if the Holocaust is historical fact or myth. Germany protests her innocence and offers huge sums for objective research. Scholars painstakingly evaluate the evidence. They cross-reference and check the records for consistency. They examine the photographs under high-powered microscopes. They review the transcripts of the Nuremberg and Eichmann trials. They read all the books about the alleged Holocaust written during the second half of the twentieth century and beyond, and they critically analyze the scholarship. And what is the result? Many scholars proclaim their *belief* that there was a Holocaust. Others insist that although the evidence is strong it is not conclusive. "How can we actually know it happened?" they say. "We have no direct evidence, and therefore, we can only surmise it." The subject remains unresolved in the academic community, and doubt is firmly and widely planted in the public mind. The Holocaust is well on its way to becoming a myth.

Ridiculous, you say? How can a preponderance of evidence be denied? Well, we don't have to go much further than the O. J. Simpson trial for the answer. O.J. did not claim temporary insanity or mitigating circumstances. His defense was outright denial, and he pulled it off. Was he guilty? How can I know? Today, there are many people who are convinced he is guilty, but a century from now they probably will be few and far between. All people will know is that doubt was established and that he was given the benefit of the doubt.

So what about my great-great-grandchildren who will be living a hundred years from now? I don't realistically expect to be around to set them straight, so what will they think? How will they know that the Holocaust really happened?

For one thing, they will have the benefit of the Jewish transferal process. We Jewish people have a great talent for transferring knowledge into the future with incredible accuracy.

It happens that I am descended on my mother's side from the Baal Shem Tov, the eighteenth-century mystic who founded the Hasidic movement in the Ukraine. The Baal Shem Tov had a lifelong desire to immigrate to the Holy Land, but when he passed away in 1760, he was still in the Ukraine. About twenty years earlier he had actually attempted the journey, but he got only as far as the Greek isles. A close brush with death persuaded him to turn back.

The Baal Shem Tov reached safety in Constantinople on the last day of Passover, and in gratitude to the Almighty he thenceforth made a feast of thanksgiving at that time every year. He also instructed that his descendants for ten generations do so as well. I am a ninth-generation descendant, and in my family, we observe this hallowed custom scrupulously. Every year, ever since I can remember, we gather around a food-laden table in the synagogue or in the home of a family member at the close of Passover, and we retell the story of the Baal Shem Tov's providential deliverance from a storm at sea.

This past Passover, it was my turn to host the "Baal Shem Tov Seudah" for my family. I also invited a number of friends and neighbors. I told the story to a rapt audience, and afterward we sang and talked and ate, not necessarily in that order. It was beautiful, as always.

The story I told is exactly as I heard it from my grandfather every year until he passed away thirty-five years ago at the age of eighty. He had heard the story from his father-in-law some sixty years earlier. (We have already jumped one century into the past!) Now, my great-grandfather heard the story from his own grandfather, who heard it from Rabbi Baruch of Medzibezh, the Baal Shem Tov's grandson, who heard it directly from the Baal Shem Tov every year as he was growing up.

In the nearly three centuries since this story took place, it passed through four trustworthy hands between the Baal Shem Tov and me, as it also did along hundreds of parallel lines of descent. I and the thousands of other descendants of the Baal Shem Tov who have received this tradition know that the Baal Shem Tov told this story at his table in the waning hours of Passover every single year after he returned to the Ukraine, as surely as if we had been sitting there ourselves. The story itself we have to believe, but we know for a fact that the Baal Shem Tov told this particular story at that particular time.

My grandchildren will know that the Holocaust took place, because they will hear about it from their parents and their teachers, who will have heard about it from their parents and teachers. Is this called knowing? It is.

How do we know anything to be true? There are essentially two ways, direct observation and secondhand knowledge. Most of what we know is from secondhand knowledge. If we were to limit ourselves to direct observation, we would know nothing of history or science or just about anything else. We could not rely on textbooks or information we hear from others. If we undergo an operation, how would we know the surgeon had gone to medical school? When we board a plane, how would we know the pilot had been trained to fly? We put our lives on the line without direct knowledge that it is safe to do so. Clearly, we must accept some secondhand knowledge in order to be able to function as normal human beings.

Still, we cannot be gullible. So how do we determine if we should give credibility to secondhand knowledge? Since we have no way of making a direct evaluation, we must do so by inference. Either the information is true or it is false. If we can show it is unreasonable to consider it false, then it is reasonable to consider it true. If it is unreasonable to believe the pilot is an impostor, then it is reasonable to step on to the plane.

So let us consider. Why would secondhand knowledge be false? There are a few possibilities. The provider of the information may be ignorant or mistaken or a liar. If we can eliminate these possibilities, then it is reasonable to assume that the information is true.

It is easy to deal with the issue of ignorance or mistakes. We just need to determine if the provider has the intelligence to get it right. If the information is simple, we can trust an average person. If it is more complex, then we would feel more confident with the testimony of an expert. If a person told you it rained yesterday, you would not think he was mistaken. But if he told you there had been an atmospheric inversion, you would want to know if he is a meteorologist.

The issue of credibility is thornier. How can we be sure information has not been deliberately fabricated? One of the strongest proofs is to hear the same information from many sources. If one person were to tell me that a train was derailed in Nebraska, I might be somewhat doubtful. But if I heard it from many people and on all the news stations, I would accept it as having happened. We do not assume that there are universal conspiracies to fool us unless we suffer from acute paranoia.

This then is how we determine the reliability of secondhand knowledge. Simple information from many sources is true. Complex information from a single inexpert source is most likely untrue. Anything that falls into the gray areas in between is subject to varying degrees of doubt.

Therefore, if countless Jewish people testify that there was a Holocaust, we can safely accept it as reliable secondhand knowledge. They cannot all be lying.

Admittedly, this may not be proof for a German youngster who is predisposed to disbelieve the Holocaust. He has no problem claiming that all the Jews who are part of this transferal process are liars and villains. Germans have accused Jews of worse things and attempted to exterminate all of us. But my grandchildren will know that Jews are wonderful people, and they will know that the transferal process is reliable and has been proved to be exceedingly accurate.

For example, take the idea of genealogies, which are quite popular today. We have been keeping genealogical records for millennia. Thousands and thousands of Jewish people can trace their ancestors for hundreds of years until they link up with some of the recorded lineages that lead all the way back to biblical times. I can do this on my father's side and my mother's. Please look at the old genealogies in Dzherba, Tunisia, and all the other genealogies on record in the Diaspora Museum in Tel Aviv. They go back thousands of years. When Queen Elizabeth's ancestors were illiterate savages in the German forests, thousands of our people had distinguished genealogies as long as my arm. And they are clearly not inventions, because they are intertwined with each other. To fabricate all of them so that they will be consistent with each other would have required a vast diabolical plot supported by a good mainframe computer at the least.

During the Temple eras priests could not participate in the Temple service unless they could prove their lineage all the way back to Aaron or one of his known descendants; as we read in Ezra (2:62), after the return from Babylon certain families "sought their genealogy scrolls but could not find them, and they were excluded from the priesthood." Furthermore, a Kohein could only marry an Israelite woman who produced a genealogy. A judge could only be appointed to the Sanhedrin if he produced a genealogy. We took these things very seriously. Even in Reform congregations today, I am sure there is little question about who is a Kohein and who is not. Jews have long memories and keep good records.

About a year ago, I read an amazing report in the *New York Times*. A team of geneticists has done an extensive study of Kohanim, similar to the Hemings-Jefferson research, and they discovered that Kohanim share one common gene, clear proof of one common ancestor. Aaron!

This is also clear proof of the efficacy of the transferal process.

We also know the teacher-to-teacher transferal process, which has been documented conscientiously throughout history all the way back to biblical times. I refer you to Raphael Halperin's *Atlas Atzei Chaim* in Hebrew. It is impossible not to be impressed by all those pages of tables and charts presenting the continuity of the teaching process through the ages in minute detail. Unfortunately, the teacher-to-teacher process cannot be confirmed by a common gene in the soul.

We, the Jewish people, have always been very focused on genealogy. A large part of the Bible is devoted to names and relationships. Read the First Book of Chronicles! The Talmud (Baba Batra 91a) identifies Abraham's mother as Amathalia the daughter of Karnebo. There is no mention of this name in the Bible, and yet the Jewish transferal process preserved it orally for fifteen hundred years! Bible critics laughed this name off as pure invention, and they proved their case by the absence of a name such as Karnebo in any Babylonian records. Well, lo and behold, archaeologists have since discovered new Babylonian records in Ebla that mention the name Karnebo as a royal family name. You say you would be "fascinated by archaeological proof of Abraham's existence." How about archaeological support of Abraham's grandfather's existence? Does that do anything for you?

And what about the accuracy of our Torah scrolls? Some years ago, a comparison was made of extant manuscript copies of the Christian Bible reproduced by monks over the centuries. They discovered over 150,000 variations. Of these, fully 400 affected the meaning of the text, and 50 actually resulted in important differences. We can assume this was not intentional, just the natural error factor resulting from a thousand years of laborious copying and recopying in dusty monastery scriptoria.

In startling contrast, an examination of Torah scrolls from all over the world, from Ireland to Siberia to isolated Yemen, all handwritten by scribes, yielded just nine instances of one-letter spelling discrepancies. Nine! And none of them affect the meaning of the text. Why is this so? Because every week we take out the scrolls and read them in public. The people follow the reading closely, and if something is wrong, they are quick to point it out.

Think about it. Here were monks sitting in the security and serenity of their scriptoria, trying to be accurate and faithful to the original, which is only half the size of the Torah, and still, they produced over a hundred thousand variations. At the same time, we oppressed and persecuted Jews, whose books were so often confiscated and incinerated, managed to reproduce our scrolls with near-perfect accuracy in far-flung communities that were not in touch with each other.

What does this tell us about the integrity of our transferal process? What does this tell us about the Jewish people?

So when I speculate about how our grandchildren will be affected by Holocaust denial, I can be sure they will not consider it a Jewish myth. But how much will they really know? How much will they really believe? I can just hear them talking. "Sure, there was a Holocaust, but the information might have become somewhat exaggerated over the years. Were there actually six million victims? Were old people, women, and children actually killed in gas chambers? Can it really be true that Nazi officers smashed babies' heads against the walls and then went back to their quarters to listen to Mozart? Did Nazi doctors really do all sorts of ghastly medical experiments on young Jewish twins? Come on, something bad must have happened, but do you expect us to believe all these outlandish stories?"

So how do we convince them? What can we possibly do to make sure our descendants never forget the Holocaust in all its horrid detail?

Only one sort of evidence is truly convincing—the testimony of many witnesses. Modern technology has shown us that documents, photographs, and even videos can be falsified. But the testimony of witnesses will always have credibility. Everything can be disputed—except for testimony. If there had been five witnesses to the Nicole Simpson murder, the person they accused, O.J. or otherwise, would most probably have been convicted.

Hearing Holocaust survivors, hundreds of thousands of them, tell the story of their experiences, hearing their solemn testimony—that is truly compelling. You cannot listen to so many people telling the same gruesome story and think they are lying or mistaken, not if they are your own people, not if you consider Jewish people credible. But nearly sixty years have passed since the Holocaust. I read in the *New York Times* that Israeli government figures show that there are only 230,000 survivors left in Israel, and that 20,000 have died since 1997. The *Times* gave no figures for the rest of the world, but you get the picture. Within a decade or two, hardly any living survivors of the Holocaust will remain. There will be no one left to give testimony, and the wheels of outright Holocaust denial or revisionism will move into higher gear.

Since our descendants will not hear the testimony of survivors, how can we preserve for them the integrity of the Holocaust record?

Years ago, I read about a proposal that would work—if it could be implemented. It goes as follows:

All the Holocaust survivors and their children are brought together from all over the world for an international convention. Difficult logistically, but possible. A major statement that gives a detailed account of the Holocaust experience is read in public in front of all the survivors, and they all bear witness to its truth and accuracy. This forms the essence of the testimony, which will henceforth be called the Shoah Manifesto.

All the survivors and their children form an organization called the Shoah Society. The purpose of this society is to perpetuate the testimony of the survivors, to keep it alive and immediate as it was on the day it was given. The members of the Society accept a set of rules. Every week, Society members congregate to pay their respects to the victims and to read sections of the Shoah Manifesto aloud. Three times a year, all Society members conduct special ceremonies. During the Festival of Liberation, they commemorate the day the survivors were liberated by eating tiny crusts of bread, as they did in the camps, and reading from the Manifesto. During the Festival of Ships, they all leave their homes and live on boats to commemorate the experiences of the displaced persons that emigrated to Israel and the United States after the Holocaust. During the Festival of the Formation of the Society, they gather in meeting halls and read the entire Manifesto in public.

Every child born into the Shoah Society has a blue number tattooed on his right forearm. As he grows up, he is taught to read the Manifesto until it becomes very familiar to him. Members of the Society, who are to be known as Shoah Witnesses, are forbidden to marry out of the Society, in order to maintain the integrity of their mission. If someone wants to join the Society, he can, as long as he accepts all its rules.

Shoah Witnesses wear yellow *Jude* stars on their outer garments, and they use no products manufactured in Germany. They also affix scrolls containing important parts of the Manifesto, in tubes wrapped in barbed wire, to their doorposts. Finally, each Shoah Witness participates in producing a handwritten scroll of the Manifesto, which is considered a major fulfillment of his mission.

The rules are precise and cannot be violated. Should someone insist on wearing a pink *Jude* star instead of a yellow one, for instance, he would be ejected from the Society; the rules clearly call for a yellow star.

The formation of the Shoah Society and all its rules are written into the Manifesto itself, together with a cardinal rule that the Manifesto may never be altered, either by addition or subtraction.

The Manifesto also calls for and describes the distribution process. Handwritten copies on parchment are to be made for every geographical group of survivors to take home with them, and they are enjoined to make more copies when they come home, thereby giving the Manifesto as wide a distribution as possible among the Shoah Witnesses.

In addition, the Manifesto instructs that it be inscribed in its entirety on a large marble slab, so that Shoah Witnesses can check the accuracy of their scrolls in the intermediate period during which the scroll is reproduced and distributed throughout the world. All this is to safeguard its integrity.

The Manifesto is completed and distributed according to the instructions inscribed within it. The living testimony of the survivors is now encapsulated in the Manifesto and preserved for the ages.

Over the years, many descendants of the survivors leave the Society, but many others remain true to the mission of their ancestors. One hundred years later, there are millions of Shoah Witnesses living in every corner of the world. Their copies of the Manifesto, millions of them, are all identical, and the Shoah Witnesses themselves are instantly recognizable to each other by their customs and traditions.

The system is tight. There is no room for falsification. When could such a lie have been introduced? How could they have gotten so many people to assume the mantle of Shoah Witnesses and to champion a Manifesto that is clearly untrue?

Granted, the testimony of the Shoah Witnesses proves there was a Holocaust. But does it prove all the details are true? Of course it does, because the Shoah Witnesses testify not only to the Holocaust itself but also to the creation of the Shoah Manifesto during the lifetime of the survivors, with their approval, and its distribution to all of them.

From that point on, the Manifesto speaks for itself, since its credentials as the genuine testimony of the survivors have been established. From that point on, whoever reads the Manifesto hears the courageous, pain-filled voices of the survivors speaking to him clearly across the chasm of years, centuries, and millennia.

Quite a creative idea, wouldn't you say? Obviously, we will not see anything of the sort take place.

All this was an analogy, of course. Something of this sort did indeed take place, not with regard to the Holocaust but with regard to God's revelation to the Jewish people and the covenant He forged with them.

You write, "Modern thought has demonstrated for me conclusively that the Torah was written by human beings. . . . A day in any decent library will allow our readers to see scores of sources documenting the evidence." You throw out this remark in such a casual way, as if any half-intelligent person would be forced to bow to the wisdom of these unspecified arguments and proofs. In one fell swoop, you have endorsed the writings of the Torah deniers as the absolute truth—even though you claim there is no absolute truth—and declared three thousand years of Jewish thought to be nothing more than falsehood. I know you claim to find moral value in the writings of the great sages of Jewish history, but they weren't coming to convey moral values. They were giving testimony to the truth of the Torah.

You understand that Holocaust deniers can obfuscate the truth with fine-sounding words and scholarly research to the point where even our own grandchildren might be confused. But you fail to see that the Torah deniers have done a similar job to the point where even some of our own people, including you, have bought into their way of thinking.

You once mentioned to me that you sense distress in my writing. You are right. Shouldn't I be distressed when I see my fellow Jews hooked by Torah deniers?

This "documented evidence" to which you refer is surely the school of so-called Higher Criticism, which denies the truth of the Torah and the archaeological record, which if anything supports the reliability of the transferal process. We need to examine this evidence briefly but sharply in future postings. For the present, however, let us talk about the evidence in favor of the Torah.

Let's begin with the Kuzari's proof, which I touched on earlier in the context of the Holocaust. It is impossible, he explains, to invent a story of national impact that an entire people supposedly witnessed and convince the direct descendants of these supposed witnesses that it is true. It simply cannot be done. People will inevitably object to it and say, "If this is true, why didn't we ever hear about it?"

The Torah relates the story of the age of revelation, forty years that spanned the spectacular Exodus from Egypt, God's revelation to the people at Mount Sinai, forty years of manna falling from Heaven, forty years of the most marvelous miracles, forty years during which God forged an everlasting covenant with the Jewish people, forty years during which the Jewish people were instructed in numerous observances that transformed their daily lives. Could someone come along and sell such a story to a people without encountering fierce resistance? "What kind of ridiculous stories are you telling us? Don't you think we would have heard about this if it were true? If all the people witnessed these miracles, why didn't my father tell me about it? My grandfather?" A myth such as this would never be accepted. The Torah makes this point in Exodus (19:9): "I will come to you in a thick cloud, so that all the people will hear when I speak to you, then they will also believe in you forever." And again in Deuteronomy (4:32): "For ask now of the early days that preceded you from the day God created people on the earth, from one end of heaven to the other, if there was ever such a great thing, or *if anything like it was ever heard. . . .*"

The introduction of Christianity or Islam faced no such difficulties. The Christian story was popularized during Paul's travels in Europe. He told them about stories without national impact that happened to undefined groups of people in a foreign country many years earlier. No one could object: "Hey, why didn't we ever hear about these things?" There were no published accounts, no formal testimonies. Why then should Romans, Corinthians, and Galatians have heard about things irrelevant to them?

The same applies to Islam. Wouldn't Mohammed have been thrilled to have God anoint him as the one true prophet before a gathering of millions of Arabs around the Qaaba Stone in Mecca? But he didn't dare make such a claim. People would have laughed him out of town. Instead, he met privately with the angel Gabriel in a cave. A low-risk story. Take it or leave it. The Koran itself claims no miraculous proof, only that its wisdom could not have been composed by an illiterate camel driver.

Wouldn't it have been convincing if Jesus had skimmed over every rooftop in Israel and Europe and blessed the people after he supposedly rose from the dead? But of course, no one would dare make such a claim. Instead, only a few people were privileged to see the empty tomb and tell the rest of the world about it. A low-risk story. Take it or leave it.

Judaism, however, dares to claim revelation, and not just any revelation but forty consecutive years of spectacular miracles. This cannot be a lie. No one would have accepted it.

Christianity and Islam, therefore, have to draw their legitimacy from Judaism's public revelation, to appropriate it for themselves by claiming to be the natural successors to Judaism. They are the ones who stand on the shoulders of our Jewish ancestors, Ammi, not you. They accept the truths of our ancestors, but they insist that they have progressed further. You, on the other hand, make our ancestors out to be deluded dupes (of whom?).

One more point about Christians and Muslims. There is an old saying that "fathers do not lie to their children." Certainly not about significant matters. Christians tell their children that Paul came and told them such-and-such stories. This is true. Paul did tell these stories. Muslims tell their children that Mohammed said he spoke to the angel Gabriel. This is also true. Mohammed did say it. Our ancestors told their children that God spoke to the entire Jewish nation. They did not lie to their children either.

Let us now take the Kuzari's powerful proof one giant step further. There is another element here besides a spectacular story that could not have been invented. There is also a book called the Torah, our own Manifesto of the Revelation Witnesses.

Have you ever wondered why Deuteronomy 31 speaks about the punishments for disobedience after we just had a very long and bone-chilling exposition of the punishments in Deuteronomy 28? Was it just sloppy editing by our semiliterate forebears who were always making blatant editorial bloopers, such as those duplicate and contradictory creation stories you found at the beginning of the Bible? (The classic commentaries on Genesis are very enlightening on this question.)

The answer is as follows. Deuteronomy 28 exhorts the people to avoid the dire consequences of disobedience. Deuteronomy 31 addresses an altogether different problem. Listen to the words. "And God said to Moses, 'Behold, you are about to go to rest with your ancestors, and these people will get up and wander off after the alien gods of the land, and they will abandon Me and violate the covenant I forged with them. My anger will flare on that day, and I will abandon them and hide My face from them, and they will be helpless, and great misfortunes and troubles will come upon them, and they will say on that day that it is because our Lord is not among us that these misfortunes have befallen us. . . .'"

This is the problem God is addressing. He knows there will be lapses among the people and that He will hide His face and all the manifestations of His Presence and let them suffer. And He knows that this will open the door to Christians and Muslims who will claim that God has canceled the covenant. (It would incidentally also open the door to heretics who will claim that there never was a covenant, that everything is a myth.) In order to defend against these eventualities, God sets up safeguards.

Let us read further. "And now, write for yourselves this poem and teach it to the people of Israel, place it in their mouths, in order that this poem will serve as My witness to the people of Israel. . . . And should it happen that great misfortunes and troubles befall them, then this poem will speak out to them as *a witness that it will not be forgotten* from their children. . . ."

The starkly beautiful poem that follows, promising the eternity of the covenant, is incorporated in the Torah. All the safeguards are also in the Torah. "You shall not add to the word I command you, nor may you subtract from it." (Deuteronomy 4:2) Shabbat and the festivals, the *mezuzah* on the door, as well as numerous other commandments and observances recall those forty years of revelation.

Here is the creation of the Manifesto. Copies of the Torah are distributed to all the tribes, and each individual Jew, in the final commandment of the Torah, is required to participate directly in producing a Torah scroll. The Manifesto itself mandates immediate and very wide distribution to preserve the testimony it contains. In addition, the Torah was inscribed on huge stone slabs and planted on the soil of the Promised Land as soon as the people crossed the Jordan River (Deuteronomy 27:2).

Here now is the Kuzari's proof in its full force. No one can now claim that the Torah was introduced hundreds of years later. First of all, why have we never heard about an event of such national importance? Second, how could such a document of living testimony be fabricated? People would have said, "If this is an authentic book, why don't we already have it? According to what is written here, it was distributed widely centuries ago to the original witnesses. There should be many thousands of these scrolls in existence. Where are they?" And they would reject it as a fake.

But they didn't reject it, did they? They embraced it, which proves that it was written and distributed right then and there, when the people stood across the Jordan River, poised to enter Canaan. These people who had just spent forty years in the Desert bore testimony to the truth of what is written in the Torah, to all the miraculous manifestations and revelations they witnessed. Their living testimony comes down to us, hermetically sealed in the Torah and protected from tampering. It is because of them, our ancestors, that we don't just believe in the truth of the Torah. We know it.

(This system was used once again during the Babylonian exile to perpetuate the memory of the Purim story. You wrote that you don't believe it happened. I believe it did. The last section of the Megillah describes the creation of the scroll and its distribution [Esther 9:30–32]: "And he sent letters to all the Jews, to the hundred and twenty-seven provinces of the kingdom of Ahasuerus . . . as Mordechai and Queen Esther had instructed them . . . and it was written in the book." It would have been impossible to publish such a book a century or two later if the scroll itself declares, at such length and in such detail, that it was already well known throughout the Jewish world right from the beginning.)

For the thousands of years since the distribution of our Manifesto, these Torah Witnesses, the Jewish people, have been the custodians of the testimony. We circumcise our children. We wear *tefillin* and *tzitzit*, and we place *mezuzot* on our doorposts. We observe Shabbat. We celebrate our festivals to commemorate those seminal years. We have transported this living testimony down though the ages, and we will carry it into the future.

True, many of our people are no longer faithful to the rules of our Society, and they have thereby relinquished their role as Witnesses. But there are enough faithful Witnesses left in the world to ensure the continued viability of the Torah. And there will always be. God promised that the Torah will never be completely forgotten.

Many people have forgotten the Torah. They have become separated from the Jewish transferal process. They have no memory of the Exodus, Mount Sinai, manna from Heaven. They believe it is all myth. But not to me, nor to any of the Witnesses. We protect the living testimony of our ancestors and are not reluctant to present it to the rest of the world. The evidence is there. All they have to do is look at it.

Earlier we discussed the Passover Seder. Have you ever wondered why more secular Jewish families have a Seder than attend Yom Kippur services? You might say it is because the Seder celebrates the birth of Jewish nationhood, but that doesn't really account for the inordinate emphasis all Jews place on it, even in the most secular *kibbutzim*. I think it is rather because the Seder is a critical element in the transferal process. It focuses on *vehigadeta levincha*, "telling the children," with an elaborate ritual, symbols, stories, and recitations. Over the centuries and millennia, this ritual has become so deeply ingrained in the Jewish psyche because of its importance that all Jews instinctively honor it— even if they don't know why.

Incidentally, do you remember telling me a while ago about a book by Lawrence Hoffman that claimed the Seder was copied from the Roman symposium? I've sought out the book and read it. Mr. Hoffman says that there was a Roman custom called the symposium in which people would get together for a meal and then settle down for some discussion. Since the Seder also features a meal and discussion, it must have been borrowed from the symposium. Mr. Hoffman then generously admits that all this is "somewhat speculative."

No, the Seder was not copied from the Romans. It was ancient before the Romans arrived on the scene. (Professor W. F. Albright proves that the Greek *alpha beta* is derived from the Hebrew *aleph bet*, because these words have meaning in Hebrew (Shabbat 104a) but not in Greek. The Greeks and Romans copied us, Ammi, not vice versa. Certainly not with something as important as the Seder.)

And there is a much more fundamental difference between the Seder and the symposium. The Seder is not a discussion. It is a transferal ritual, the formal fulfillment of "telling the children," repeated year after year, century after century, at first over the paschal sacrifice and afterward in the present form. It follows exactly the formula described in the Torah (Exodus 13:8): "And when your son asks you tomorrow, saying, 'What is this?' then you shall say to him, 'With strength of hand did God take us out of Egypt, of the house of bondage.'" Many more verses describe the Seder. It is the living transferal process of Judaism, and it will survive as long as we survive.

Listen to Psalms describe the transferal process (78:3–6). "Things we heard and have come to know, things our fathers have told us. We will not conceal them from the children, we declare God's praises to the next generation, His power and the wonders He performed. He installed testimonies in Jacob, set Teachings in Israel, which He commanded our fathers to tell their sons. Let the next generation know, let the sons to be born grow up and tell it to their own children."

The Holocaust too will be remembered only because of the extreme integrity of the Jewish transferal process. We have heard the testimony of the witnesses, and we know that the books and textbooks are the truth. Our grandchildren will accept them only because they know that our people and our transferal process are deserving of their trust.

There are also other strong proofs of the authenticity of the Torah.

First, if the Torah is no more than a manufactured founding document full of imaginative legends and myths, why does it treat the Jewish people so harshly? Why are their flaws examined at length and their virtues glossed over so quickly? The Jewish people spent forty years in the Desert, and we read at length about the shameful incidents of the Golden Calf, the Spies, the Korach Rebellion, the constant willfulness and obstinacy of the "stiff-necked" people. All these things took place during a two-year period. But what about the other thirty-eight years? Virtual silence. A quick glance into the Book of Judges gives the impression that the first four centuries in Israel were ceaselessly violent and sinful. But if you look more closely, you notice that every once in a while we are told, "And the land was tranquil for eighty years." Or, "And the land was tranquil for forty years." One sentence for the worthy generations, chapters for the unworthy. Surely this goes beyond the limits of even the worst Jewish self-deprecation.

And how about the law of the sabbatical year (for the land, not for professors and rabbis)? Let's look into Leviticus (25:2–21): "When you come into the land that I give you, then shall the land rest, a sabbath for God. Six years shall you plant your field and six years shall you prune your vineyard, and gather in its produce. But in the seventh year, there shall be a sabbath of rest for the land, a sabbath for God, you shall not plant your field nor prune your vineyard. . . . And if you shall say, 'What will we eat in the seventh year? Behold, we cannot plant nor gather in our produce,' then I will command My blessing for you in the sixth year, and it will yield enough produce for three years."

Hmm, as you would say.

Does this sound like something people would make up? Will it win them votes in the next election? And how exactly did they plan to deliver on the three-for-one crop in the sixth year?

And what about the annual pilgrimages to Jerusalem? Let's read in Exodus (34:24), "And no man will covet your land when you go up to see the face of God your Lord three times a year." All the people are to leave their lands unprotected and make the pilgrimage to Jerusalem. But don't worry, says God, I'll make sure no one takes advantage of your absence. This is really some kind of guarantee. Who would write such a thing and why? And how did they expect to deliver on this wild promise?

There are numerous proofs of this sort, Ammi. If you need more, I will gladly supply them.

I just want to go on record with two other categories of proof.

One is the very nature of the ideology expounded in the Torah. These were totally alien concepts to the pagan world into which they were being introduced. Love your neighbor as yourself. Be sensitive to widows and orphans. Leave a corner of your field for poor people. Where does all this come from? Who would dare propose such things in the pagan world? And why would anyone accept it?

Finally, I want to talk about prophecy. There is a famous story in which the Kaiser asks Bismarck, "Can you prove the existence of God?" Bismarck replies, "The Jews, your majesty. The Jews."

Our survival as a people despite our separation from our homeland, despite the hostility of our powerful neighbors, despite all the persecution and slaughter, is truly a miracle. I think you, Ammi, also mentioned that you see the divine hand in this. Who in his right mind could have imagined such a thing? And who in his right mind would have thought that today there would be millions of Jews living in Israel? The Christians were very shaken by the capture of Jerusalem in the Six-Day War. Their own prophecies assured them that the Jews would never return to Israel, but it happened! Yes, the Jewish people have survived and prospered against all odds. Who could have predicted such a thing?

Wonder of wonders, let us read from Leviticus 26: "And [if you disobey Me] I will destroy your high places and cut down your sun-pillars and cast your carcasses upon the carcasses of your idols. And I will lay waste your cities and devastate your sanctuaries. . . . And I will bring your land into desolation and your enemies that dwell in it shall be astonished by it. And I will scatter you among the nations and I will unsheathe the sword after you. . . . And yet for all that, when they are in the land of their enemies I will not reject them nor will I abhor them to destroy them utterly and to break My covenant with them, for I am God their Lord."

What an amazingly accurate and uncanny prediction of the next few thousand years of Jewish history! What an incredibly bold prediction of Jewish survival when by all rights we should have long disappeared! I think this prophecy is almost as miraculous as Jewish survival itself. This was not written by men. It couldn't have been.

"Prediction," writes Professor Wilhelm Jerusalem in his *Introduction to Philosophy*, "is the highest standard of proof."

I have a number of other comments regarding your last posting. I will leave them for next time. I have written enough for now.

Warmest regards,
Yosef

P.S. You mentioned that we have to do 613 *mitzvot* every day. In fact, most of these do not apply to everyday life. The only ones that really impact our lifestyle in a major way are Shabbat, festivals, and kosher.

But all *mitzvot,* if performed in the right spirit, deliver enough joy and fulfillment to make any inconvenience worthwhile.

June 6, 2000

Dear Ammi,

I was pleased to read, in your posting of May 23, your positive comments about the "minor temple" of Orthodox home life and the good fortune of all those who enjoy this blessing. I was also pleased that you discerned in my posting a genuine respect for women, which I certainly have. (I got a good chuckle from your first sentence, which deftly sidestepped some of my main arguments.)

You say that my portrayal of Orthodox life is idealized, and once again you are right. It is what an Orthodox home should be, although it sometimes is not. I haven't conducted a survey. Nonetheless, based on my own experience with friends, family, and associates, the idealized portrayal is quite commonplace.

We certainly have our share of problems in the Orthodox community. The Torah sets up a paradigm for us. Those who adhere to it more closely are the fortunate ones. Others may develop patterns of abuse. We do not condone them, nor do we excuse them. They are the symptoms of failure rather than success at Orthodox life.

You say Orthodox women stay in abusive marriages longer than other women. I would not dispute that. The same also applies to Orthodox men. In the Orthodox community, very great efforts are invested in saving troubled marriages. The Talmud tells us (Gittin 90b) that "when a man and a woman divorce even the altar in the Temple sheds tears over them." We do everything we can to avert the pain and suffering of divorce, especially for the children, who invariably suffer terrible but often unexpressed guilt and trauma as a result of a breakup.

"If the household you are describing is voluntary," you wrote, "I am happy for those who choose to live this way." Let me rephrase your implicit question. What if an Orthodox woman chooses to give her career priority over raising a Jewish family while remaining fully Torah-observant? Would that be allowed?

The answer is yes. Believe it or not, the Torah embraces quite a bit of pluralism, as long as no commandments are broken. There are many issues on which the Torah and the Sages recognize different approaches; sometimes they recommend one over the other, and sometimes both are fine. As you say, the preferred and recommended model for Orthodox women "creates an encouraging environment to sustain Jewish life into the next generation"; it helps us sink deep roots and forge strong family ties. Nonetheless, there are many careerist Orthodox women, and they fit comfortably into the community. Moreover, as members of the community, they participate in its warmth, stability, sense of purpose, and intense Jewishness, so that an Orthodox "career woman" will not really be identical to a Reform one.

There is pluralism in Orthodoxy. The Orthodox umbrella stretches out over Hasidim, Mitnagdim, Lubavitchers, Litvishers, *baalei teshuvah,* Sephardim, Ashkenazim, Yekkies, Young Israel, Mizrachi, Modern Orthodox, scholars, mystics, professors, doctors, scientists, tycoons, grocers, and numerous others of every shade and stripe. We are truly a rainbow coalition. Everyone is encouraged to give expression to his or her own inner voice within the parameters of Halakhah. Only those who deny the divine origin of the Torah and the supremacy of the Oral Law step out from under the umbrella.

Your pluralism, Ammi, also has its limits. It is really only a question of degree. You would not accept Jews for Jesus under your pluralist umbrella, would you? But you do accept those who deny the basic tenets of traditional Jewish belief. We, however, do not recognize these views as authentically Jewish, although we certainly accept all Jews as our brothers.

You keep repeating that you are the majority and will continue to be the majority. I beg to differ. Reform has a low birth rate (1.72) and a high assimilation rate (53 percent). Orthodoxy has a high birth rate (*charedi,* 6.4; *dati,* 3.23) and a low (but still way too high) assimilation rate (3 percent across the board). The pendulum is clearly swinging in the other direction. A demographic study that appeared in *Moment* in 1996 has calculated that over a span of four generations 200 *charedi* Orthodox Jews will increase to 5,175, and 200 *dati* Orthodox Jews will increase to 692. Over this same time period, 200 Reform Jews will dwindle to 27. Ouch!

Even if you allow for a substantial margin of error, the numbers are mind-numbing. This is much more than the Orthodox becoming a majority. It is a population implosion, a formula for extinction, Heaven forbid.

It is encouraging to hear about young Reform mothers so intent on their children getting a Jewish education. They are to be commended for recognizing that their children need to be anchored to a meaningful value system if their Jewishness is to have relevance when they grow up. So they bring their children to the Temple school, but for some inexplicable reason, they cannot stop a 53 percent intermarriage rate. Something is seriously wrong.

I cannot agree with you that Reform people "study Judaism and are observant to the best of their abilities." They can do better, much better; they were just never taught to do better. Their rabbis assure them that their reinterpreted Judaism gives them the autonomy to do as they please; there are no rules and restrictions. They give their people a bloodless shadow of the Judaism for which our ancestors were ready to lay down their lives, and often did.

By the way, I am troubled by your inclination to discourage large families because of financial considerations. We are a depleted nation; genocide and assimilation have reduced our numbers drastically. You should be thanking all those people who are having large families and offering them subsidies to encourage them to continue to do so.

You make a point of mentioning that most Orthodox institutions survive through the generosity of non-Orthodox families. You have a tendency to make these rash generalizations, and I question the research that led to this statement. But let us even say you are right. What's the point? That the Orthodox beneficiaries of non-Orthodox largesse should be thankful? I'm sure they are, and genuinely so. These people give money to Orthodox institutions because, like you, they recognize the importance of a robust Orthodox community for the future of the Jewish people. Some of them may also feel that, even if they are not so observant, supporting Orthodox institutions will get them on God's good side; and who's to say that it won't? They are giving their money with their eyes wide open.

You also seem to think it is inequitable for Orthodox charity to remain in the Orthodox community, with very little going to non-Jewish and non-Orthodox causes. When it comes to charity, the Talmud spells out the system of priorities very clearly. "The poor of your own city come first." That makes sense, doesn't it? Don't go sending money to the starving masses in Bangladesh if your neighbor is starving as well. Take care of him first, and then worry about what to do with the rest of the money.

The Orthodox community pays billions of dollars annually in property taxes and state and federal taxes allocated for education, but we do not use the public schools. We want our children to get a solid Torah education. We want them to be taught morality, to be told the difference between right and wrong, unlike the morality-neutral public schools that have produced such horrors in recent years. And we don't want them asking for Christmas trees to be like their gentile friends and eventually marrying those friends. Our taxes are, in effect, subsidizing non-Orthodox and non-Jewish education.

An Orthodox family starts with a distinct disadvantage compared to a secular family. How is a family with five or six children supposed to pay tuition to cover the actual costs of their education? The cost for primary and secondary education can easily top $30,000 to $40,000 a year! Very few families can handle such expenses. We need to mobilize all our resources to pay our teachers competitive salaries and build viable schools with airy classrooms, well-equipped laboratories, libraries, and spacious playgrounds. This is where the bulk of our charity should and does go. Charity begins at home.

MORE ON WOMEN

But let us get back to the central issue we are discussing, the role of the woman in Jewish life. You threw a few quotations at me, as you've done before, and once again I have to say that you do injustice to the classic sources. You take a few words here and there out of context and ignore the broad scope. Honestly now, does the Talmud hold women in high regard or low regard? It is either one or the other. I think that if you look at the big picture you will see with perfect clarity that the Talmud holds women in the highest regard, even though it was written at a time when pagan society considered women mere chattels. You yourself quoted many of the sources in your posting, in addition to those I quoted in mine. Shouldn't you look beyond the superficiality of the seemingly negative sources you quoted?

For instance, you mention that the Talmud links women to witchcraft. That sounds like a real put-down. But is the Talmud out to put down women? Heaven forbid. Look at all the praise and the admiration. So what does this mean? Simply that women are more drawn to the occult than are men. Even today, far more women than men check their horoscopes. In societies that practice witchcraft, therefore, women would probably be more susceptible to the influence. Does that mean women are witches? Please.

You mention that the Talmud compares Deborah to a wasp. Check your sources. Did that have anything to do with her being a woman? Nothing at all. It refers to her taking undue advantage of the prerogatives of her high office. But why don't you look at the positive? Here was a woman who, twenty-five hundred years ago, was freely elected the national leader, a Judge of Israel, a tribute to her greatness. The Talmud is full of admiration for her and considers her among the greatest people in Jewish history.

You quote from Maimonides that if a woman refuses to carry out her wifely duties she should be chastised, even with rods. First of all, this refers to the courts, not the husband, and if you noticed, the Ra'avad protests that rods are not used on women, only on men. But what is the issue here? It is based on a passage in the Talmud (Ketubot 61a). According to Rashi, it discusses the wife's obligation to make herself attractive to her husband, and that it is simply advice without coercion; the particular duties mentioned would not be applicable in our day, but others would take their place. According to Maimonides, it refers to her obligation to do at least a few basic household duties if she is living at her husband's expense and not bringing money into the household. This is enforceable. She has the option, however, of saying, *"Eini nizonit ve'eini osah.* I will support myself, and I will not do any work for you."* If she wants to be independent, she certainly can.

You quote from Sotah (3:4) that "whoever teaches his daughter Torah teaches her obscenity." I actually quoted the same *mishnah* in my posting, but I translated it as "teaches her to be duplicitous," according to the explanation of the Talmud (Sotah 21b) that defines *tiflut* as *armumiut,* duplicity. That is what I meant by "a little knowledge is a dangerous thing." She may use it for duplicitous purposes.

So, you ask, why isn't "a little bit of knowledge" a dangerous thing for those men who are not going to become talmudic scholars? Why do we encourage them to study *daf yomi* (one page of the Talmud every day)? Because men are obligated to study the Oral Law, we encourage them to do so, even if they begin with only a little bit. Hopefully, it will work itself up into more once they get into it. One of my neighbors is a very busy computer technician. He started learning *daf yomi* and became so absorbed that he spends hours preparing, studying, and reviewing his daily *daf.* In seven and a half years, he will finish the entire Talmud, and over his lifetime, may he live long and be well, he will do so a number of times. He will probably also study a few tractates in much greater depth. This is our model for a Jewish layman.

You ask me if you are correct in assuming that I have no problem with a woman who chooses Talmud over the home. And if she chooses Talmud, couldn't she do as well as men? And if so, couldn't she become a communal leader?

Do I have problem with it? No, I do not. A woman is not forbidden to study Talmud if she so chooses, and there is no reason she cannot do as well as a man. But a communal leader? With that I do have a problem. I think I explained it sufficiently in my last posting. There is no point in going over the same ground again. Theoretically, of course, it is possible for another Deborah to come along.

You know, Ammi, you make it sound as if we're the ones who are restricting women from the Torah, while you come along as gallant knights on white horses to give our Jewish damsels in distress—finally— the opportunity to learn Torah. Nothing could be further from the truth.

Let us talk a little bit about Talmud scholarship. The type of learning that takes place in *yeshivot* has no parallel in the intellectual world. It is the penetration of the word of God to the cellular and molecular level; the deeper you go, the more depth unfolds in front of your eyes.

In most *yeshivot* that follow the Lithuanian method, one page of the Talmud is studied during the entire four-hour morning session daily for two to three weeks. That's some seventy-five hours of mind-bending study on one single folio of the Talmud. Do you understand what that means? The work is done in a partner system, called *chavrutot*. Two young men will study together for this entire period and take apart that single page of the Talmud, analyzing each statement, tracing the strands of reasoning and following them where they interconnect with other *sugyot* elsewhere in the same tractate or in other tractates.

They will go through the commentaries of Rashi and the Tosafists, the Rif, the Rosh, the Ramban, the Rashba, the Ritva, the Maharsha, and many others. They will follow the development of the concepts in the works of Maimonides and the commentaries of Maggid Mishneh, Kessef Mishneh, and Lechem Mishneh. The more adventurous will go through the commentaries of Mishneh Lemelech as well. Then they will see how all the strands come together in the Shulchan Aruch, according to the elucidations of the Sema, the Shach, the Ketzot Hachoshen, and the Netivot Hamishpat and, of course, the incomparable genius of the Vilna Gaon.

And when the *chavrutot* have finished—in other words, scratched the surface—they move on to the next folio, and the process begins again.

You, Ammi, who supposedly champion opening the Talmud to women are not offering any women this option. On the contrary, you have taken it away from the men as well. Opening up a volume of the Talmud, reading the words and translating them is not Talmud scholarship. Scouring the Talmud and compiling lists of quotations that can be misinterpreted out of context and thrown in the face of the Orthodox is not Talmud scholarship. Vanessa Ochs reading a page of the Talmud in Israel with a male study partner is not Talmud scholarship. There is an old Russian joke that Stalin made all Russians equal—by making them all poor. Do you want to make women equal by making all Jews Torah-poor?

Well, I'll have you know that Orthodox women are not Torah-poor. The average Orthodox woman who has gone through the entire system of Torah education—elementary, high school, and seminary—and taken her studies seriously has a much deeper and broader knowledge of the Torah and the classic commentaries and works than many Reform rabbis—male or female. She knows Chumash and Tanach, in the original, with the major commentaries, which also gives her a grasp of the midrashic and talmudic sources. She knows Halakhah very well. And she's been introduced to the works of Maimonides, Rabbeinu Bachya, the Kuzari, the Maharal, Rabbi Moshe Chaim Luzzatto, the Mussar masters, and many others.

Women do not study the Talmud on the *yeshivah* level, because it is not obligatory for them to do so. Since it is only voluntary, it does not take precedence over other priorities and obligations. As for practical Halakhah applications, you cannot derive them yourself from the Talmud in any case. You must go through the authorities of the Shulchan Aruch. But that doesn't mean that a woman is deprived of a high level of Torah scholarship.

You may not know this, but Orthodox girls are far ahead of Orthodox boys in some of these subjects. For instance, very few Orthodox boys have the in-depth knowledge of the Prophets so common among our girls. It is just not possible, on a mass scale, to do both. Because the boys are trained so intensely in the type of Talmud scholarship I described, they pay the price in other areas of the Torah. Hopefully, they will make it up on their own.

Orthodox women derive plenty of intellectual satisfaction from the Torah. Many of them maintain their high level of Torah education in later life through classes and lectures, and by reading a lot. They also derive plenty of spiritual satisfaction from building their minor temples and raising their children to love God and follow in the footsteps of their ancestors.

You say there is not much spare time left over for "other interests" for a woman taking care of five or six children. Well, this is only a problem if you don't really value what you are doing on a profound level. Would you tell a painter to produce fewer works of art so that he will have more spare time for "other interests"? An Orthodox mother sees her children as her living works of art in every facet of their personalities imaginable. She sees her life's work—building her home and making it worthy of hosting the Divine Presence—a pursuit of the highest order. And although it is hard work, most Orthodox women still find time to teach or work in other professions or businesses. True, some women may not be able to find time to pursue "other interests." But there are priorities.

A mother hears her little daughter crying from the other room. The little girl was frightened by a bad dream, and she is trembling. The mother hugs her child and whispers comforting words in her ear. She says, "Don't worry, sweetheart. Daddy and Mommy are in the next room. We love you." The trembling subsides. The mother tucks the little girl in and kisses her. She closes her eyes and falls into a peaceful sleep.

What an incredible magic moment this is! What a moment of pure holiness! And would it be any less magical, any less holy or any less inspiring if this little girl were her fifth child?

For an Orthodox woman who chooses to have a large family, each child is such a stellar creation, such an important achievement, that she is ready to forgo some other interests for this transcendent fulfillment.

My best regards to your family.

Yosef

———————

August 2, 2000

Dear Ammi,

I am looking forward to your return from your July vacation and the resumption of our correspondence. Summers get in the way of progress, but they are important. You have to take a break sometime.

It's really your turn to speak now, since I've sent the last two postings, but I want to make a few comments before we continue. During this break, I've reread some of our earlier postings, and I couldn't help noticing how often you use the word "fundamentalist" when referring to me or other Orthodox thinkers. In your April 28 posting, you wrote, "I use the term 'fundamentalist' not in a derogatory manner. . . . [T]here are many fundamentalists who are good, decent and peace-loving people."

In my experience, when someone says "I'm not trying to be difficult," get ready for a difficult time. When someone tells you "I don't mean to be offensive," prepare to be offended. When someone says "I don't mean to use the term 'fundamentalist' in a derogatory manner" and that some of you are actually "good, decent and peace-loving," you can hear the Reform spin doctors at work.

Until we began this project, I was not attuned to Reform–Orthodox polemics, but I've been catching up on my reading. There appears to be a lot of contentiousness, invective, and labeling on both sides. Your colleagues have appropriated for themselves the high-sounding labels of pluralist, egalitarian, progressive, inclusive, and modern, and they have assigned derogatory labels such as fundamentalist to the Orthodox. The Orthodox label the Reform heretics and moral relativists.

What's the point, Ammi? Am I supposed to argue with you that I am not a fundamentalist? You know as well as I do that I am no fundamentalist. My position is based on solid reason and logic, as I believe I demonstrated to you. If anything, I could argue that you are a fundamentalist Darwinist, since you accept the theory of evolution as gospel even though you really don't know that much about it. If it's written in *On the Origin of Species,* it must be the truth.

In fact, the trend in the scientific community has been to reject traditional evolution. In fact, new advances in molecular biochemistry have just about blown the theory to pieces. In fact, Darwin himself admitted to getting "cold shudders" every time he thought about complex organs such as the eye that cannot be explained by evolution. And yet you cling to the theory. Isn't that secular fundamentalism? I suggest you read Michael Denton's excellent *Evolution: A Theory in Crisis.* Don't worry, the man is no creationist (another label). It's all first-rate science.

Between you and me, my good friend, you are not such a pluralist either. You also have boundaries, which is as it should be. As for a movement that engenders assimilation, shouldn't it be considered "regressive" rather than "progressive"? Squabbling over labels will get us nowhere.

Haven't we come to a point in our friendship where we can speak openly and directly without hiding behind labels? You write in your March 23 posting, "I am interested in getting on to other issues. You recently returned from Israel. Are you a Zionist?" Is this how to initiate a dialogue about Israel? By bandying about another label?

Ammi, I propose that from this point on we both abandon labels and stick to substance. Labels are weapons. We should not seek to inflict wounds. We should henceforth communicate as good friends that have serious differences of opinion.

My best regards to your family.

Yosef

August 4, 2000

Yosef:

I was pleased to read your latest note and to be reassured that you have not lost your fighting spirit. I was worried that the summer might mellow you a bit.

If you do not consider yourself a "fundamentalist," that is okay with me. Call yourself whatever you want, or nothing. Tell me how you want your views characterized, and I will have an opportunity to respond. I believe in giving people the right to define themselves.

You are a bit too defensive in your resistance to characterizations. I agree that labeling people is often used for derogatory purposes and should, in those cases, be avoided and condemned. All too often, accusations like "racism," "sexism," "homophobia," are thrown at people in an effort to end any reasonable debate by impugning the character of the other. I also agree that from time to time labeling is an exercise in intellectual laziness, when reasoned argument fails.

But that does not imply that we cannot attempt to characterize viewpoints. Social and political discourse is only possible if we allow ourselves to broadly characterize a philosophy, implicitly acknowledging that such characterizations are broad and general, and might not apply to all circumstances. Thus terms like "liberal," "conservative," "democrat," "republican," "royalist," "socialist," "Marxist," "communist," "secularist," "humanist," "theist," are appropriate terms that make social discourse understandable and possible. Few people take offense at these characterizations, if, in fact, in broad terms they describe their views.

In this vein, I used the term "fundamentalist" to characterize your approach to the interpretation of texts. My understanding of your position is that you interpret sacred writings in a "fundamental" way. Perhaps it is more palatable for you to describe your approach as "literal." In any case, as I mentioned to you earlier, I did not use the term "fundamentalist" in a derogatory manner. To the extent that your resistance to the characterization of "fundamentalist" reveals your disgust with the actions of—what else can I say—some fundamentalists, I am reassured.

Are you suggesting that the term "Zionist" is also a derogatory label? "Is this how to initiate a dialogue about Israel?" you ask. The State of Israel is the consequence and fulfillment of the ideology known as Zionism, and the manifestation of the political movement known as the Zionist movement. You consider that "bandying about another label"?!

There are many ultra-Orthodox Jews (Is that also a label? If so, which word—"ultra," "Orthodox" or "Jews"?) who proudly proclaim themselves to be anti-Zionists. Some of them—like the Lubavitcher Rebbe—never set foot in Israel. Others—like Neturei Karta—align themselves politically with some of the most severe opponents of Jews and Israel. Some ultra-Orthodox Jews have joined forces with Louis Farrakhan.

Given this, and mindful of your visit to Israel, I was curious whether you are a Zionist. Do you believe in the idea of the restoration of Jewish sovereignty in the Land of Israel after two thousand years of wandering? Are you a supporter of that idea? Do you work to enhance and strengthen that idea? Many "fervently Orthodox" Jews (is this a better characterization?) do not.

The Declaration of the Establishment of the State of Israel proclaims: "In the year 1897, at the summons of the spiritual father of the Jewish state, Theodor Herzl, the First Zionist Congress convened and proclaimed the right of the Jewish people to national rebirth in its own country." Zionism—the Zionist idea—is the philosophical underpinning of the State of Israel.

As you know, many Orthodox Jews were—and still are—opposed to Zionism for theological reasons. Are you?

Shabbat Shalom,

Ammi

August 6, 2000

Dear Ammi,

Welcome back. It seems the summer has left you in good form as well.

You are quite right that some labels are necessary. As you point out, I am a Jew. This is accurate. I would like to draw the line, however, between nouns and adjectives. For this book, in the spirit of friendship, let us limit ourselves to those terms that identify who we are. I am an Orthodox Jew. You are a Reform Jew. But let's steer clear of adjectival terms that describe and characterize, such as "egalitarian" and "heretical."

I would also ask you to refrain from using the ultra-Orthodox label, which has negative extremist connotations. I assure you it was not coined by us. Even the word Orthodox is not of our choosing. We practice Judaism the way it has been practiced for thousands of years—proudly, sincerely, without compromise, without revision, without equivocation. Perhaps then you should call us Classical Jews. Yes, I think I like that. Classical Judaism. It has an accurate ring to it. Otherwise, Torah Judaism might be a good label, if you need one. Or how about simply observant Jews? Or Observant Jews, if you wish.

You raise many valid issues about Israel and Zionism. I have strong opinions about them, as you can imagine. As for the word "Zionist," it is a label that many people define differently. For instance, the militant settlers on the West Bank consider themselves the true Zionists. You don't agree. So do we have to launch our discussion by defining the word "Zionist"? I think it is a relatively minor consideration. By the way, is the word "Zionist" a noun label or an adjective label? An intriguing question, don't you think? We have much to talk about. But I will wait my turn.

Warmest regards.

Yosef

December 8, 2000

Yosef:

It's good to get back into the flow. I am responding to your June 6 essay, which, in turn, is a response to my May 23 piece.

In your lengthy response to me ostensibly about the role of women, you have raised a number of additional points. Let me deal with those first and then relate to your expanded views on the role of women in Judaism:

TEXT CITATION

Please note again your impatience with my text citation. You write, "You throw a few quotations at me . . . and once again I have to say that you do injustice to the classic sources." After making this point, Yosef, you then throw a few quotations at me, demonstrating the "proper" approach to the classic sources.

The issue for you cannot be the citation of classical texts. You and I agree that Jewish discussion begins with the Torah and must be grounded in the classic texts. Thus texts must be relied upon and cited to establish a position that constitutes an authentic expression of Jewish values. You have done this throughout our discussions. Were I not to cite texts, you would then criticize me, properly, for not relating to Jewish tradition. No discussion about Judaism, and no decision about Jewish values, can be conducted without relating to the texts. Any such discussion or decision, by definition, will be limited because the discussion could be endless—as evidenced by the ongoing interpretations offered by every generation of Jews during the past two thousand years.

What I think really gets you going is that it is I, a Reform rabbi, who is citing the texts. You understand, correctly, that whoever has access to, and can pronounce authoritatively upon, the classical texts, has **power.** It is not only about *Torah lishmah*—the study of Torah for its own sake. It is also about power and authority.

If Reform, Conservative, and even Orthodox rabbis you do not approve of can use texts to support a position that is different from yours, that implies a degree of authority in them that you are unprepared to recognize.

It is this question of power that I think is at the heart of your approach to the role of women and many other communal issues. It is not "what does the text say," but "who has the authority" to interpret the texts for the community. For you it is only Orthodox men, which, of course, will dictate a certain approach to communal standards. (It is even narrower than that, because every Orthodox community has its own circle of deciders.)

PLURALISM

I laughed out loud when I read your assertion that "there is pluralism in Orthodoxy." Here is a wonderful example of the contributions of the Reform movement to the entire Jewish people that we discussed in an earlier exchange. We have been so successful in persuading Jews of the centrality of pluralism that even Orthodox and ultra-Orthodox Jews feel that they must measure and justify their approach to Judaism through this concept. After all, if you were against pluralism you would not claim that "there is pluralism in Orthodoxy." Thus even the Orthodox world now feels that it must use the vocabulary of pluralism.

Of course, you are right that there is some tolerance for various approaches within Orthodoxy. There is also great intolerance even within the Orthodox world for differing Orthodox approaches. Some of these disputes are legendary, as, for example, between the Hasidim and the Mitnagdim, the mystics and the rationalists, Satmar and Lubavitch, the modernists and the ultra-Orthodox. There were periods when even marriage was discouraged between members of these different groups. In the past, they burned each other's books, excommunicated one another, and informed on each other.

But the real issue, as you know quite well, is that there is essentially no tolerance for different theological views granted by the Orthodox community to the non-Orthodox community. As you say, there is an "umbrella" of the divine origin of the Torah and the supremacy of the Oral Law. Those who step outside it get rained upon by a torrent of theological and communal intolerance. As you write, "We do not recognize these views [those outside the umbrella] as authentically Jewish."

The problem here is not in the establishment of standards. Pluralism does not imply lack of standards. You stated correctly that we in the Reform movement also reject many beliefs that we consider not Jewish, as in the Jews for Jesus example that you cited. We are in agreement that establishing standards is a necessary element of Judaism, and those who do not meet these standards are not Jewish.

You are entitled therefore to establish standards—red lines. The problem is not in the drawing of the red lines, it is where you draw them. And here the Orthodox community has a serious problem. The further to the right you go in Orthodoxy, the more serious is the problem.

You have drawn the line in such a way as to write out the overwhelming majority—at least 90 percent—of world Jewry. What happened to the supposedly critical value of *Ahavat Yisrael*—love of the Jewish people? What happened to the central value of *Klal Yisrael*—the covenant of the Jewish people? The distinction you try to make, that while you "do not recognize these views as authentically Jewish, [you] accept all Jews as brothers," does not wash. Most Jews will see right through that. You mean that you accept these Jews as "brothers" because their mothers happened to be Jewish, but you reject everything about their philosophy of Judaism? You embrace them as members of the tribe because of a halakhic technicality, but you reject the authenticity of everything about them that forms their Jewish expression and loyalty to Jewish tradition and the Jewish people?

You mean that even in your most enlightened and tolerant moments—those moments of pluralism that you claim exist in the Orthodox world—there is nothing authentically Jewish that you can recognize in the philosophy of the other 90 percent of your people? Not one thing?

I sense something better in you and many in the Orthodox world. I sense a struggle to confront this very tension. First, I think that many of you have doubts about your own beliefs. It cannot be any other way. To be human is to doubt. And if you have your own doubts, how can you not extend the same prerogative to others? Second, I believe, or would like to believe, that many in the Orthodox world do recognize the sincerity and value of those in the non-Orthodox world. Acknowledging it publicly might be another matter. I think that many in the Orthodox world understand that to draw the line so as to exclude 90 percent of Jews is too great a burden to place upon Jewish theology and Jewish destiny.

This, I think, partially explains the constant reference by Orthodox spokesmen, raised by you too, to the various surveys supposedly demonstrating the triumph of Orthodoxy and the decline of non-Orthodoxy. You cite with evident approval the studies detailing the high birth rate in the Orthodox community as compared with the low one in the non-Orthodox community that, added to assimilation rates, lead to projections that within four generations huge numbers of Orthodox Jews will remain as compared to almost no non-Orthodox Jews. I think that it is almost as if you are leaning on the ultimate triumph of Ortho-doxy as a crutch to deal with your writing off most of the rest of world Jewry. If you can say to yourselves, "Yes, we are writing them off, and yes, it would be intolerable if it were permanent, but, rest assured, within four generations we will replace all those whom we have written off," then you might be better able to deal with the consequences of your narrowly drawn standards.

I am not a statistician. I am sure that many social scientists can pre-sent flaws in the research and different projections than those cited in the studies you mention. For the moment at least, the Reform move-ment is growing at a rapid pace. But this much I do know: No matter how many times people tried to project the ultimate demise of the Jews, it proved to be erroneous. The first reference to the Jews outside the Bible is from the Mernephtah Stele of 1235 B.C.E. There, King Merne-ptah of Egypt boasted that "Israel is laid waste." From the first appear-ance of the Jews, projections of our demise have been constant, and quite exaggerated.

A word of advice: Do not pin your hopes on the current projections. Deal with the issues of the day. We have many challenges in the Jewish world. They challenge all of us, and we are all part of the solution. Even from your perspective, there are not enough of us to allow ourselves the luxury of writing off millions of our people. I am greatly troubled about assimilation in America. I believe, though, that we will survive, and that four generations from now there will be more than 27 non-Orthodox Jews. I believe this, Yosef, because I believe in the ingenuity and will to live of the Jewish people.

And I also believe in God. God wants the Jews to survive. We are God's people. To disappear is a contradiction in terms. This is what our tradition tells us, and in this respect I intuit and believe our tradition to be right.

LARGE FAMILIES

It should be clear to you, from everything I have written, that I am in favor of large families. You entirely missed my point if you concluded that I am inclined "to discourage large families." I myself come from a fairly large family. I believe like you do that we are a depleted nation. We need lots of Jewish children.

I do think that there comes a point in parents' lives that the decision whether to have more children will be informed by increasingly complex family circumstances. There are many considerations, including, but not limited to, and often not primarily, financial.

About the financial component, it is up to the individuals involved to determine its relative weight. But if you are suggesting that it has no weight at all, then I disagree, because that throws too much of the burden of caring for these children on the community. I, like you, seek to encourage Jewish parents to have children, and am therefore supportive of certain subsidies and other communal gestures. For example, the Jewish community should subsidize Jewish education, which is currently too costly for many parents.

The question here, as in many other instances, is a question of degree. What is the degree of the financial responsibility that the parents assume for having children, versus the responsibility of the community? As generous as the community might be, I am suggesting to you that the primary responsibility is on the parents. The decision to have more children should be informed, *inter alia,* by the financial status of the family. They have to be able to afford having more children.

In Israel the government offers substantial subsidies to encourage families to have more children. There, the ultra-Orthodox community preaches to the rest of the state that it is doing more for Israel and world Jewry than everyone else, in part because of the large families they are raising. In addition to a check that all families receive before they leave the hospital with their child, the ultra-Orthodox community swaggers into Parliament and annually demands hundreds of millions of non-Orthodox taxpayer dollars for other subsidies. They need money for every stage of the child's development, justified by the same argument you make: It is the ultra-Orthodox families that are keeping Judaism alive. Often Orthodox yeshivas have far superior facilities, including smaller class sizes, than the public schools educating most of the citizens. Most of the taxes—the source of the state's funds—are supplied by non-Orthodox Jews to support a subsidy system that distorts Jewish values and creates a dependency upon the state harmful to both the ultra-Orthodox and non-Orthodox communities. An entire underclass is created because of this notion that everyone should pay exorbitantly for the decision of the few to create large families. Isn't that precisely what conservative people rail against in this country?

Ultra-Orthodox temerity extends beyond childhood into adulthood. Thus they argue that since ultra-Orthodox young men are doing more for the security of Israel by studying and praying than are soldiers on the front lines, they should be exempt from army service that is compulsory for everyone else. And while the state is at it, these ultra-Orthodox men, many of whom are draft dodgers, should be paid more than combat pay to pray and study.

And it gets curiouser and curiouser. Most ultra-Orthodox communities are not even loyal to the state giving them these subsidies. Most of their members are not Zionists. They do not recite the national anthem. They do not recognize the Israeli flag. They do not serve in the army. They are antagonistic to the central institutions of the state. They repeatedly declare that they observe God's laws, not man's laws. Thus the perverse situation is created in which non-Orthodox citizens of the state, loyal to its central democratic institutions, are heavily subsidizing other citizens who are antagonistic to the state and make no secret of their desire to dismantle its central institutions.

Sometimes, I think that only the Jews could have devised this type of Alice in Wonderland reality.

CHARITY

You cited the talmudic dictum "The poor of your own city come first." There you go again. I could say to you, as you have said to me, you throw a few quotations at me, as you've done before, and once again I have to say that you do injustice to the classic sources. You take a few words here and there out of context and ignore the broad scope. I could say that, but I won't!

I will, however, make a couple of points: First, Judaism is both particularism and universalism. Through the Jewish particular, the universal aspirations of all mankind are manifested. We learn this from the moment God selected Abraham, stating "all the peoples of the earth shall bless themselves through you." While it might be true that your starving neighbor demands more attention, it does not follow that the starving masses in Bangladesh deserve no attention. Remember that Jewish obligations extend to the "stranger, for you were strangers in the Land of Egypt." Also, if only to maintain good relations with non-Jews, Jewish tradition encouraged giving charity to gentiles. (Maimonides, Yad, Matanot Aniyim, Chap. 7)

Second, even if the needs of your own community come first, it does not follow that the needs of the entire Jewish people are not of high priority. Orthodox Jews, like all other Jews, have an obligation to support the charitable needs of the entire Jewish community, not only "those of their own town." You too have an obligation to support the central philanthropic bodies of the Jewish community. You say, "Charity begins at home." But nowhere have I read that charity ends at home.

Again, I wish to be very careful here. There are many Orthodox Jews that are exceedingly charitable to general Jewish causes. But the impression you yourself are giving is that most Orthodox (at least ultra-Orthodox) charity stays in the local community or is given outside the local community to another Orthodox institution. You seek to rationalize or justify this by stating that you pay "billions of dollars in property taxes and state and federal taxes"—as if you are the only ones who pay these taxes. You protest that the costs of education are expensive—as if it is not expensive for everyone else. You complain that "our taxes are, in effect, subsidizing non-Orthodox and non-Jewish education." (The ultra-Orthodox in Israel have no problem accepting subsidies through the taxes of those who disagree with them, and with whom, in turn, they disagree.)

Are you really trying to claim that through your taxes to the local and federal government you are discharging your obligation to support the broader Jewish community? That is preposterous. Are you lumping non-Orthodox Jewish children with gentile children? Where is your concern for Klal Yisrael? If you are concerned about assimilation, why don't you help to invest in non-Orthodox Jewish day schools? They can play a critical role in stemming the assimilatory trends you decry. Yosef, on so many levels, including charity, you act as if you have already abandoned Klal Yisrael. Where is your sense of Jewish community? Aren't the needs of non-Orthodox Jewish senior citizens important to you? What about absorbing new non-Orthodox Jewish immigrants? What about non-Orthodox Jewish orphans, battered women, or just plain poor folks? Does the lame excuse that the needs of your community come first take care of it for you?

THE ROLE OF WOMEN

Yosef, you start out by conceding that your "portrayal of Orthodox life is idealized." You then proceed to state that the "idealized portrayal is quite commonplace." In the absence of the arrival of the messiah it cannot be both. Either your portrayal is idealized or it is not. I do not doubt that some people try to live the lifestyle you describe. I find your confidence in the popularity and superiority of this lifestyle misplaced.

You write: "Let me rephrase your implicit question. What if an Orthodox woman chooses to give her career priority over raising a Jewish family while remaining fully Torah-observant? Would that be allowed?" That was not my implicit question. I had no implicit question. I simply wanted to emphasize that I am happy for all those people who live a lifestyle that makes sense to them and gives them satisfaction. I am particularly pleased that the lifestyle you describe is apparently successful in transmitting Jewish identity to the next generation.

However, since you raised it, let me respond. You say that there are many careerist Orthodox women and they fit comfortably in the community. You suggest that there is considerable latitude for women to decide their roles—as long as no commands are broken.

Yosef, either Orthodox women are equal or they are not. After reading your full description, I think that you have argued that men and women are not equal; that they have different roles, and thus women are precluded from certain choices. Women's role is to be the minister of internal affairs of their families. You have said that women cannot be communal leaders no matter how brilliant, qualified, or temperamentally suited they might be. This is a man's role. I am not really sure why you have so argued. After all, you cite positively the example of the biblical Deborah, and you speculate that it is theoretically possible for another Deborah to come along. So if it is theoretically possible, what is your objection?

Despite your assertion that you adequately dealt with this last time, it is not at all clear to me. You seem to be wavering between arguing that there is something inherent within the characteristics of women that preclude them from communal leadership, and the position that they have a different role. You write that "simply(!) . . . women are more drawn to the occult than are men." At the same time, you argue that Jewish tradition holds women in high regard and that they have in the past, and thus they can in the future hold positions of leadership—but only theoretically.

My best understanding of your position is that women are precluded from communal leadership primarily because of the issue of modesty. It is not modest for men to see women in positions of leadership. It is not modest for men to see women praying alongside them.

My answer is twofold: First, your argument is not persuasive for most people. During Israeli Prime Minister Golda Meir's term, there was a mass rapist on the loose. Her well-meaning male advisors suggested to her that she should impose a curfew on all women after dark. Her response was that if the problem was with a male rapist, why curfew the women? She suggested that it might be wiser to curfew all of the men. In the same vein, some people might say that if men have a problem with modesty, why not preclude them from communal leadership? They might then get over it.

Even in the Orthodox community, your argument is getting harder and harder to support. There is a fascinating development within Orthodoxy that is encouraging the assumption of communal leadership by women, and there is even talk of ordaining Orthodox women as rabbis. Currently, the discussions are taking place within the more moderate Orthodox circles, but you know these things have a way of spreading. (Here is another great contribution of the Reform movement to the Jewish people.)

Second, if the question is primarily one of modesty, I am sure that Jewish law, with all of its ingenuity and creativity, could devise a way to deal with this issue and allow women to assume communal leadership. That must be so because there were women leaders in the past. Were the issues of modesty different then? If Deborah's leadership was consistent with Jewish law, then why not the leadership of modern women? Was Deborah's leadership within the constraints of modesty while all modern women's are not? Is there no concrete case beyond the "theoretical" possibility? Surely, Jewish law can find a solution to the question of modesty, if we have had, in our past, precedents of women's leadership.

You wrote in your May 1 essay, "In a casual conversation between an attractive man and an attractive woman, the man's thoughts will easily turn in a libidinous direction, but if the woman is not masculinized, hers will not." How do you know all this? Have you asked enough men and women to ascertain whether this is true? You then use this assumption, highly problematic in its own right, to justify putting women behind a *mekhitzah* and not men. You write: "Putting men behind the *mekhitzah* and having women conduct the services accomplishes nothing. But with women behind the *mekhitzah,* men have no problem concentrating on their communication with God without the slightest improper thought or feeling."

No, I think that it is really a question of power. I think that Orthodox men cannot fathom sharing communal power with women. You ask, "Does the Talmud hold women in high regard or low regard?" I think that the answer is both, and that you are incorrect when you state, "It is either one or the other." We have cited passages from the Talmud and other commentary that indicate a complicated relationship toward women. To offer a few more examples:

The Talmud contains some beautiful, touching statements about women and wives: "A man must always be wary of wronging his wife . . . the punishment for wronging her is nearby (will soon follow)." "If your wife is shorter than you, bend down and whisper (i.e., listen to her)." (Baba Metzia 59a) But on the same page we also read, "He who follows a woman's advice will end up in hell."

On the one hand, we read, "A man who has no wife lives without joy . . . blessing . . . goodness . . . and peace" (Yevamot 62b) and "We can infer how fine a good wife is, for the Torah is symbolized by her." (Yevamot 63b) But on the same page, we find, "It is a pious deed (mitzvah) to divorce a bad wife." (The man determines what constitutes a "bad" wife.) We can marvel at the great respect shown to women and the honor men must show their wives, while also reading: "A man may do whatever he wants with his wife [during intercourse]; it may be compared to meat bought from the butcher . . . if he wants to eat it salted, he can do so; if he wants to eat it roasted he can do so; if he wants to eat it boiled he can do so." (Nedarim 20b)

We can read such touching statements in the Talmud as "When Rabbi Joseph heard the footsteps of his mother, he said 'I shall arise before the approaching shekhinah,' (presence of God)." (Kiddushin 31b) But we can also read, "A woman is like a leather jug full of excrement, whose opening is full of blood, yet everyone [men] chases after her." (Shabbat 152a)

The point here is not to suggest that all interpretations of all commentators are followed, but to demonstrate that the tradition's approach is complex. There is a stream of thought within the tradition that is derogatory of some female characteristics that it presumes to understand.

I see this approach all the time and it leads to dangerous actions. For example, Orthodox legislators recently introduced in Israel's Parliament an extremely troubling and even obscene bill entitled: "Defense of the Western Wall." The bill calls for seven years' imprisonment(!) for any woman who performs a religious act at the Western Wall that includes "taking out the Torah and reading from it, shofar blowing, donning of talit or tefillin." The bill is directed not primarily at those "inauthentic" Reform or Conservative Jews. What really enraged the Orthodox legislators was that Orthodox women sought to pray at the Western Wall—in the women's section and in a manner that they consider to be halakhically sound.

See, Yosef, why we need pluralism? Do you understand how dangerous fundamentalism can be? Can you appreciate the arrogance of those who are convinced that they have knowledge of "absolute truth," and with this "knowledge" seek to impose it upon everyone else? Religious fundamentalism discussed in the classroom or constrained within isolated communities is one thing. Religious fundamentalism given political expression and power creates extremism that will ultimately destroy the goodness of society and suck out its free spirit.

The Western Wall bill, not yet law, is supported by all of the ultra-Orthodox parties in the Knesset, representing hundreds of thousands of ultra-Orthodox Jews in Israel. What approach would you say this reveals about Orthodoxy and women? Is it one of respect? Is it, as you insist is reflected "with perfect clarity" in the Talmud, one of "high regard"?

Let me make a few brief additional comments:

Damsels in distress. You write that I make it sound as if we are rescuing your Jewish damsels in distress by finally giving them the opportunity to learn Torah.

Please try to follow my argument. I do not doubt that Orthodox girls study in school. I am pleased that adult Orthodox women may also study, although as I wrote before, due to the respective roles of women and men in the house, women have little spare time to do so. (That, however, is their choice and I support their right to choose for themselves how they want to live.)

The question is one of obligation. The very act of exempting women from certain obligations that men assume becomes the basis for different—and unequal—treatment. You have defined women's role in such a way as to exclude their study at the highest level, that of men ("A woman does not come to the study house," Moed Katan 18a.) You have discouraged women from pursuing their intellectual talents (as in Eliezer's reply to a woman who asked a good question on scriptures: "Women's wisdom is only with a spindle," Yomah 66b). You have prevented women from reaping important fruits of their study, communal leadership. ("A man may be appointed the leader of the community, but not a woman," Sifre Deuteronomy Piska 157.)

If Orthodox women feel that they do not need to be "rescued," fine. Many non-Orthodox women and increasing numbers of Orthodox women, however, do feel that they have been liberated to maximize their potential within the Jewish community as a result of the more open thinking we have introduced into the Jewish world. Ask them. I can give you names.

"A mother hears her little daughter crying." I appreciate your description of a mother comforting her child after a bad dream. I agree with you that it is a magical moment of deep pleasure. You make it sound as if only Orthodox mothers comfort their children. Other mothers also do this. Yosef, even men do this. I know because I have done it myself.

One final thought: What precisely did you mean when you wrote that "the Talmud holds women in the highest regard, even though it was written at a time when pagan society considered women mere chattels?" You have been asserting throughout as an article of faith that the Talmud was transmitted from God to Sinai and was received whole and pure during the talmudic period, and represents God's will. What difference then does it make when it was actually put to paper? According to you the Talmud is timeless, no? Its values about women originate at Sinai.

Why then do you feel you have to justify the value of the Talmud within its historical context of pagan society? I know why I would want to do that. I have made the point that the Talmud is the product of hundreds of years of development in reaction to, and part of, Jewish and general society.

But you? I thought your point was that the Talmud is ahistorical. I thought you said that there is absolute truth. Standards never change because they come from God. Therefore, the very comparison to pagan times is irrelevant.

You know what I think? Perhaps there is an element of doubt within you. That, of course, is fine with me. As the prophet Micah recommended, one should "walk humbly with your God."

Ammi

Chanukah, 2000

Dear Yosef:

I send this posting to you as my Chanukah gift. I hope you enjoy it! I must be going soft on you. I thoroughly enjoyed the uplifting description of your beliefs. There are a few comments that I will make at the end of this essay in reaction to some specific points you raise, but by and large I would like to simply let your description stand. It is a good description of Orthodoxy.

I am not really interested in persuading you to alter your Orthodox philosophy. Really, I am not. I want Orthodoxy and Orthodox Jews around. We need each other. It is precisely because I believe that so much of religion involves the human element that I concede my (and your) fallibility regarding the search to discern God's will. It is the spectrum of understanding and the sum total of Jewish history and experience that best serves this search. Jews have always had different interpretations of the sacred texts. I find this not to be a source of weakness, but one of strength. This characteristic has served us well in reenergizing Judaism in every generation and ensuring its vitality. It is one secret to our longevity.

The Midrash says: "Just as the *etrog* has taste as well as fragrance, so Israel has among them those who possess learning and good deeds. Just as the palm tree has taste but no fragrance, so Israel has among them those who possess learning but no good deeds. Just as the myrtle has fragrance but no taste, so Israel has among them those who possess good deeds but not learning. Just as the willow has no taste and no fragrance, so Israel has among them those who possess neither learning nor good deeds. What does the Holy One do? He says, 'Let them all be tied together in one band and they will atone for each other. If you have done so, then at that instant I am exalted.'" (Leviticus Rabbah 30:12)

We are a people with differing characteristics and understandings. But we are all bound together in history and destiny. We need each other and our differing understandings of Judaism. It keeps us honest, refreshed, and vital. God exalts in these differences.

The religious task is best articulated in the book of Deuteronomy: "And now Israel, what does the Lord your God demand of you?" (10:12) The fundamental characteristic of the religious person is the search to discern the will of God. What does God demand of us?

"Only[!] this," states Deuteronomy. "To revere the Lord your God, to walk only in His paths, to love Him, and to serve the Lord your God with all your heart and soul."

"Do what is right and good in the sight of God." (Deuteronomy 6:18)

The religious person assumes the existence of God. But how to discern what is "right and good in God's sight?" How to discover the will of God?

For the Jew, the starting point is the Torah. Indeed, Deuteronomy itself states: "keep[ing] the Lord's commandments and laws which I enjoin upon you today."

But what are these laws and commandments? How do we apply them? Who tells us how they relate to differing circumstances? Who interprets them? What happens if laws and commandments conflict? What happens if they are impossible to observe? How should we respond to our sense of conscience and reason—also God-given—that some laws are out of date, impractical, or worse, unethical?

Yosef, I think that you and I agree that these questions are answered by human beings. "If a case is too baffling for you to decide . . . you shall . . . appear before . . . the magistrate in charge at the time and present your problem. When they have announced to you the verdict . . . you shall carry out the verdict. . . ." (Deuteronomy 17:8–12)

Even if you believe with perfect faith in the literal transmission of the Torah from God to Moses and ultimately to our generation, I think we will agree that the Judaism we practice today is not at all the Judaism practiced in biblical times. Rather, it is the Judaism of successive generations of Jews who interpreted the Bible, who pronounced verdicts, expounded upon and expanded points of law, custom, tradition, and theology throughout our history.

The starting point is the Bible because that is where our people's search for God begins. In our search, we cannot deny clear evidence or reason. The case for human involvement in the authorship of the Torah is overwhelming. Volumes have been written; and in this respect I wrote in one of my earlier pieces, let our readers review the evidence for themselves and decide.

To assert human involvement in the authorship and redaction of the Bible is not to suggest that there is no underlying truth to the episodes and context described therein. For example, to assert human authorship of the Torah is not to deny a history of slavery in Egypt. Archaeologists are discovering finds that suggest or confirm the occurrence of many of the events described in the Bible.

More important, to acknowledge human involvement in the authorship of the Bible is not to deny the presence of God within it. The Bible reflects our search for and encounter with God. I agree with Rabbi Hananyah, who wrote in the Mishnah: "When two people sit and words of Torah pass between them the presence of God rests among them." (Pirke Avot 3:2) God is in the texts. When we study them, the Divine Presence and Will become clearer, so that slowly, generation after generation, it might be possible to comprehend the will of God. The key is to engage the process seriously. "Study Torah again and again, turn it over and over, for everything is contained in it." (Ibid., 5:22)

Thus "Torah"—the ongoing process of explanation, explication, and argumentation—has been emphasized more in our tradition than the concept of "the Torah"—meaning the five books of Moses. Orthodoxy asserts that the Pentateuch was literally dictated by God to Moses. The Torah itself never made this claim or that the five books of Moses constitute an integral unit. When the word *torah* is used in the Bible it means a specific rule or law. To the best of my knowledge, all Jews affirm that "Torah" explains "the Torah." It is through this process that our partnership with God is manifested and His will might become clearer.

Thus, I wrote, for example, that for me the importance of the Book of Genesis is not in its literal recitation of how the world was created. A literal reading of Genesis will lead one to conclude that the world is 5761 years old. In this context, I wrote that I see no need to contort and distort reason to a fundamentalist, or if you prefer, literal, reading of the biblical text every time a dinosaur bone is discovered. Rather, I am much more interested in the beliefs flowing from Genesis, discovered or elucidated through the human-divine process of Torah.

This process produced revolutionary teachings: There is a God. God is a creator. God is outside of nature, and nature is subservient to God. There is a universal order to the universe. Human beings are the pinnacle of creation, made in the image of God. Man, however, is not God, and is thus subject to a higher order. Genesis teaches that human beings should strive to imitate God, to be God's partner, but that we can be arrogant. Genesis teaches that human beings have free will, and that part of this freedom includes our capacity to choose evil. We are capable of murder, but we are each other's keeper.

Genesis teaches that God is just ("Will not the judge of all the earth deal justly?" 18:25) and therefore human beings must do justice. Human beings and societies are perfectible. We can become holy ("You should be holy for I am holy," Leviticus 19:2). We learn from Genesis that life is good, that there is meaning and purpose to human existence. We learn from Genesis the importance of rest.

To read the Bible literally is to underestimate its timelessness and overestimate your own abilities. The Bible does not claim to be a history textbook. It does not claim to be a science thesis. It does not even claim to be a comprehensive book of laws. Rather, we have understood the Bible to be the record of our people's encounter with God. It speaks in the language of human beings. As such even you should concede that it contains truths that are indecipherable by we who have only a limited understanding.

Our tradition teaches that people experience revelation differently. "The divine word spoke to each and every person according to his particular capacity." (Pesikta d'Rav Kahana 12:25) There is no "one," "authoritative," or "literal" understanding. "Just as a hammer strikes the rock and it shatters into many pieces, so does a single verse [of Torah] yield many meanings." (Sanhedrin 34a)

While postbiblical tradition took for granted the direct transmission of the Torah, it did not, by and large, succumb to the temptation of literalism. A literal reading of the Bible freezes revelation in one time and place, and the rabbis knew that this approach would cause Judaism to atrophy. Whoever studies Torah and does not revise it is like a planter who does not reap.

What was good for one generation is not necessarily good for another. The Mishnah asks: "Why are the words of the individual sage recorded along with those of the majority? After all, is not the halakhah decided according to the majority opinion? Because a court may [someday] prefer the opinion of the individual sage and it may decide to rely on it." (Eduyot 1:5)

Who decided that the most literal reading of the Bible is the most accurate or sophisticated? It could very well be the opposite. Literal readers of the Bible have been responsible for some of humanity's worst abuses. Slavery was most vociferously defended in this country by clergymen. In *The Adventures of Huckleberry Finn,* Mark Twain describes the struggle between literalism and conscience when Huck Finn believes it to be his religious duty to turn in the runaway slave Jim, who was the property of Miss Watson.

"The more I [Huck Finn] studied about this, the more my conscience went to grinding me, and the more wicked and low-down and ornery I got to feeling. And at last, when it hit me all of a sudden that here was the plain hand of Providence slapping me in the face and letting me know my wickedness was being watched all the time from up there in heaven, whilst I was stealing a poor old woman's nigger. . . . Something inside me kept saying, 'There was the Sunday school you could a gone to it; and if you'd a done it they'd a learnt you, there, that people that acts as I'd been acting about that nigger goes to everlasting fire. . . .' So I got a piece of paper and a pencil, all glad and excited, and set down and wrote: *Miss Watson your runaway nigger Jim is down here two mile below Pikesville. . . .* I took it up and held it in my hand. I was a-trembling, because I'd got to decide, for ever, betwixt two things, and I knowed it. I studied a minute, sort of holding my breath, and then says to myself: 'All right, then, I'll go to hell'—and tore it up." (Chap. 31)

Conscience is from God, and defines the human condition. It is, in part, what the Bible refers to when it asserts that we were made in the image of God. Animals do not have a conscience. Therefore, when we have a conflict between the law and conscience, between traditional standards and contemporary conscience, how should we decide? When Javert arrests Valjean in the name of justice and law for stealing a loaf of bread to feed his starving family, does this further the will of God? "We are never done with conscience," wrote Victor Hugo. "It is bottomless, being God. We cast into this pit the labor of our whole life, we cast in our fortune, we cast in our riches, we cast in our success, we cast in our liberty, or our country, we cast in our well being, we cast in our repose, we cast in our happiness. More! More! More! Empty the vase! Turn out the urn! We must at last cast in our heart."

Jewish tradition was very concerned with the tendency to read Torah literally. Yes, talmudic rabbis claimed an oral tradition of transmission extending back to Moses at Sinai, but they did so more out of a need to establish the authority of the rabbis to interpret the law than out of a desire to instill a literal reading of texts. How in the world could literalism have been the norm when the Talmud explodes with disputes and conflicting interpretations on the same verse? Layer upon layer of commentary, code, responsa, Midrash, liturgy, and philosophy were added through the centuries.

To the Talmud's great credit, it never attempted to hide these arguments. Quite the contrary, it reveled in them. Argument and controversy did not at all frighten Judaism. If controversies were for the sake of Heaven, for the purpose of penetrating deeper meanings and discerning God's will, they had a salutary and cumulative effect. "Any controversy that is for the sake of Heaven is destined to endure." (Pirke Avot 5:17) In this way we could, in fact, get closer to God, warming ourselves by the light of Torah.

We read in the Midrash, "Torah is fire, given in fire and comparable to fire. What is the nature of fire? If one comes too near to it one gets burned. If one keeps too far from it one gets cold. The only thing to do is to warm himself against its flame." (Mekhilta Bakhodesh, Chap. 4)

There are those who read sacred texts so literally as to lose all sense of proportion, moderation, or reason. They have a scorched-earth theology. They alone possess absolute truth. The Midrash cautioned them against the foreign fires of arrogance, intolerance, and closed-mindedness. On the other hand, there are those who are so removed from tradition's warmth as to have lost all sense of wonder and mystery about the universe. The Midrash implies that they could use some warming by the fires of Torah's inspiration. The proper relationship is to come close to Torah but to be temperate, moderate, and reasonable.

Ultimate truth exists—we call it God—but it is not fully ascertainable or understandable by human beings. We can only warm ourselves. We cannot come too close. We are limited. We are not God. The more we study and experience, individually and as a people, the more wisdom and understanding we acquire, but we humans will never be able to say "Now I understand absolute truth"—at least not until some new kind of messianic existence dawns. Human beings are limited. The Torah is not. Incomplete truth is human; absolute truth is God. "Why was the Torah given in the wilderness? Just as the wilderness has no limit so the words of the Torah have no limit." (Pesikta d'Rav Kahana 12:20)

Here then is the significance of the talmudic passage discussed earlier about Rabbi Eliezer's dispute with the Sages. (Baba Metzia 59b) A heavenly voice descended to the earth proclaiming that Eliezer was correct in his interpretation. For heaven's sake, what could be more powerful than a heavenly voice justifying Eliezer's interpretation? "Sorry," said the Sages, "the Torah is not in the heavens."

Human beings now interpret the Torah. Even a heavenly voice won't do. Absolute truth, as proclaimed by the heavenly voice, is rejected. We humans must uncover Torah's meaning. One moment of revelation at Sinai was deemphasized in favor of human interpretation, which is continuous, and requires study and understanding by human beings. Even if we do not penetrate what you call "ultimate truth," this process (not any process, but *this* process) gets us on the right path. It is what God wants. The will of God is to be found and exercised by the people. And lo and behold, the people could even overrule the heavens. This exercise of power by the people, even if it was wrong on the question of the law itself, was sanctioned by tradition.

And my, how the rabbis took advantage of this. They employed many devices to change biblical law, custom, and standards. They amended the Written Law. They clarified it. They extended it. They modified it. They abrogated it. They legislated on matters not written in the Torah. They innovated. All of this changed the law to such an extent that even the Talmud concedes that Moses himself did not recognize the laws that he supposedly pronounced. (Menachot 29b)

To state that the Torah is not in the heavens is not to deny the existence of God. It is not to deny the presence of God in the encounter between Man and Torah. It is to assert that Torah is a tool for human living and understanding. Similarly, to concede human involvement in the writing of the Bible is not to deny the existence of God in the texts. But if the task is left to us to discern God's will, it follows that all of our human frailties and limitations will be brought to the effort. This is not to say that we cannot believe in certain truths emanating from God. I reject the view that asserts that all opinions have equal weight or validity. We have accumulated millennia of wisdom where we are entitled to conclude that tradition, history, experience, reason, discernment, moral judgment, and finally intuition of divine origin and will make a belief "true" or "self-evident." It is a truth that is filtered through human understanding. That, we are told, is what God wants. Torah was revealed for human use, not for the angels. The angels don't need Torah.

Discerning the will of God is at best a partially human endeavor. Our faith never knew an infallible human being. We have no pope or God in human form. Thus the act of discerning God's will cries out for theological modesty.

Our tradition was actually quite modest about its dogmatic assertions. "It is not in our power to explain why the wicked are at ease, or why the righteous suffer." (Pirke Avot 4:15) Yes, we always had, and still do have, certain basic beliefs, violation or rejection of which render the rejecter outside the Jewish faith. But we tended not to be so dogmatic about our beliefs. We were much more concerned with how we act.

"Study is not the chief thing but deeds." (Ibid., 1:17) "Anyone whose deeds exceed his wisdom, his wisdom shall endure. Anyone whose wisdom exceeds his deeds, his wisdom shall not endure." (Ibid., 3:9) One whose wisdom exceeds his deeds is likened to a tree with many branches but few roots. One whose deeds exceed his wisdom is like a tree with few branches but many roots, so that the wind cannot move it. (Ibid., 3:17)

Even in conversion, where you would think that the harshest test of faith would be imposed, our tradition is surprisingly lenient. "If a man desires to convert . . . he is . . . told . . . don't you know that Israel is persecuted and oppressed. . . . If he replies I know and yet am unworthy he is accepted forthwith and given instruction in some of the minor and major commandments. . . . He is told of the punishment for the transgression of the commands . . . and . . . the reward for their fulfillment." (Yevamot 47a–b)

Of course, there is no suggestion that beliefs are unimportant or that a convert need not know anything. But two ideas are emphasized here that are of particular importance. First, the tradition distinguishes between commandments. There are minor and major commands. Not all commands are of equal weight. Second, there is no comprehensive theological exam necessary for conversion. We do not overwhelm the convert with information or details. We do not expect converts to have mastered Jewish theology and to have penetrated the truths of existence. The key to conversion is the desire to cast your lot with the destiny of the Jewish people and the acceptance of the yoke of commandments—that is—the idea that Jews are bound by behavioral expectations and standards.

Judaism was particularly insistent on the centrality of Jewish peoplehood. Perhaps Judaism's most revolutionary thought was the notion that the entire people is holy. Revelation did not occur to one human being or one caste. All of the people experienced revelation and they assumed all of the responsibilities freely, responding "all that the Lord has spoken we will faithfully do!" (Exodus 24:7) No other faith makes such a claim. As Abraham Joshua Heschel wrote: "And if you ask what was it like when the people stood at Sinai hearing God's voice, the answer will be 'Like no other event in the history of man.' There are countless legends, myths, reports, but none of them tells of a whole people witnessing an event such as Sinai." (*God in Search of Man* [Farrar, Straus & Giroux], p. 189)

The Jewish people is unique—"a kingdom of priests and a holy nation." (Exodus 19:6) God chose to single out the Jewish people for a special task—to bring the reality of God to the world, "to perfect the world under the sovereignty of God." (Prayer Book) "I will make of you a great nation and I will bless you. . . . And all the families of the earth shall bless themselves through you." (Genesis 12:2–3)

The Jewish people was selected by God to testify to His presence and to further His will. "For I have singled [Abraham] out that he may instruct his children and his posterity to keep the way of the Lord by doing what is just and right." (Genesis 18:19) "This is My servant whom I uphold, My chosen one in whom I delight. I have put My spirit upon him. He shall teach the true way to the nations. . . . I created you and appointed you a covenant people, a light to the nations, opening eyes deprived of light." (Isaiah 42)

The Bible is essentially the record of the covenant. Only the first eleven chapters of Genesis, a mere sliver of the sacred texts, describe universal events. All of the rest of the Bible describes events that relate to the Jewish people. The Bible's concern is first particular—the Jewish people—that practices a universal purpose: to perfect the world.

Thus the covenant between God and the Jewish people forms the heart of Judaism. This covenant is not for the purpose of self-aggrandizement or expansion. Anyone if they so choose can join the Jewish people. The Torah was given in the middle of the desert, openly and in public, states the tradition, so that anyone wishing to accept it could come and accept it. (Mekhilta Bakhodesh) Why one would want to join the Jewish people is another matter. It is hard to be a Jew: "You alone have I singled out of all the families of the earth. That is why I will call you to account for all your iniquities." (Amos 3:2)

The selection of the Jewish people was one of God's ways of bringing revelation to humanity. The existence of the Jewish people testifies to the existence of God.

The covenant was made for all time, not only with those standing at Sinai but also "with those who are not with us here this day." (Deuteronomy 29:15) It is an everlasting covenant that cannot be abrogated. As bleak as things might look for the Jews, God cannot abandon His covenant with the Jewish people, "for the word of God is always fulfilled." (Isaiah 40:8) It would be a contradiction in terms for the Jews to be wiped out and disappear from the universe. "I will not wholly wipe out the House of Jacob. . . . On that day I will set up again the fallen booth of David. . . . I will restore My people Israel. They shall rebuild ruined cities and inhabit them; they shall plant vineyards and drink their wine; they shall till gardens and eat their fruit. And I will plant them upon their soil, nevermore to be uprooted from the soil I have given them." (Amos 9)

God loves the Jewish people and the Jews love God. "You are precious to Me, and I love you." (Isaiah 43:4) Tradition considered the relationship between God and the Jewish people as a cosmic love affair. "God came from Sinai to receive Israel as a bridegroom comes forth to meet the bride." (Mekhilta Bakhodesh, Chap. 3) Thus even in our darkest hours when the world seems cold and godless, God is with the Jewish people: "When you pass through water I will be with you; through streams they shall not overwhelm you." (Isaiah 43:2)

The covenant with God imposes a special sacred relationship between Jews. There is a solemn bond carried through the ages. "Israel is a spiritual order in which the human and the ultimate, the natural and the holy, enter a lasting covenant. For us Jews there can be no fellowship with God without the fellowship with the people Israel. Abandoning Israel, we desert God. Jewish existence is not only the adherence to particular doctrines and observances but primarily the living in the spiritual order of the Jewish people, the living in the Jews of the past and with the Jews of the present. Our share in holiness we acquire by living in the Jewish community. What we do as individuals is a trivial episode, what we attain as Israel causes us to grow into the infinite." (Heschel, p. 423)

Yosef, this is where I find some of Orthodoxy so troubling. I now feel mostly sadness. Some Orthodox Jews and some of those speaking in the name of Orthodoxy have violated our faith in the most fundamental way. They have given up on the Jewish people. If God has not given up on the Jews, then what gives you the right?

Somewhere along the line, you have lost so much that is precious and dear. You have redefined Judaism in terms of absolutes. True Jew or sinner. Believer or heretic. Absolute truth or falsehood. Somewhere along the line you forgot or minimized one of the central pillars of Judaism, the covenant of the Jewish people. It is no longer, What are the commonalties, the shared experiences, the common history and destiny of our people that characterize Orthodox discussion? Rather, it is, Who has the true belief and who is a liar or heretic? Let us protect ourselves from those who blaspheme the name of God.

In this spirit, Rabbi Moshe Feinstein, perhaps the greatest of Orthodox decisors of the twentieth century, forbade the conducting of Orthodox services anywhere within a Conservative synagogue. "It is well-known that they (Conservative Jews) are kofrim—deniers of many Torah laws." "Most Conservative and Reform rabbis are assumed to be deniers of God and His Torah." "All the people buried in Reform cemeteries are evildoers who have denied our holy Torah." (Responsa, Orah Hayim ii. 50, iv. 91, and Yoreh De'ah, iii. 149, as quoted by Kellner in *Must a Jew Believe in Anything?*)

In this effort to emphasize the inviolability of beliefs over the sanctity of the Jewish people, there is more in common between Orthodoxy and Reform than you think. Early in Reform history, the Classical Reformers also deemphasized Jewish peoplehood: "We consider ourselves no longer a nation, but a religious community." (Pittsburgh Platform) This belief, foreign to Judaism, had the same disastrous consequences for our movement that it will have for Orthodoxy.

Had we continued down this road, we would have become marginalized, and ultimately cast aside by world Jewry. Continue down this road and you too will become marginalized, ghettoized, as some Orthodox sects are already. No fertility projection will save us from the historic consequences of Orthodoxy's disastrous shift in emphasis.

The implication for Orthodoxy of claiming to possess absolute truth is to consider inauthentic everyone else. No people, no social setting, can operate on the basis of absolutes. Tradition recognizes that where there is absolute truth there is no peace. And where there is peace, there is no absolute truth. There is a wonderful *midrash* about the creation of Adam. When God was about to create Adam, the ministering angels formed two groups. Love and Righteousness urged God to create human beings. They are capable of, and will do, acts of love and righteousness, they insisted. Peace and Truth urged God not to create Man because he is capable of, and will do, acts of war and falsehood. The angels were split evenly on whether to create human beings. What did God do? He took truth and cast it to the ground. The vote was then 2 to 1 in favor of creating Adam, and thus Man was born. (Midrash Rabbah) Absolute truth cannot exist in a human setting. Even God recognized that it must give way if there will be human life.

You make it sound as if Orthodoxy says: "Accept in totality the dogma that every word of the Written and Oral Law was dictated by God at Sinai, or you are a sinner (fine distinctions that you try to make about recognizing the Jewishness of the sinner because of his birth to a Jewish mother but denying his religious authenticity notwithstanding). If you do not accept our understanding of absolute truth, ipso facto and by definition you are ignorant or a heretic. If only you knew what we know."

All of the knowledge in the world does not necessarily bring you any closer to wisdom or understanding. "What is said of someone who studies Torah and Mishnah . . . but does not deal honorably and does not speak pleasantly with people? 'Woe to that person who studied Torah. Woe to his father who taught him Torah. Woe to his teacher who taught him Torah.'" (Yomah 86a) What is the good of study, what is the good of knowledge if it brings you no closer to, or might actually distance you from, understanding? When I hear some ultra-Orthodox Jews lecturing the world about how much they know and how ignorant everyone else is, I am reminded of what was said of the graduates of the elite French universities: "They know everything, unfortunately they don't know anything else."

Numerous ties bind the Jewish people to Torah that go beyond the fundamentalist belief in revelation. To state the obvious, Torah—including the Talmud and post-talmudic writings—is ours. We have loved it, nurtured it, expanded it and expounded upon it, embraced it, and died for it for three thousand years. Torah is what Jews do. The Talmud relates Akiva's parable, which he related shortly before the Romans executed him for violating their decree forbidding the teaching of Torah. Akiva compared the Jewish people's attachment to Torah to that of a fish to water. Torah is Israel's natural element, as water is to a fish, he said. While in water there are many dangers, but out of water the fish will die. (Berachot 61b) We can no longer live without Torah than a fish can live on dry land. Akiva gave his life for Torah, as did so many other Jews in our history who had not one view, but a myriad of beliefs on revelation.

Torah for the Jews is life itself. In this sense there is no difference in the approaches of Orthodox and non-Orthodox Jews. Yes, we have certain basic beliefs that we must insist upon, denial of which renders one outside the tent. But there is no need to obsess over ways to characterize millions of our already depleted people (your words) as inauthentic and write them out of our common destiny. We should be spending our days figuring out ways to embrace as many Jews as possible. We should do so not merely because it is useful, but because it is our sacred task inherited from Sinai.

We must recognize that there will be a wide divergence in the manner that Jews think about and practice Judaism. That, in and of itself, is not at all deleterious. Quite the contrary, it reflects a maturity and vitality about us. It has always been that way.

Contemporary understandings about the role of reason, science, democracy, pluralism, egalitarianism, critical analysis, like it or not, will inform and influence large swaths of our people. I can make the case that these concepts are approved of, and might even have their source, in the Bible and postbiblical tradition. But even if you disagree, there is no point in denying that they define the reality of our day.

Freedom is a good thing. Reason is a good thing. Autonomy is a good thing. Like all good things, they can be taken to extremes. So our role is to balance each other out, to keep each other honest; to criticize and rebuke one another but always to love one's fellow Jew as oneself. (Leviticus 19)

In this way, communities can have wide differences of customs and practices. We are seeking "irresistible unity" (Churchill) without uniformity. Communities should feel entitled to innovate. They should be encouraged to exercise the highest degree of autonomy consistent with the basic parameters and obligations of Jewish peoplehood. Just as the Jewish people has an obligation to acknowledge and respect human creativity, differences and innovation, so too the innovator has an obligation to acknowledge the parameters of Jewish peoplehood and the limitations to his autonomy that it imposes.

Yosef, as I mentioned at the outset, I think your description of your beliefs should more or less stand as is. Let me make a number of brief comments.

"EXACTLY AS I HEARD IT"

You write of the very beautiful and moving story of the Baal Shem Tov that you recite every year at Passover. It is a great example of the power of memory and transmission, so important to our people. You write, "The story I told is exactly as I heard it from my grandfather every year. . . . He had heard the story from his father-in-law some sixty years earlier."

Yosef, if the story has any complexity to it at all, and unless that story is written down, it is well-nigh impossible for you to have told it "*exactly*" as you heard it from your grandfather. Even a storyteller's intonation and emphases change the meaning. Further, the more times a story is told orally, the more it becomes corrupted. Details are forgotten; others are added as embellishments. Can you imagine what happens to a story that by now, as you say, is told by thousands of other descendants over 250 years? Do they all tell it *"exactly"* alike? This does not imply that the underlying story did not happen; that there was a man known as the Baal Shem Tov and that he told a similar story on Passover, and that he instructed his descendants to tell it and that it was similar to the content you recite now.

Furthermore, I think that by now you probably have more insights than the first time you told it. You have a deeper understanding of the significance because not only do you know what the Baal Shem Tov knew, but also, in the meantime, 250 years of history have transpired.

"FABRICATED"

You write, "How can we be sure that information has not been deliberately fabricated?"

Any lawyer knows that eyewitness accounts are notoriously unreliable. Trials are often about conflicting testimonies to the same witnessed event. In many legal systems, including Jewish law, this is the reason that more than one witness is desirable, if not often required. It is not a question of deliberate fabrication. People simply see things differently. Was Jesus really resurrected, or did his followers deliberately fabricate this? Did Mohammed really ascend to Heaven, or was this deliberately fabricated? Maybe much more complicated dynamics are going on.

"HOLOCAUST AND TORAH DENIERS"

You write, "You understand that Holocaust deniers can obfuscate the truth . . . but you fail to see that the Torah deniers have done a similar job to the point where even some of our own people, including you, have bought into their way of thinking."

Yosef, I understand your point, but be careful how you think it through and phrase it. First, I have not denied Torah, as detailed extensively. Second, you aren't equating different understandings of revelation with Holocaust denial, are you?

"THE EVIDENCE IN FAVOR OF THE TORAH"

You write, "It is impossible . . . to invent a story . . . that an entire people supposedly witnessed. . . ."

That is an enclosed circular argument that goes something like this: How do we know that revelation occurred in the manner described in the Bible? Because the Bible says so. Where is the proof? The Bible says that 600,000 adults witnessed revelation. Would 600,000 people lie?

Now as I have detailed in this essay, I too believe that the entire people received revelation. I have given some reasons, but I acknowledge that at some point, where reason ends and faith begins, I have taken a leap of faith. The so-called proof you cite based upon Yehudah Halevi is not sufficient. It convinces those who are already convinced.

FORTY YEARS OF MIRACLES

You write, "Judaism . . . dares to claim revelation, and not just any revelation but forty consecutive years of spectacular miracles. This cannot be a lie. No one would have accepted it."

See my comments above.

CHRISTIANITY, ISLAM, AND NON-ORTHODOX JUDAISM

You write, "Christianity and Islam . . . draw their legitimacy from Judaism's public revelation. . . . They are the ones who stand on the shoulders of our Jewish ancestors, Ammi, not you."

Yosef, is your argument that Christianity and Islam are closer to Judaism than Reform, Conservative, or Reconstructionist Judaism?

PURIM

You write, "You wrote that you don't believe it [the Purim story] happened."

I did not write that. I wrote, "I and most Jews celebrate Purim not because we believe in the literal biblical rendition, but because it is an opportunity to celebrate Jewish survival in the face of anti-Semitism."

I am less concerned with whether events really happened in the manner described in the Bible than with the lessons we learn. The Purim story is as relevant today as when it purports to occur because of the values it teaches. Discovering these values is the primary way we extract ongoing meaning from biblical passages. I do not read these passages as if reading a history textbook. (You could have also added Jonah's fishy experience to this principle.) Even history books are notoriously unreliable. History is also a human endeavor and is often written by the winners. Inevitably, it too is not fully objective or absolute truth.

FAITHFUL WITNESSES

You write, "There are enough faithful Witnesses left in the world to ensure the continued viability of the Torah."

By "faithful Witnesses," I gather you mean Orthodox Jews. Does that mean that everyone else is either not a witness or is not faithful?

Ammi

———

December 22, 2000

Dear Ammi,

On the issue of women, I feel like we're doing laps, but let's have another go at it if you wish. There are essentially four issues that touch on gender equality. Let me summarize briefly.

1. In the traditional model of Jewish family life, the man has primary responsibility for the livelihood and the woman for household and children. This model does not sit well with secular Western society, in which people live primarily for themselves (while being kind to others, of course). Since the overriding secular goal is individual achievement and gratification, people are by definition competing with each other. Everyone is playing the game of life, and it is only fair that the playing field should be level. Everyone looks into everyone else's plate and says, "Why can't I have the same thing? It's not fair!" And rightfully so.

But let us think for a moment about the air force. Imagine the navigator of a warplane saying to the pilot, "Why should you have all the fun? Let's be fair. Today, you be the pilot and I'll be the navigator. Tomorrow, I'll be the pilot and you the navigator." Do you think this argument is valid? I should hope not. Fairness is not the issue here. When two people are focused on one common goal, the issue is not equality but success.

Judaism expects us to come together for the common goal of sparking and sustaining the spiritual growth of our families, of serving as role models for the world, of bringing people to a deeper appreciation of the meaning of life. As God's chosen people, we are meant to take our responsibility seriously. This does not mean we should run around preaching to the rest of the world; they will just look at us as sanctimonious windbags and hate us all the more for it. It means that we should build homes and communities in which Torah study, observance, ideals and values are the guiding lights. Before God gave the Torah to the Jewish people, He articulated the common goal in a nutshell. We are to be "a kingdom of priests, a holy nation." (Exodus 19:6) We are all expected to promote this common goal.

On an individual basis, traditional roles are recommended, not mandatory. The Jewish woman must look into her own heart and decide how to bridge the two worlds in which she lives without violating the inviolable; she can decide for herself how to apportion her life between career and family. If she feels driven to become the president of a *Fortune* 500 company, she can do so.

With regard to the assignment of privileges within the family, according to the guidelines of the Talmud, the wife takes precedence in personal needs, while the husband takes precedence in ceremonial roles as the titular head of the family. If both husband and wife need new clothes and there is just enough money for one set, the wife gets the money, while the husband gets to make Kiddush for the family in his old suit. This is the recommended paradigm. It is not mandatory.

2. As for the *mekhitzah,* the intent is not to push women to "the back of the bus." In fact, in many synagogues the *mekhitzah* runs right down the middle, dividing the chamber right and left rather than front and back. Rather, it is to create a separation between the sexes so that the time spent in the synagogue will be a spiritual rather than a social experience.

In *Jew vs. Jew,* Samuel Freedman writes about a couple who left a non-Orthodox congregation in Los Angeles to join a Modern Orthodox *shul.* In an ironic twist, the wife found that the *mekhitzah* gave her a refreshing "sense of continuity and female solidarity"; it had enhanced the spirituality of the prayer experience for her. But for some people, the grass is always greener on the other side of the *mekhitzah.*

3. As a rule, the Torah defines and assigns the respective roles in public ritual. For example, the hereditary Kohanim serve as the priestly caste of the Jewish people. They are the first called to the Torah, and the ones who pronounce the priestly blessing over the people. Is this fair? Is this equality? Are all Kohanim holier than us common Jews? Now, a liberal-minded person might say that a merit-based priesthood would be superior to a hereditary one, but the Torah explicitly disagrees. Judaism does not provide the latitude for role reversals in the realm of public ritual.

By the same token, in matters of public ritual, the Sages assigned the roles of cantor, reader, and the like to men in imitation of the Temple ritual and for reasons of modesty as well.

I understand that some women may have powerful spiritual aspirations that they feel would be best expressed in a man's role. But the fact of the matter is that if we try to remake Judaism to our tastes and specifications we create something new and different, an ersatz Judaism that delegitimizes the Torah, the Talmud, and thousands of years of Jewish scholarship, practice, and tradition. This is not the Judaism for which our ancestors lived and died. At best, it bears only a pale superficial resemblance to it.

You write, "The very act of exempting women from certain obligations that men assume becomes the basis for different and unequal treatment." Listen to yourself. Your statement effectively negates the Written Law, the Talmud, and the Shulchan Aruch. The price of equality, according to you, is to become Reform. Tell me, Ammi, how does Reform achieve equality with regard to the obligations spelled out in the Torah? By the wife putting on *tefillin,* for example, or by the husband ceasing to do so?

4. Finally, there is the issue of female rabbis and communal leaders. Although women are not obligated to study Torah, such a thing is theoretically possible, and in fact, it has happened from time to time, as in the case of Deborah. Even if a woman should attain the requisite scholarship, the issue of modesty would remain a major hurdle. In our times, of course, women who aspire to be communal teachers and leaders can do so through the print media, as numerous Orthodox women have done very effectively.

You find it hard to relate to these difficulties, because female Reform rabbis do not encounter such obstacles. The vaunted Reform autonomy frees you from any real need for serious Torah scholarship, and modesty is apparently not one of your concerns.

For us, however, modesty is a major concern. You challenge my statement that "a man's thoughts are more likely [than a woman's] to turn in libidinous directions" and wonder how I know this. Talmudic and rabbinic sources are replete with this idea; it forms the basis for many *halakhot* in the Shulchan Aruch. You disagree. As in all issues, I'm sure your view on this matter is based on contemporary Western thought and mores. This leaves me in a quandary. Should I accept the opinion of the Sages whose wisdom and guidance produced the rock-solid institution of the traditional Jewish family? Or should I accept the opinion of your contemporary thinkers whose values have led to promiscuity, teenage pregnancy, infidelity, high divorce rates, the breakdown of the family—the ultimate debasement and denigration of women on an unprecedented scale?

Modesty is a difficult concept for people raised in America, where a casual hug and kiss between near strangers are as meaningless as a handshake, where women walk half-clad on the streets in the summertime. Queen Elizabeth wouldn't be caught dead dressed like that. Well, my wife and daughter are more distinguished than the queen; they are descended from the biblical patriarchs and matriarchs, and they choose to dress and behave accordingly.

In the final analysis, classic Judaism is not perfectly compatible with modern Western values. As in all areas of life, choices must be made. Do we want authentic Judaism, the kind that endured with uninterrupted continuity for thousands of years, the kind that provided inspiration and fulfillment to innumerable Jewish people throughout the ages, the kind for which people have given their lives? And if so, are we prepared to integrate into our lives only those Western values that are not antithetical to Judaism? Or do we want a full, Western-style secular life with just enough Jewishness to give it the patina of tradition, kosher-style deli rather than authentically kosher deli?

By the way, Ammi, most Orthodox women are doing just fine, thank you. They are poised, respected, and fulfilled and are not plagued by a sense of inequality. Although you keep dropping smug little remarks about how your kind of egalitarianism is seeping into the Orthodox world, you are living in a pipe dream.

Which brings us to the "Women of the Wall" and other nominally Orthodox mavericks whose "names [you] can supply." I am sure you can, since they would probably fit on a couple of pieces of paper.

You cite the bill introduced in the Knesset called "Defense of the Western Wall" as an example of Orthodox intolerance, of the attempt "to impose [Orthodox standards] upon everyone else." You mention that this bill calls for women to be imprisoned for seven years if they don a *tallit* at the Wall! It is beyond credibility.

Now, I know that the Western Wall is one of the main arenas of your dedicated activism in Israel, and that the issue of pluralism at the Wall is very near and dear to your heart. At the same time, not being politically active myself, and since I have little knowledge and less understanding of the intricacies of Israeli politics, I asked a friend at Agudath Israel to enlighten me. He explained that absolutely no one wants any woman to sit in jail for even one minute for donning a *tallit* at the Wall, but that the prohibition is to be temporarily included in a broader law, which carries a penalty of imprisonment, until a better law can be written. I guess this is another example of the unfortunate and often bizarre vagaries of Israeli law and politics, which you yourself described to me at length over lunch last summer. Please, I don't want to debate this particular law with you. I grant that the way it is written is silly. No one will argue the point.

I would, however, like to address the larger issue of so-called pluralism at the Wall. My friend at Agudath Israel faxed me some material, including some by non-Orthodox Jews. I would like to share these with you.

Here is a piece from the *Forward* by the secular writer Hillel Halkin: "Where exactly does it say in Reform or Conservative Judaism that it is a religious commandment for women to don prayer shawls at the Western Wall? Were they to come to the Wall without prayer shawls as a simple gesture of respect for the traditions of the place, against what sacred principles of their faith would they be sinning? Are there no other places to practice Jewish feminism in the world, in Israel or even in Jerusalem that they must do it at the one site where it most infuriates large numbers of other Jews? Would it be quibbling to point out that twenty years ago Conservative women did not even wear prayer shawls in their own synagogues, and that not so much longer ago than that even the men in Reform temples did not wear prayer shawls in their synagogues?

"This is the nub of the matter. What really motivates the behavior of Jews like those . . . or the Jewish feminist group called Women of the Wall . . . is not religious need. It is religious politics, which is something very different. Of course, since Orthodoxy in Israel plays (and very successfully) at religious politics, it would be hypocritical to condemn Reform and Conservative for doing the same. . . . At the same time, however, one's heart does not go out to political manipulators in quite the same way that it goes out to religious martyrs. At least mine doesn't."

And here is a letter to the editor from the New York *Jewish Week*: "As a member of a Reform congregation, I must respond to many letters and articles on incidents that have taken place at the Western Wall. Please consider that Jewish practice and tradition from time immemorial have been for men and women to pray separately. This practice, still carried on by the Orthodox, has extended to the Wall, and it is a practice that has been respected by Israelis. Is it unreasonable to permit our Orthodox brethren to continue in this tradition, given their steadfast, unwavering, fervent devotion to this sacred place for centuries before the Conservative and Reform movements even existed?

"The Orthodox agree that the [Wall] is the property of Klal Yisrael, not just the Orthodox. . . . They do not ask those who come to stand before the Wall if they are Reform, Conservative or even Jewish. They ask only that men cover their heads and women pray in an area of the Wall separate from the men. Is it really asking that much from the Conservative and Reform to adhere to a centuries-old tradition?

"Our rabbis and Jewish leaders have a far larger challenge than how we visit the Wall. They must assist our American Jewish community in finding its place in the battle for Jewish continuity. The battle for our Jewish souls, tradition, culture and religion is here in the United States. The leaders and rabbis are taking the easy way out as they try to have us devalue, even hate the Orthodox at the expense of putting our own house in order."

I couldn't have said it better myself.

Yosef

PART THREE

January 1, 2001

Dear Ammi,

It seems you feel compelled by "clear evidence and reason" to deny that Moses wrote the Torah at God's behest. You would rather espouse the theories of the Bible critics who see the Torah as an imperfectly edited composite of ancient and not so ancient records of Jewish mythology. You state again and again that "volumes have been written . . . let the readers review the evidence for themselves and decide."

Well, then, let us start with you. How many of these dusty volumes have you investigated carefully? And if you yourself didn't do so, do you honestly expect others to plow through them and decide on their reliability? No, what you've done is a clever lawyer's trick. Point to a stack of thick books and declare that the "clear evidence" is all there, relying on the power of suggestion to "prove" your point

Don't invest so much faith in these Bible critics, Ammi. They aren't worthy of it. Professor Yechezkel Kaufman, a secular Bible critic, puts it very well in *A History of the Jewish Faith* (Hebrew): "Biblical criticism finds itself today in a unique situation. There is a dominant theory, yet no one knows why it dominates. In the history of ideas, theories or concepts based on certain accepted principles often enjoy a disembodied existence long after those principles have been discredited. This is exactly what happened to the scientific study of the Bible in our times. . . . [In the nineteenth century,] Wellhausen . . . based his theories on an interlocking system of proofs that seemed to complement each other, forming layers of solid intellectual foundations upon which he erected the definitive edifice of his ideas. In the meantime, however, these foundations disintegrated one by one. The proofs were refuted outright or at least seriously questioned. The scholars of the Wellhausen school were forced to admit that most of the proofs do not hold up under scrutiny. Nonetheless, they did not abandon the conclusions."

Such is the nature of pseudoscience. Someone tosses out a bit of wild speculation, and by the time it goes around the block, it is an accepted fact; no one has the time or the inclination to check it out. I used to wonder at the accepted chronology of the Egyptian pharaohs; for instance, Thutmose I reigned from 1493 to 1481 B.C.E. I asked a friend, a history professor at a university in New York, how they pin down the dates with such amazing accuracy. He told me that some academic takes a guess, and by the time it gets into the secondary and tertiary sources, it's just a fact. Who's going to check it out?

I'm sure you know that the original Native Americans migrated from Siberia to Alaska across a land bridge that existed where the Bering Strait is now. It is a well-known fact. I suggest you read *Red Earth, White Lies,* by Vine Deloria, Jr., the eminent Native American author, which just tears this idea to shreds, but you'll still find it in all the textbooks.

You and I both know that virtually none of our readers will "review the evidence for themselves." So let us deal with some of the issues you raised. You wrote in an earlier posting: "Why would God have dictated to Moses two creation stories—one where the world and beasts were created first and Man last, and another where Man is created first? Why one passage where Man and Woman are created together, as equals, and another where Man is created alone and first?"

Let us check the classic sources. The Midrash, quoted by Rashi, explains that the first account is general, while the second zeroes in on the man in the Garden of Eden and mentions only details of creation relevant to the story. A very reasonable reading of the texts. Now, if the second story is a duplicate account, as you seem to believe, why is there no mention of the creation of the sun, moon, and stars? Why is there no mention of the creation of the fishes of the sea, only the animals and the birds? According to the Midrash, however, this is not really a creation story. Therefore, the animals and birds are mentioned in the context of Adam giving them names, but since Adam did not name the fishes, they are not mentioned.

M. D. Cassuto, the prominent secular Bible scholar, also understands the "second creation account" in this way. "The subject of this chapter is the story of the Garden of Eden, and as a preface, Scripture repeats the creation story, focusing on the creation of man. The account differs from the first, but there are no contradictions, just additional details."

For some reason, however, you seem more comfortable subscribing to the view of the Bible critics that the Torah was assembled from assorted documents, and that a duplicate creation story somehow slipped through. Well, Ammi, do you think our ancestors, those brilliant primitives who produced the most powerful and magnificent piece of literature in history, ever heard of proofreading? If our hypothetical chief editor had just let his proofreaders take a look at it, they would have told him, "Sir! Big blooper right here in the first chapter. Send it back to the typesetter!"

One of the famous ideas of Julius Wellhausen and his German school of Bible criticism is the Documentary Hypothesis, the theory that the Torah is woven together from the J and E documents among others. These great minds noticed that the Bible sometimes refers to God by the J name and sometimes by the E name. They scratched their heads in bafflement. And then they had a flash of dazzling insight. There must have been different documents referring to different deities, and the hypothetical editors who blended them, in their usual sloppy style, failed to make them consistent.

Check it out, Ammi. I am not kidding you. This sort of reasoning is at the foundation of Bible criticism. This is, of course, absurd. The Midrash (Mekhilta Beshalakh) explains that the J name is used when the attribute of mercy is active and the E name when the attribute of strict justice is active. Every eight-year-old child in Hebrew school has always known this basic principle. But what can you expect from German academics who didn't learn Hebrew until they were in college, had no access to the Oral Torah, and never bothered to ask Jewish schoolteachers for the answer?

When I attended the International Book Fair in Moscow in 1987, a professor of English from the University of Tbilisi in Soviet Georgia struck up a conversation with me. He told me he had written a two-volume dictionary of American slang, and he wanted to check out a few things.

"Can I ask you a question?" he asked.

"Sure, go ahead."

"Do you know what 'ticked off' means?"

"Of course I do," I said. "It means 'annoyed.'"

He shook his head. "No. It means 'exhausted.'"

It was my turn to shake my head. "It means 'annoyed.'"

"I'm afraid you're wrong. I have made an extensive study of the expression, and all the evidence indicates that it means 'exhausted.'"

"Tell me," I said, "have you ever been to the United States?"

"No. But what difference does it make?"

"All the difference," I said.

Every street urchin in the United States knows more about American slang than this hapless fellow in his study in Tbilisi. And every child in Hebrew school knows more about the Torah than these self-appointed Bible critics.

You have to consider the Bible critics in their historical context. They had an agenda. In the nineteenth century, after the fall of Napoleon, German nationalism sought expression in its pagan Teutonic roots, and it struggled to break away from the albatross of Christianity. The political and cultural mission of Wellhausen and the other Bible critics was to discredit the Christian Bible and the foundation upon which it rests—the Jewish Bible. Every time they found a redundancy, an anomaly, or any of the other plentiful signals that call out so eloquently to Talmudists, these critics immediately discerned imperfect editing, multiple authors, and all sorts of textual flaws. Of course, it never occurred to them that the shortcomings might be in their own understanding. In the end, their specious conclusions were accepted as scientific fact, and religion was undermined.

But what about you, Ammi? Why should you parrot the enemies of Judaism and the Jewish people? I am not concerned about the decline of Judeo-Christian values in Germany, but I am concerned about all the Jews who thought that being modern meant swallowing the bitter pill of German devaluation of the Jewish heritage. It doesn't matter that you couch your German-inspired reading of the Torah and Jewish history in pretty words and glib platitudes. The plain fact is that you and other Jews like you, who have been persuaded by the German Bible critics and their successors, exemplify a tragic defeat for our people.

Even among the Bible critics themselves, many thoughtful scholars are abandoning the Documentary Hypothesis. Listen to Cassuto on the subject: "Among the proofs that many scholars bring to support the hypothesis that the Torah is a composite drawn from multiple sources, it is worthwhile to pay special attention to the interchanging of divine names. . . . Recent research has established that there is no basis for the hypothesis that [this] is an indication of multiple sources. . . . All in all, these critical theories create more difficulties than they purport to solve."

Listen to Henri Blocher in *Révélation des Origines: Le Début de la Genèse* (French). "The critics, when they judge the internal phenomena [of the Bible], project into it their customs as modern Western readers and neglect all we know today of the writing customs of Biblical times. The taste for repetition, the structure of a global statement, repeated with development, the replacement of a word by its synonyms, especially the change of a divine name in a text (i.e., the names of Osiris on the stele of Ikhernofret), are well attested characteristics of ancient Middle Eastern texts. . . . The Biblical text, as it is, agrees with the literary canons of its time."

Listen to W. F. Albright in *Archaeology and the Religion of Israel*. "The Mosaic tradition is so consistent . . . so congruent with our independent knowledge of the religious development of the Near East in the late second millennium B.C. that only hypercritical pseudo-rationalism can reject its essential historicity."

Listen to Dr. Yohanan Aharoni, in *Canaanite Israel during the Period of Israeli Occupation*. "Recent archaeological discoveries have decisively changed the entire approach of Bible critics. They now appreciate the Torah as a historical document of the highest caliber. . . . No authors or editors could have put together or invented these stories hundreds of years after they happened."

Finally, a team of Israeli and German Bible critics (reported in the *Zeitschrift für die Alttestamentaliche Wissenschaft*) conducted a computer analysis of the style and language of the Bible. Although no author is rigidly consistent in the usage of word forms and stylistic expression, a reasonable percentage of similarity can be expected. For instance, the internal percentage of similarity of Kant's works is 22, and no one questions that the works were all produced by Kant. The internal percentage of similarity of Goethe's works is just 8, and still, no one questions his authorship of all of them. The researchers discovered that the internal percentage of similarity between the J and E documents is 82! There is, therefore, no question that they are the product of one author.

So you see, Ammi, I've taken your advice and checked out some of those "volumes" of yours. I could bring you numerous additional sources if you wish, but I think this is enough. The preponderance of evidence supports the unity of the Torah's authorship, which places it way back in antiquity and actually proves its authenticity. How could such a fiction have been foisted on people who were practically contemporaries of the events described? Could you pass off a bogus issue of *Time* magazine whose cover story reported that an atom bomb had leveled Washington during World War II and whose publisher's message reported that copies of that issue had been distributed hot off the presses to every household, school, and library in America?

The disdainful disregard of Jewish sources so prevalent in Bible criticism is also evident in secular interpretations of Jewish history. There is a fast day called Asarah b'Tevet, which memorializes the Babylonian siege of Jerusalem about two and a half millennia ago. I don't know if Reform still honors this memorial, but I am sure you have heard of it. In the special Selichot for the fast day, we recall another tragic event that took place a few centuries later on the eighth of the month of Tevet. In about 250 B.C.E., King Ptolemy of Egypt summoned seventy Jewish elders to Alexandria and ordered them to translate the Torah into Greek for his library; the result, known as the Septuagint, was considered a national tragedy. This event is also recorded as an awful tragedy in Megillat Taanit, composed during Mishnaic times, not more than a century or two after the fact. Modern secular historians, however, maintain that the mostly Greek-speaking Jewish people of Alexandria inspired the translation because they wanted to show their Greek neighbors that they also had a book of wisdom. This explanation, which completely ignores Jewish sources, can only be based on speculation, yet it has entered the history books as established fact.

Why the Sages considered the Septuagint a national tragedy is a subject for a separate discussion. But I want to know which side you take on this question, Ammi. Do you walk in lockstep with the orthodox secular establishment, as do just about all the secular Jewish historians, or do you give credence to the explanation given by our ancestors when the national memory of the event was still fresh?

It does not surprise me that the secular Bible critics and historians have no regard for the Jewish national memory, but I am disappointed that you are not sensitive to it.

THE BAAL SHEM TOV STORY

Regarding my analogy of the Baal Shem Tov story, you point out that it may have changed somewhat over the years, especially since I now tell the story in light of the 250 years of history that have since transpired. This is not so, since the telling of the story is a ritualistic, uninterrupted, fifteen-minute narration. The words are not exactly the same, but the content never varies. Only afterward do discussions, if any, take place.

But even if you do not find my Baal Shem Tov story reliable, would you be more impressed if a few hundred families, all descended from the Baal Shem Tov, also observed the same annual ritual on the last day of Passover and told the identical story? Would you find the story so easy to dismiss? I doubt it. (You see? I also have doubt about some things.) Well, what if millions of people not only tell the same story but actually have it deeply embedded in the fabric of their lives, their regular observances, and their periodic festivals and celebrations? How can you dismiss the memory of millions of people? The transmission of the Torah is the most vivid memory of the entire Jewish nation.

You write that "any lawyer knows that eyewitness accounts are notoriously unreliable. . . . In many legal systems, including Jewish law, that is the reason more than one witness is desirable, if not often required." Exactly. One is not reliable, but two are. How about several million? I should think that just about eliminates the margin of error. This is precisely the parallel to the Holocaust. The deniers can impugn the testimony of individual survivors but not the testimony of tens of thousands.

CONCLUSIVE PROOF

I demonstrated to you that the Torah provides conclusive proof of its own authenticity by stating (Exodus 19:9), "I will come to you in a thick cloud, so that all the people will hear when I speak to you, then they will also believe in you forever." I then presented to you Rabbi Yehudah Halevi's illuminating explanation of how the presence of "all the people" at revelation would ensure that they would "believe in you forever." But you casually dismiss this classic proof as circular reasoning. ("How do we know that revelation occurred in the manner described in the Bible? Because the Bible says so.") It seems you missed the point completely. Is that really what you thought the great Jewish philosopher was saying? Do you take him for a fool?

Let me explain it again. Of course the Torah's own statements cannot prove its veracity. But we can make some empirical observations. The Torah, which claims that millions of Jews witnessed revelation, was accepted as the truth by virtually all Jewish people for thousands of years. This in itself is the proof. Otherwise, why would people have accepted the Torah? The people on whom this hoax was being perpetrated would surely have objected, "According to this book, these events happened in full view of millions of people. How come we never heard about them?"

In my posting, I added another powerful facet and clarification of this proof, which is based on material from the archives of the Arachim Institute in Israel. Since the Torah describes how it was distributed to all the original witnesses, it must have been in circulation from the very beginning. Otherwise, how could a book that makes such claims be introduced at a later time? Surely the people about to be duped would have objected, "According to this book, it has been in circulation since the beginning. How come we never got this book?"

Just imagine a book that claims that a people witnessed numerous incredible miracles, not once, not twice, but constantly for an entire generation! Just imagine that this same book claims it was immediately distributed to all the millions of witnesses who are enjoined to carry it with them and read it all the time. Just imagine that this same book reports that from that day on all the miraculous events should be memorialized by numerous national observances. Just imagine that the book warns (Deuteronomy 4:2), "You shall not add to the word I command you, nor may you subtract from it." Can you fabricate such a book and introduce it to people who have never heard of it? Impossible! You see, Ammi, the proof is not the testimony of the book, but rather the nature of the book itself, which makes it impossible to fabricate.

A similar device was used in the chronicle of the Purim story. The final third of the Book of Esther describes in great detail its own wide and immediate dissemination to all the far-flung communities that were delivered from the Persian decree of extermination. This served as a guarantee that its authenticity could not be legitimately questioned, for if it were introduced at a later time, no one would accept it. "Look!" people would say. "It is written right here in the book that all the communities received copies immediately after the event. How come we never heard the story or saw the scrolls?"

You ask if, in my opinion, "Christianity and Islam are closer to Judaism than Reform, Conservative, or Reconstructionist Judaism." Christianity and Islam accept the truth of revelation described in the Torah but claim that future, nonpublic revelations superseded it. You, on the other hand, maintain by intuition that we are the chosen people, but you do not accept the Torah's description of revelation as actual fact nor its laws as legally binding. Both these viewpoints are distant from Judaism—and from each other—but the feelings that resonate in your heart are unquestionably Jewish. I'll address that at greater length in a separate posting.

THE TORAH ACCORDING TO HUCKLEBERRY FINN

Look where your views have led you, Ammi. By denying that the Torah as written is the word of God, you take for yourself the right to judge it, to decide that "some laws are out-of-date, impractical, or worse, unethical."

First of all, the example you give of the Torah's alleged lack of ethics is another of your misrepresentations. You point specifically to slavery and follow up with a touching quotation from *Huckleberry Finn*. How nice, but totally off the point. Your reading of the Torah matches Huckleberry's, but you are both equally misinformed.

Do you think the Torah condones American slavery? Do you think the Torah approves of black people being abducted from their villages in Africa, stuffed into the stinking holds of slave ships and sold on the block in America? Are you unaware that the Torah demands the death penalty for "one who abducts a man and sells him"? (Exodus 21:16) The American enslavement of the black people was a despicable crime, a capital offense.

Now for the facts. According to the Torah, kings have the power to enslave prisoners of war or criminals, and even then, theirs is no more than an indentured status that does not extend to the children. (Maimonides, Yad, Avadim 9:4–5) The only slavery that has permanence is when it constitutes the first step in the process of conversion to Judaism. When a gentile slave is acquired by a Jew, he is ritually purified and circumcised just like any other convert, but he does not assume full Jewish status. By joining a Jewish household as a servant, he becomes an associate member of the covenant of Abraham and assumes some of its obligations; this status also extends to his children. If, however, the slave refuses to accept these limited obligations to Torah observance, his master cannot keep him. (Ibid., 8:12)

Furthermore, a slave who enters the covenant is considered a human being. If his master injures him, he automatically goes free. (Ibid., 5:4) Furthermore, killing anyone's slave is punishable by death. (Ibid., Rotze'ach 2:10) Furthermore, if a slave living in the Diaspora wants to live in Israel, his master is obliged to immigrate with him or sell him to someone else who will take him there. (Ibid., Avadim 8:9) Furthermore, if a slave living in the Diaspora runs away to Israel, his master is obligated to set him free; the emancipated slave must then indemnify his former master when he can afford it. (Ibid., 8:10) Furthermore, if a Jew living in Israel sells his slave to a master in the Diaspora, the slave goes free with no indemnification whatsoever. (Ibid., 8:6)

Does this sound like black slavery in America, Ammi? In fact, I don't think we should demean these people who enter the covenant by calling them slaves. The Hebrew word is *eved,* and I think "servant" would be a more appropriate translation, just as the Torah describes Moses as the *eved* of God (Deuteronomy 34:5), which you would translate as "servant," not "slave."

But wait. This is not all. Listen to how the master is required to treat his servant. I quote Maimonides (Yad, Avadim 9:5): "One should be kind and righteous and not lay a heavy burden on one's servant nor cause him pain. One should provide him with all kinds of food and drink; the early Sages used to share all their courses with their servants. . . . Similarly, one must not demean them by deed or word; Scripture allows servitude but not disgrace. One should not yell at them or express anger. Rather, one should speak softly and listen to their grievances. This is specifically mentioned among the pleasant ways on which Job prided himself (Job 31:13), 'Had I disdained the just cause of my manservant and maidservant when they challenged me, what could I have said when the Lord rose up? What could I have answered Him when He remembered? For the One who made him made me in the belly, the same One prepared us in the womb.'"

We can go into this much more deeply, but this is not the place for it. In the meantime, bounce this off Huckleberry Finn, Ammi. You would certainly ease his conscience about helping the runaway Jim.

But there is a much deeper problem here than your misreading of the Torah's stand on slavery. Who gave you the right to judge the ethics of the Torah? Don't you realize that to call the Torah unethical is a contradiction in terms? If even the smallest part of the Torah is unethical, then it could not have come from God, not by revelation, not by intuition. With what does that leave you, Ammi, but a worthless roll of parchment, an artifact from the distant, primitive past? Did Abraham question God's ethics when He told him to bind Isaac for a sacrifice? Would you have? Are you more ethical than God Himself?

Over the course of millennia, hundreds of thousands, perhaps even millions, of great Jewish scholars and thinkers, the people on whose shoulders you claim to stand, have revered the Torah and considered each word sacrosanct. Along come Reform rabbis, their bellies full of newfound wisdom, and declare the Torah unethical? I am aghast.

Be well, my friend.

Yosef

January 14, 2001
Dear Ammi,

In your last posting you referred back to earlier comments of yours (April 2000) that supposedly established your credentials as an enlightened, thoroughly modern man while implying that I and others like me are hopelessly mired in medieval obscurantism. I beg to differ.

DISFIGURING REASON

You wrote: "The fundamentalist viewpoint that the world is less than six thousand years old because that is what Genesis implies is irrational to me. I have no interest in disfiguring reason and twisting myself into theological contortions every time a dinosaur bone is discovered."

Personally, I do not claim to know the age of the earth with any degree of certainty, not because there is a conflict between the Torah and science, but because there are conflicting views among the scientists themselves. If science should prove conclusively that the earth is billions of years old, that is fine with me. Genesis would still not be disproved. Classical Judaism is based on the interpretations of the Oral Law; it is incorrect to take issue with the text based on what a literal reading "implies" to you (remember "an eye for an eye"?). Nachmanides, commenting on the first verse of the Torah, states very clearly that Genesis gives us no inkling of the creation process, nor is it meant to do so. The Tosafists explain (Rosh Hashanah 8a) that biblical chronology begins after creation; the entire process of creation took place prior to the first day of Year One. Moreover, the Torah reveals nothing about the relative passage of time during the pre-biblical period. (See Dr. Gerald Schroeder in *Genesis and the Big Bang.*) So how old is the earth according to our measurement of time? Is it five thousand years old? Five million? Five billion? I don't know. But you apparently do.

It seems our roles are suddenly reversed. You have contended all along that there is no certainty in this world, and you have chided me for my own need for certainty. Yet amazingly, a dinosaur bone convinces you beyond the shadow of a doubt that the earth is hundreds of millions or even billions of years old. Frankly, I am puzzled. How exactly does the discovery of a dinosaur bone prove the extreme antiquity of the earth with such absolute certainty? Has science somehow removed all your doubts?

I know that the textbooks provide hard information on the age of the earth down to the decimal points, Ammi, but don't invest so much faith in them. They change all the time. For many years, the textbooks preached Aristotle's theory of a static universe; the idea of an expanding universe with an origin was considered "disfiguring reason." But today, science is convinced the universe is expanding. Are you absolutely certain the prevailing scientific opinion will be the same a hundred years from now? For hundreds of years, scientists swore by Newtonian physics; then Einstein turned physics on its head. Are you absolutely certain Einstein will still be as authoritative a hundred years from now?

Physics, for instance, is a fairly exact science. Its hypotheses can be subjected to the scientific method; scientists can observe phenomena firsthand and conduct experiments. And yet, although physics can improve society and advance technology, it still cannot tell us what causes gravity; the machines continue to work, but the theories change.

On the other hand, geology and evolutionary biology, which attempt to determine the origins of the natural world, are far from exact sciences. There are no time machines to help us observe what took place in antiquity, nor can we test hypotheses by experimentation. We can only construct theories on the basis of fragmentary evidence. And as the body of evidence grows and mathematical analysis progresses, the theories constantly change (and are duly recorded in the textbooks as fact). Classical Darwinism was very popular in the scientific community a century ago; it was considered an obvious fact. But the theory was so flawed that it eventually gave way to neo-Darwinism, the synthetic theory, which then became the new fact. Today the fashionable hypothesis is punctuated equilibrium as opposed to gradualism. Do you think we might have a different fact one hundred years from now? Or have we determined, once and for all, the final absolute truth of evolutionary biology?

So let us talk about geology. There is no conclusive scientific proof to any estimate of the earth's age. The common measurements based on the half-life of the uranium or potassium isotope or any of the other radiogenic geological chronometers are far from accurate (see Richard Milton's *Shattering the Myths of Darwinism*). But even if we stipulate the integrity of the measurements, their validity rests on the assumption that, in the famous words of Archibald Geikie, "the present is the key to the past," that no global cataclysmic upheavals ever occurred, that all change is the result of the steady drip-drip of placid time.

What right do we have to make this kind of an assumption? If the Shoemaker-Levy Comet collided with Jupiter in 1994, why couldn't such a thing have happened to the earth, not only once but even a number of times? And if the earth did experience such cataclysms in the dim past, the effects on the topography, climate, and environment of the earth would have been so extreme as to render all standard geological dating completely meaningless.

This is not just idle talk, Ammi. There is plenty of evidence of major upheavals in natural history. What caused the sudden extinction of the dinosaurs and mammoths? Why was the flesh of frozen prehistoric mammoths edible in the last century? Doesn't that suggest that whatever killed them quick-froze them as well? Why are there no signs of Ice Age glaciers in Siberia, the coldest place on earth? How do we account for continental drift? Why is there a deserted but well-preserved city in the Andes Mountains two and a half miles above sea level, where nothing grows and there is hardly any air to breathe? Doesn't this suggest that the mountains rose during historical times after the city had been built? In fact, a study by Helmut de Terra of the Carnegie Institute and T. T. Paterson of Harvard concluded that the Himalayas reached their present lofty height during the historical period.

So why do many scientists deny the possibility of historical cataclysms? Because without virtually unlimited amounts of time, the Darwinian theory of evolution in any of its forms or revisions would collapse.

Now, evolution undoubtedly takes place on some level. Over a span of generations, a species will get taller or shorter, darker or lighter, and so forth, depending on numerous biological factors; influenza bugs may evolve to the point where they are immune to last year's drugs, and of course, the resistant bugs will replace the susceptible ones through natural selection. This is called microevolution.

But is speciation also a fact? Can one species morph into another through evolution by random mutations? Can amoebae evolve into fish, which evolve into monkeys, which in turn evolve into humans? Can macroevolution happen? Darwinists believe it can and does happen, that life arose from a "primordial soup" and progressed through astronomical numbers of highly improbable random mutations, which were then molded into different species by natural selection. According to the Darwinists, there is no intelligent design in the universe. Human beings are a fortuitous accident, no more than overgrown, sentient amoebae, the product of random mutations. God, if He exists, is a disinterested First Cause who set the game in motion and sat back to watch the fun without any direct involvement. According to the Darwinists, people do not have souls, just as amoebae do not. There is no higher meaning to life, nor is there an afterlife. Prayer is pointless.

But what about the science of Darwinism? Is it sound? Actually, it is quite poor. If a cancer researcher were to apply for a project grant based on Darwinist-quality science, he wouldn't get a plugged nickel.

First of all, it appears to be a mathematical impossibility. Dr. Lee Spetner, in *Not by Chance!* makes an interesting calculation. If you were to flip 150 coins, what are your chances of having them all come up heads? The answer is 1 in 10^{45}. This is an astronomical number. If 10,000,000,000 computers were to run simulated coin flips for 3,000 years, they would not reach that number. We would, therefore, call it an impossibility. The chance of the random emergence of a new species, according to Dr. Spetner, is 1 in $3.6 \times 10^{2,738}$!

Furthermore, since it would take countless random steps to effect any significant Darwinian change, there should be numerous fossils of the intermediate forms. Darwin assured his readers that exploration would fill the gaps in the fossil record. Well, 150 years have since passed. Museums the world over are full of fossils, but the gaps are as gaping as ever. The intermediate forms have still not been found. Where are all the semigiraffes with medium-sized necks?

Then there is the problem of complex organs such as the human eye, with its extremely intricate mechanisms for receiving, processing, and transmitting images, none of which is efficient except as part of the whole, not to mention the capacity of the brain to interpret those images. Darwin himself wrote in On the Origin of Species, "[T]he belief that an organ so perfect as the eye could have been formed by natural selection is enough to stagger anyone. . . . I have felt the difficulty far too keenly to be surprised at others hesitating to extend the principle of natural selection to so startling a length." The desperate explanations offered by Darwinist apologists are embarrassingly lame; they are sophistry rather than science. Talk about "disfiguring reason"!

Moreover, recent advances in molecular biochemistry, as Michael Denton explains in Evolution: A Theory in Crisis, have torpedoed Darwinism from a different direction. Darwin assumed that evolution began with simple organisms like the amoeba, but modern science has discovered that on the molecular level amoebae are as complex as any other organism. So where are the "simple organisms" that came out of the "primordial soup"? There are none.

So why do Darwinists believe as they do in spite of all the problems with the theory? Because of the doctrine of naturalism, the belief that all observed phenomena can and must be explained by natural causes. Naturalism is not science; there is no scientific proof that God has no place in the natural world, that the world is not the product of intelligent design or that there is no divine providence. Naturalism is a creed, an atheistic philosophy. But if we banish God from nature, how do we explain its fantastic biological complexity? Darwinism attempts to supply an answer of sorts, albeit an admittedly far-fetched one.

In The Blind Watchmaker, the famous Oxford evolutionist Richard Dawkins writes, "An atheist before Darwin could have said, 'I have no explanation for complex biological design. All I know is that God is not a good explanation, so we must wait and hope [for] a better one.' I can't help feeling that such a position, although logically sound, would have left one feeling pretty unsatisfied. . . . Darwin made it possible to be an intellectually fulfilled atheist." There it is—the philosophical foundation of Darwinism. Intellectually fulfilling atheism.

Darwinists do not really have good solutions for the numerous difficulties and inconsistencies of the theory. For the most part, they defend it by calling its detractors dirty names, such as creationist or fundamentalist, and making other *ad hominem* attacks. Then they present a series of species with similar features and increasing sophistication as proof of evolution, when in actuality it proves not descent but similarity; if a Lexus and a Ford both have transmissions and CD players, does that prove that the Lexus is descended from the Ford? Darwinists have no scientific proof that random macroevolution ever took place. Their proof, if you can call it that, is philosophical. They argue that, given enough time, it could conceivably have happened, and since there is no other remotely viable explanation, then it must have happened. God, as Dawkins has informed us, is not a viable explanation.

Given enough time—those are the key words. By their own admission, Darwinists need practically endless stretches of time for their speculations to have even the slightest chance of ever having occurred, not thousands, not millions, but billions of years. Therefore, it is critical to the Darwinists that geological time be stretched to its outermost limits.

This alliance of Darwinist biologists and geologists has imposed its views on the public. "So successful has this promotional campaign been," writes Richard Milton, "that today almost everyone, including scientists working in other fields, has been led to believe that radioactive dating is . . . well nigh unassailable because of the universal constancy of radioactive decay. In fact, none of these widely held beliefs is supported by the evidence."

Today almost everyone believes with certainty that the earth is 4.6 billion years old. Even you, Ammi, spring to this conclusion with absolute certainty whenever you hear of a dinosaur bone.

Now, I know that you are not a Darwinist, Ammi. You assured me you believe in creation, the soul, and an afterlife. You also told me you believe God directs evolution. I agree. If so, there is no need for you to disfigure reason by assuming extreme antiquity when a dinosaur bone is discovered.

By the way, your daughter will be taught some form of Darwinism in high school and college. Do you think it would be prudent to point out to her that Darwinism is antithetical to your religious beliefs?

All the best,

Yosef

February 14, 2001

Dear Ammi,

It comes as no surprise that citations from the classical texts have become a major bone of contention between us. You are miffed that I object to your use of talmudic and midrashic quotations to promote your agenda, and I am miffed that you consistently distort or present them out of context.

Moreover, you accuse me of objecting because "it is I, a Reform rabbi, who is citing the texts. You understand, correctly, that whoever has access to, and can pronounce authoritatively upon, the classical texts, has **power**" (the last word in boldface type for extreme emphasis). Really, Ammi, it is not about power. I want no power over you. It is all about "pronouncing authoritatively upon the classical texts," as you so aptly put it. You are not interested in pronouncing authoritatively on the Torah and Talmud. You are not interested in discovering their internal truth. You are only interested in distorting and exploiting them to further your agenda. So let us have this out once and for all. Let us put your "authoritative pronouncements" to the test.

In the very same posting in which you define our discussion as a political power struggle rather than an intellectual exchange, you toss in two more appalling distortions designed to misrepresent the Talmud's attitude toward women.

You quote the Talmud's statement (Shabbat 152a) that a woman is like a "jug full of excrement whose opening is full of blood yet men chase after her" as a denigration of women. Very well, let us view this statement in its context. Is it true or is it taken out of context and distorted? The Talmud states: "Rav Kahana said: 'What is the meaning of that which is written (Psalms 33:9), "For He spoke, and it came to be"? This refers to women. And [the conclusion of the verse], "He commanded, and it endured"? This refers to children.' There is a [*beraita*] teaching: 'A woman is like a jug full of excrement whose opening is full of blood yet all chase after her.'"

Rav Kahana states that the attraction to women and the desire to have children are essentially illogical. Physical desires help keep a person alive, but emotional needs are not essential for survival. A man is drawn to food because he is hungry, to water because he is thirsty, but why should he be drawn to a woman? And why should he want to invest so much wealth, energy, and endless patience in raising children? It is only because God decreed that it be so. "For He spoke, and it came to be" that a man should be drawn to women. "He commanded, and it endured" that he should want children. The Talmud supports this statement with the *beraita* that "a woman is like a jug . . . ," pointing up the irrationality of the attraction to a body whose beauty is only skin-deep, a skin that covers a decidedly unattractive mass of organs, sinews, excrement, and blood.

The Talmud was written when it was uncommon for women to pursue men, something just as irrational. For our own times, we can draw the corollary, with full Talmudic authority, that a man is like a "jug full of excrement whose opening is full of semen yet women chase after him."

The attitude revealed in this talmudic statement is actually the exact opposite of your distortion. Since it clearly took a special divine decree to generate sexual attraction and the desire to procreate, they must have been designed for a higher purpose. As the Talmud tells us (Sotah 17a), "When a man and a woman marry, the Divine Presence rests between them."

Incidentally, you wonder why I wrote that "the Talmud holds women in the highest regard, even though it was written at a time when pagan society considered women mere chattels." Why did I have to "justify the value of the Talmud within its historical context" if its values are timeless? I was saying that the historical context of the Talmud, from which it was such a radical departure, is a strong proof that it is indeed divine and timeless.

I was also shocked by your scandalous distortion of the talmudic statement that "a woman is like meat that can be eaten salted, roasted or boiled." You give the impression that the Talmud encourages a caveman attitude toward women when nothing could be further from the truth. The Talmud is merely stating that there are no restrictions in the physical expression of the marriage relationship (see Maimonides, Yad, Issurei Be'ah 21:9). As for the caveman attitude, the Talmud states (Pesachim 49b), "Marrying off one's daughter to an ignoramus is like throwing her to the lions. Just as a lion pounces and devours shamelessly, so are the ignorant violent, rapacious and shameless." Elsewhere, the Talmud warns (Eruvin 100b) of the terrible consequences of coerced relations. Talmudic and rabbinic writings repeatedly urge husband and wife to relax together and exchange tender words before consummation so that the act will be a sanctified expression of intimacy and love, an act of spiritual giving rather than carnal pleasure-taking (Maimonides, Yad, De'ot 5:4).

Then, after splattering the Talmud with mud, you piously state that "the tradition's approach is complex." When a scholar calls something complex, he means something intricate but consistent. But you don't really mean complex, do you? You mean contradictory. Your superficial reading of the texts and lack of scope present you with numerous conflicts, but you do not respect the texts enough to make an in-depth study to discover the consistency in the words of the Sages. You would rather view the Talmud as a mass of contradictions that may be freely conscripted into your Reform arsenal. And to add insult to injury, you demand equal access to the time-honored authority that flows from the Talmud.

What gives you the right to interpret the Talmud? Would you presume to interpret X-rays or offer medical diagnoses without proper training? Would you presume to offer judicial rulings with no law degree, without checking the precedents and case law? So why do you feel entitled to play fast and loose with the classical texts? Are you suggesting that all Jews be given scholastic autonomy with regard to the classical texts, that we all be allowed to interpret them as advocating our own points of view regardless of what the Sages actually meant?

Approach the Talmud as a scholar, study and ponder, as your (pre-Reform) ancestors and mine have done for thousands of years, expend the intense intellectual effort that talmudic scholarship demands, see the entire picture of the Talmud, and you will discover the beautiful and consistent system of thought that gives it indestructible life.

You quote from the Talmud (Yevamot 47a) that a prospective convert is "given instruction in some of the minor and major commandments." From this you draw the Reform conclusion that "the tradition distinguishes between commandments. There are minor and major commands. Not all commands are of equal weight." And therefore, I gather, not all must be observed, correct?

If this is true, why bother at all to tell the convert about the "minor" commands? Why not concentrate on the important "major" commands? Furthermore, does it concern you that your interpretation is inconsistent with the Mishnaic instruction (Pirke Avot 2:1) to be "as heedful of a minor command as of a major one, because you do not know the relative rewards of the commands"? Clearly, all commands are equally important; major and minor refer to the deed, not the obligation. Therefore, the prospective convert is given a representative sampling of both the major and the minor—a sort of cross-section of Judaism.

More than once, you quote from the Talmud (Sanhedrin 34a) that "just as a hammer strikes the rock and shatters it into many pieces, so does a single verse [of Torah] yield many meanings." More than once, you quote from the Midrash (Pesikta d'Rav Kahana 12:25) that "the divine word spoke to each and every person according to his particular capacity." From these sources, you infer that the Talmud views all interpretations as valid, including yours. Do you really think the Sages of the Talmud considered every silly flight of fancy a "piece of the rock" of Torah? Do you really think even one Sage of the Talmud would have validated the Reform interpretation that it is sufficient to keep the Sabbath or observe dietary laws "in the spiritual sense" alone? So what do we do with the entire Tractate Shabbat, the second largest in the Talmud? Toss it into the wastebasket?

I can just imagine you saying to your daughter, "Do your homework, sweetheart, and be in bed by nine-thirty." And your daughter replies, "You know, Daddy, surely you only want me to do homework in the conceptual sense of reinforcing the principles and values I encounter in school. But to sit down and actually open books and cover paper after paper with writing is so . . . so . . . so totally twentieth century! So I'll just read some Victor Hugo, Mark Twain, and perhaps some poetry. It's just as good. As for going to sleep at nine-thirty, I think that would be anachronistic, a vestige from the nineteenth century when expensive candles were used for illumination and there were no telephones or on-line chat rooms. But I understand that you want me to go to sleep, and I definitely will. Eventually."

When God said, "Do not eat the flesh of the swine," you take it in the spiritual sense. When God said, "Do not perform labors on the Sabbath," you take it in the spiritual sense. How about when He said, "Do not commit adultery"? Do you also take that in the spiritual sense? This you call Torah?

You quote from the Midrash: "Torah is fire, given in fire and comparable to fire. What is the nature of fire? If one comes too near to it one gets burned. If one keeps too far from it one gets cold. The only thing to do is to warm oneself against its flame." (Mekhilta Bakhodesh 4) From this, you infer that "the proper relationship is to come close to Torah, but to be temperate, moderate, and reasonable." Are you suggesting that Reform's disregard for the commandments is appropriately "temperate, moderate, and reasonable"? Are you suggesting that the Sages who composed this Midrash approved of Reform? Are you kidding?

Actually, the Midrash is referring to someone like you. It is stating that one who studies Torah and presumes to interpret it must be extremely wary of inadvertent (let alone deliberate!) distortions; the Talmud states (Yomah 85b) that Yom Kippur does not atone for the sin of misinterpreting the Torah. And yet we are still obliged to study Torah. Therefore, we should approach it as we would a fire—with great care.

You quote from the Mishnah (Eduyot 1:5): "Why are the words of the individual sages recorded along with those of the majority? After all, is not the Halakhah decided according to the majority opinion? Because a court may [someday] prefer the opinion of the individual sage and it may decide to rely on it." From this, you infer that "what was good for one generation is not necessarily good for another." Are you saying that the laws change with the times? That is an incorrect reading of the Mishnah, which anticipates possible changes in the prevailing legal opinion, not social conditions, just as the judicial outlook of the Supreme Court may vary from time to time; Talmudic rulings are not decided by the prevailing political or social fashions. Read the rest of the *mishnah:* "For a court cannot overturn the ruling of an earlier court unless it is greater [than the first] in wisdom and numbers." The additional weight of an earlier minority opinion can shift the judicial balance in favor of the later court.

What has any of this to do with you? Are you claiming for yourself the right to overturn earlier rulings of the talmudic Sages? Are you a Sage? Are you "greater in wisdom" than the Sages of the Talmud?

You have never met an Orthodox sage—people like Rabbi Aaron Kotler, Rabbi Yaakov Kamenetsky, and Rabbi Shlomo Zalman Auerbach of blessed memory, people whose knowledge is as vast as the sky and whose wisdom is as deep as the sea, who are the embodiment of Torah and love for the Jewish people, who live for God and Klal Yisrael and are completely above greed, lust, and personal ambition. You don't know that these sort of people can exist, but many of your constituents do. In times of financial or family crisis, many of them come running to the holy Orthodox sages for advice and blessings, because they recognize that these wise and compassionate people are the closest approximation to angels on this earth. These are, and have always been, our treasured and revered leaders. There are such people today, Ammi, and if you wish, it would be my honor and pleasure to introduce you to some of them. Then you would at least have some point of reference for the Sages of the Talmud, who were much greater still.

You write, "We need each other and our differing understandings of Judaism. It keeps us honest, refreshed, and vital. *God exalts in these differences* [emphasis added]." Oh, really? And how do you know this? Is this another feat of your extraordinary intuition? It is just preposterous. On one side, we have the Sages of the Talmud who would put a man to death for idol worship, and on the other side, we have Ammi et al. who feel that observance is at best optional, that no religious transgression should be punished by death. Can God exalt in such a difference? Does He exalt when the Sages put the idolater to death and smile when you pat him on the back? What kind of ridiculous God have you invented?

I agree that "we need each other," but I absolutely deny that we need "our differing understandings of Judaism." We just need the truth.

Ammi, I understand the Sadducees who gained control of the reins of power in the government and the Temple and simply rejected and ignored the restrictions of the Oral Law, calling it all a pack of lies. But look at what you are doing. You call the Oral Law a rabbinic invention, and yet you constantly quote from the Talmud as the alleged justification for your approach to Judaism. You remind me of the Stalinist distortion of the original communist idea in George Orwell's *Animal Farm:* "All men are created equal, but some are more equal than others."

You write, "I think we will agree that the Judaism we practice today is not at all the Judaism practiced in biblical times." We will agree on nothing of the sort. We wear the same *tallit* and *tefillin* as we did then. We keep the same Shabbat and festivals with all their observances and laws. We follow the same dietary laws. We live by the same commandments, values, and principles. All that has changed is that rabbinic courts added precautionary laws as "a fence around the Torah." But the Torah inside that fence has never changed nor will it ever change. It has survived all sorts of adversity throughout the ages. It will survive Reform as well.

Halevi, in *Dorot Harishonim: The Biblical Era* (pp. 33–67), brings numerous proofs that the people observed both the Written Law and the Oral Law during biblical times. I will quote just two of them. When King Saul notices that David is absent from the official meal in honor of Rosh Chodesh (the New Month), he asks (I Samuel 20:27), "Why hasn't [he] come to the meal, neither yesterday nor today?" Now, a two-day Rosh Chodesh is only possible if it depends on a visual sighting of the moon, something mentioned not in the Written Law but in the Talmud (Rosh Hashanah 30b). In another example, the prophet Jeremiah states (17:21), "So said God, 'Watch yourselves, and do not carry burdens on the Sabbath day and bring them into the gates of Jerusalem.'" Carrying on Shabbat is mentioned only in the Oral Law. There are many more proofs if you care to look them up.

You write, "[T]almudic rabbis claimed an oral tradition of transmission extending back to Moses at Sinai, but they did so more out of a need to establish the authority of the rabbis to interpret the law than out of a desire to instill a literal reading of texts." In other words, it was a cynical power grab based on a deliberate falsification. Hmm. What's this with the power fixation, Ammi? And if you really believe this, how can you respect the Talmud and value its wisdom? And besides, if the Talmud was a big lie perpetrated by the Sages, why were Rabbi Akiva and so many other Sages willing to die a martyr's death for it? Does that make sense? If the Sages wanted power, they should have become Sadducees!

Furthermore, your remarks are contradictory (or perhaps complex?).

If the rabbis "interpret" the law, then they are not reading it "literally." We've been through this before when we discussed "an eye for an eye," and I proved to you that the Torah did not mean this to be taken literally. Please refer to those postings to refresh your memory. The whole point of the Talmud is that the Written Law cannot be read literally without the interpretations of the Oral Law. The Sadducees and Karaites, who rejected the Oral Law, were literalists. We are not. You yourself acknowledge this when you write, "How in the world could literalism have been the norm when the Talmud explodes with disputes and conflicting interpretations on the same verse?" Exactly.

So let us talk a little about the Oral Law.

Ammi, I think even you would be forced to admit there must have been some kind of oral transmission along with the Written Law. Otherwise, how would we make heads or tails of it? We wouldn't even be able to read it. Since the letters in the Torah scrolls come without markings, the cantillation and vowel marks used by all Jews all over the world must have come down to us by oral transmission. The Talmud relates (Shabbat 31a) that a gentile who refused to accept the Oral Law asked Hillel to convert him to Judaism. "Fine," said Hillel, and he began to teach him the Hebrew letters—*aleph, bet, gimmel,* and so on. The next day, Hillel showed him a totally different letter for an *aleph.* "That's not what you told me yesterday!" the prospective convert objected. "Exactly!" said Hillel. "Just as you must rely on me for this, you must also rely on me for all of the Oral Law as well." Without the oral transmission, we cannot even identify the letters.

Furthermore, many laws in the Torah are simply not self-explanatory. The Torah tells us to wear *tefillin,* but it fails to describe them. Should they be square or round, black or pink, large or small, leather or metal? No information is given. How were we meant to fulfill this and similar commandments if there was no parallel oral teaching?

We know that kosher meat is obtained by *shechitah,* ritual slaughter. But how are we supposed to slaughter the animals? By shooting them? The Torah states (Deuteronomy 12:21), "You may slaughter your cattle and sheep that God will have given you *in the manner I have prescribed* [emphasis added]." The Talmud explains (Chulin 28a) that God instructed Moses that animals must be slaughtered by cutting through the trachea and esophagus. Notice that the Written Law calls for slaughter in the "manner I have prescribed." The Written Law is clearly referring to the Oral Law!

So we know there must have been an Oral Law, but you may wonder if the vast body of talmudic material is indeed the same Oral Law that must have accompanied the Written Law or if it is something else altogether, a fabrication of the Sages. Now then, since we have absolutely no record of any other Oral Law, it would be only reasonable to assume that the Talmud is indeed the Oral Law that existed from the beginning, as it claims to be. But there are much stronger proofs.

The key feature of talmudic scholarship—as those even casually familiar with it will attest—is not analysis, not originality, not creativity, but consistency. The quest for consistency is the overriding imperative of the Talmud itself and of all the rabbinic commentaries that develop its concepts. This quest mandates that all superficial inconsistencies must be resolved and thereby gives rise to the great surge of analysis, logic, original thought, and sheer genius that characterize Talmudic scholarship.

In every *sugya* (talmudic discussion)—and there are thousands—the Sages pounce on every law, rule, or statement and challenge it. Is it consistent with the Written Law? Is it consistent with the Oral Law—with all sixty-three tractates in the six Orders of the Mishnah, with all the *beraitot,* with all the Gemara? For instance, in analyzing the legal definition of theft, the Talmud explores (Baba Kama 70b) the acquisition of movable property, the transfer of a bill of divorce, and the prohibition against carrying from one domain to another on Shabbat. The Talmud understands that there are logical rules defining possession and that these principles must function consistently in all areas where possession plays a role.

No opinion is valid unless it is consistent with every area of talmudic law, no matter how remotely related. This is what makes talmudic scholarship so vital and exciting. Everything has to fit. And it does!

Once a statement is proved consistent with the entire Written Law and Oral Law, it is examined for consistency with rigorous rules of logic and exegesis. Finally, it must be consistent with established practice among the observant (*puk chazi ma ama devar*). Once it passes all three tests, the statement can be used to determine Halakhah.

Now tell me, Ammi, is it even remotely possible that humans could create such a vast body of incredibly consistent material and deliver it to the people full-blown? You must admit that it would be utterly impossible to find consistency among all the innumerable speeches delivered in Congress or all the innumerable rulings of American judges over the last two centuries; every lawyer knows you can find case law to support just about any legal position. And yet the bedrock law of the Talmud is entirely consistent; there are no disputes about the basic principles. A brigade of Einsteins could not have fabricated such a unified body of knowledge that encompasses all of life.

Furthermore, the institution of *semichah*—ordination—guaranteed the integrity of the transmission process of the Oral Law. The *semichah* could only be administered by a sage who had himself received *semichah* from an earlier sage. All important judicial roles required *semichah,* making it a critical element in Jewish communal life, and there was no way to obtain it other than to connect to this chain. In this manner, the chain of transmission extends faithfully and scrupulously all the way back to the first *semichah,* which is recorded in Numbers (27:18): "And God said to Moses, 'Take Joshua bin Nun, a man of spirit, and lay your hands [*vesamachta*] upon him.'" Maimonides, in his introduction to the Mishnah, chronicles the entire chain of ordination in precise detail.

According to the Talmud (Ketubot 17a), *semichah* was conferred in a public ceremony with great fanfare. This public scrutiny was apparently an indispensable feature of the process. The Talmud relates (Sanhedrin 14a) that the "evil empire" (Rome, not the Soviet Union) outlawed the practice of *semichah* on penalty of death to the entire town in which it took place. (The Romans apparently appreciated the critical role of *semichah* in guaranteeing the integrity of the Oral Law.) Rabbi Yehudah ben Bava took five of his disciples—Rabbi Meir, Rabbi Yehudah, Rabbi Shimon, Rabbi Yosi, and Rabbi Eleazar ben Shamua—out into the fields and gave them *semichah*. Because it was a public ceremony, the Romans caught wind of it and came charging after them. Rabbi Yehudah ben Bava told his newly ordained disciples to flee while he held off their pursuers. He was run through by Roman lances and perished in a pool of his own blood.

Why did Rabbi Yehudah ben Bava and his disciples risk their lives by conducting a public *semichah* ceremony? Wouldn't it have been more prudent to have a secret ceremony in a dark cellar with no one else present? Clearly, the *semichah* ceremony needed to be performed in full public view to guarantee the integrity and authenticity of the process. A *semichah* given behind closed doors would carry no weight. With no alternative to a public ceremony, Rabbi Yehudah ben Bava risked his life so that the chain of transmission of the Oral Law would remain intact.

So this is the established process of talmudic ordination. An aspiring sage must become expert in the Oral Law. Then he must be ordained by another sage who has himself been ordained by an ordained sage and so on all the way back. And the ordination ceremony must be performed in public! Such a process must be genuine, because an invention would necessarily violate its own rules.

All these safeguards guaranteed the integrity of the Oral Law. Nonetheless, as political and social conditions grew increasingly unstable, the Sages feared it might be forgotten, and they decided to commit it to paper, creating the Talmud. They began with the Mishnah, which is exceedingly terse but nonetheless provides more information than the Written Law does. Ultimately, as the political situation deteriorated even further and the danger of forgetfulness and error loomed, they added a synopsis of the talmudic debates—the Gemara.

You once asked me, "[Do] you really believe that the thousands of pages in the Talmud were literally transcribed by Moses on Sinai?" Of course not. The Sages spent their lives learning, memorizing, absorbing, pondering, analyzing, and explicating the Oral Law transmitted from Moses, and when the times forced them to record it, they used their own words.

So how do we reconcile an authoritative chain of oral transmission with a Talmud that, in your words, "explodes with disputes and conflicting interpretations of the same verse"?

The Oral Law is composed of a vast number of laws, principles, and rules that complement the Written Law. But their application to new situations leaves room for wide judicial creativity. As long as a ruling in a new situation is completely consistent with all the principles of the Oral Law, it is valid. Moreover, it now becomes part of the Oral Law and can be used to develop further applications. We see the same pattern in mathematics and science, which develop theorems from existing principles and then use these new theorems to develop further theorems without retracing all the original steps. It is an efficient method that makes for great intellectual vitality and integrity.

The talmudic method and the post-talmudic development of Halakhah right up to the present make for a living Torah. Let us say a question arises regarding genetic engineering. The answer can be found in the Talmud. How? We investigate the basic principles of the Oral Law that affect every aspect of the question, we examine the talmudic method of applying these principles to new situations, and we extend that process to the situations that arise in our own times.

But logic does not always guarantee a single solution to a new situation. For example, say we are told that a row has eleven tiles and that the row changes from one color to another somewhere in the middle. These are the givens. We now observe that the first five tiles are white, the last five are black, and the middle one is missing. What color must the missing tile be? It can be white. It can be black. It can be half white and half black. It can be three-quarters white and one-quarter black, or vice versa. And so on. All these answers are valid; they are consistent with the givens. Each creates a transition from one color to another. The missing tile cannot be red, green, or yellow, because that would introduce a third color into the row. Nor can we leave the missing space empty, because that would give us ten tiles instead of eleven. These answers would be inconsistent with the givens and, therefore, rejected.

The same applies to the Oral Law. In many situations, there may be any number of logical solutions to the application of the Law. If they fit the criteria of consistency with the existing laws and principles, they are all true and valid, and they become integrated into the Oral Law. As the Talmud declares (Eruvin 13b), *"Elu va'elu divrei Elohim chaim.* Both these and these are the living word of God." Future Talmudic scholars will study all the conflicting opinions, because they are all Torah. They are all truth.

But practically speaking, what are we supposed to do when we have conflicting opinions regarding one legal question? Are we free to choose whichever we like simply because they are both valid Torah opinions?

No, says the Torah. There is only one valid practical application of the Oral Law, and the Torah provides the rule by which to find it. "The verdict follows the majority." (Exodus 23:2) When it comes to practice, majority rules. This does not mean that the majority is right and the minority wrong, just as we do not find the correct answers to questions of history, philosophy, mathematics, science, and medicine by taking a vote. It means that the Torah gives us a strict rule to use in cases where the talmudic debate does not produce a universally accepted solution. Otherwise, there would be chaos. Nonetheless, we fulfill our obligation to study Torah even when we review, analyze, and dissect the minority opinions. They are genuine Torah views, but they do not govern our practice.

If you think this through carefully, we can resolve another of the problems you have encountered. You write that the Sages "changed the Law to such an extent that even the Talmud concedes (Menachot 29b) that Moses himself did not recognize the laws that he supposedly pronounced." We have discussed this passage once before, and I explained at the time that according to Rashi's commentary Moses had not yet received the Torah. I think we should go into it a little more deeply. Let us take another look.

> [Moses] went and sat at the end of the eighteenth row [of Rabbi Akiva's disciples], but he could not understand what they were saying. He was crestfallen. Then [Rabbi Akiva and his disciples] continued on to another subject.
> His disciples asked [Rabbi Akiva]: "How do you know this?"
> He said to them: "It is a law given to Moses on Sinai."
> [When Moses heard this], he felt reassured.

You draw the conclusion that Rabbi Akiva had taken such liberties with the laws that even Moses could not recognize them. But why don't you take a closer look at the very end of the citation? Rabbi Akiva tells his disciples that his source is "a law given to Moses on Sinai." Moses hears this reply and is reassured. Was Rabbi Akiva lying? And if so, why was Moses reassured by an obvious lie? And if Rabbi Akiva was telling the truth, why didn't Moses recognize the laws? Furthermore, why didn't Rabbi Akiva's disciples question his sources earlier in the discourse?

It seems clear that Rabbi Akiva was applying his logic to a situation the Oral Law did not address. Moses could not follow the discussion, because he was unfamiliar with the fifteen hundred years of cumulative intellectual development that had created an intricate and complex legal edifice by Rabbi Akiva's time. But then Rabbi Akiva introduced a new piece of information that was not an outgrowth of the logical process. "How do you know that?" asked his disciples. Rabbi Akiva gave his source as "a law given to Moses on Sinai."

Imagine Euclid, the father of geometry, attending a lecture in advanced civil engineering. The schematics and concepts developed from his principles would probably be too intricate for him to follow effortlessly, but the entire edifice would nonetheless rest on his principles and axioms.

Similarly, when Moses heard that the starting points for all logical discourses were laws transmitted through him, he was reassured. The Sages had no authority to create new biblical law, but they had full authority to draw new applications from existing Mosaic laws.

An excellent example is the Talmudic passage (Baba Metzia 59b) you've brought up once before and cite again in your recent posting. Rabbi Eliezer and the Sages disagree regarding "the oven of *achnai*." A heavenly voice agrees with Rabbi Eliezer. "The Torah is not in the heavens," say the Sages. God laughs and says, "My children have bested Me."

This talmudic passage really seems to have excited you. "For Heaven's sake," you write, "what could be more powerful than a heavenly voice justifying Eliezer's interpretation? 'Sorry,' said the Sages, 'the Torah is not in the heavens.' Human beings now interpret the Torah. Even a heavenly voice won't do. Absolute truth, as proclaimed by the heavenly voice, is rejected." Obviously, you think you have found here the license to reject absolute truth. Congratulations.

But really, Ammi, if the heavenly voice had been God's revelation of absolute truth, how could the Sages have dared defy His expressed will? If God had declared Rabbi Eliezer right and the Sages mistaken, would they have defied His judgment? Can a human being win an argument against omniscient God? If that is what you think, the God whose existence you intuit is decidedly primitive.

Clearly, God never meant to say the Sages had erred, that their opinion was inconsistent with the Oral Law. The Talmud points out that the debate spanned every conceivable argument, and still the disputants could not find consensus; no one could bring a proof the other could not refute. In other words, both views were consistent with the Oral Law; both were valid expressions of Torah. So practically speaking, what do we do? We know the Torah's instructions. "The verdict follows the majority." The view of the Sages prevails.

Rabbi Eliezer, however, called upon the heavens to back him up, and God endorsed his view. Now, if God was saying the Sages had erred, He should have pointed up their inconsistency, and their opinion would have collapsed by itself. But there really was no inconsistency; it would have been untrue to say the Sages had erred. God did not address the issue of consistency in the Oral Law. He addressed the determination of the practical ruling, saying, "Why do you oppose Rabbi Eliezer when the Halakhah should always be like him?"

Therefore, the Sages argued correctly, "The Torah is not in the heavens." They did not mean that God was wrong and they were right. They meant that the Torah gives us a hard-and-fast rule for determining the practical application of the Oral Law in case of an unresolved dispute. Majority rules! God Himself had decreed that the Torah is immutable, that even prophets who work miracles cannot change the Torah's rules. "Do not heed that prophet ... for God your Lord is testing you." (Deuteronomy 13:4) The heavenly voice supporting Rabbi Eliezer was a test. The majority opinion consistent with the Oral Law prevails.

You write, "We must recognize that there will be a wide divergence in the manner that Jews think about and practice Judaism. ... It has always been that way." Wrong. The divergence has always been in the scope of judicial creativity that the Oral Law provides within the boundaries of consistency—as long as none of its basic principles is violated. But you have diverged yourself right out of the picture. Every single sage in the Talmud would have been scandalized and outraged by the practices of Reform, and I dare you to contend otherwise. On whose shoulders are you standing, my good friend?

One more word about your aversion to truth. You write, "There is a wonderful *midrash* about the creation of Adam. ... Love and Righteousness urged God to create human beings. ... Peace and Truth urged God not to. ... The angels were split evenly. ... What did God do? He took Truth and cast it to the ground. The vote was then 2 to 1 in favor of creating Adam, and thus Man was born. (Midrash Rabbah) Absolute truth cannot exist in a human setting. Even God recognized that it must give way if there will be human life." How gleeful you become when you find a source that seems to devalue truth.

But does the Midrash really say what you claim it does, Ammi? You inadvertently omitted the end of the citation, which supports its thesis with a quote from Psalms, "Truth sprouts from the earth, righteousness is observed from the heavens." (85:12) According to you, the Psalmist must be coming to bury truth, which "cannot exist in a human setting." Are you correct? Let us take a look. "Truth sprouts from the earth." If the Psalmist meant to bury truth, why does it "sprout from the earth"? Even worse, you have skewed the quote. The Midrash does not say, "The vote was then 2 to 1," as you quoted. That was merely the way you understood it, and you took the liberty of inserting your incorrect interpretation into the quote itself.

Let us also take a look at a sampling of references to truth in the Psalms. Has the Psalmist indeed given up on truth? "Guide me by Your truth, teach me, for You are the Lord of my salvation." (25:5) "For Your kindness is before my eyes, and I walk by Your truth." (26:3) "Dispatch Your light and Your truth, they will lead me, they will bring me to Your holy mountain, to Your dwelling place." (43:3) "Behold, You desired truth in my inner thoughts, You gave me wisdom in my private heart." (51:8) "Your Teaching is the truth." (119:142) There are many more. Obviously, truth is alive and well in the Psalms.

So what does the Midrash mean? The Vilna Gaon explains that Truth objected to the creation of humans because they would find it so difficult to discover truth. God responded by "casting Truth down to the earth." In other words, he entrusted Truth to the Sages so that all their scrupulously formulated rulings would be the "living word of God"; even if they could not reach consensus, all judicial views consistent with the basic principles of the entire Written Law and Oral Law would have the force of truth. Truth would sprout, blossom and flourish in the minds of the Sages.

Ammi, you deny the existence of a discoverable truth because that would be an obstacle to the policy of "anything goes." Nonetheless, you demand the authority to interpret and reinterpret the Torah and the Talmud into oblivion. You have no hard-and-fast doctrines, not even a reliable moral compass. You blow hot and cold with the prevailing relativist winds of contemporary society. Where is intellectual and moral integrity? Where are sacred religious principles?

Let me quote from a Reform responsum (5751.4) that appears on an official Reform Web site: "In 1990, a congregation in Cincinnati, Ohio, applied for membership in UAHC. This congregation practices 'Judaism with a humanistic perspective' . . . its liturgy deletes any and all mention of God. . . . Their philosophy doesn't admit of either Covenant or commandments. The responsa committee, in response to this application, denied (*although not unanimously* [emphasis added]) that this congregation was a Reform congregation. Rabbi Gunther Plaut, chair of the committee at the time, wrote: 'Persons of varying shadings of belief or unbelief, practice or non-practice, may belong to UAHC congregations as individuals, and we respect their rights. But it is different when they come as a congregation whose declared principles are at fundamental variance with the historic God-orientation of Reform Judaism. . . . But should we not open the gates wide enough to admit even such concepts into our fold? Are not diversity and inclusiveness a hallmark of Reform? To this we would reply: *yesh gevul*, there are limits. Reform Judaism cannot be everything, or it will be nothing. The argument that we ourselves are excluded by the Orthodox and therefore should not keep others out who wish to join us has an attractive sound to it. Taken to its inevitable conclusion, however, we would end up with a Reform Judaism in which Reform determines what Judaism is and not the other way around.'"

Apparently, Reform does not have unlimited flexibility (although this is not a unanimous opinion). You also have a *gevul*, a limit, but look where it is! At the outright denial of God, for Heaven's sake! And you dare demand authority to interpret the Torah and the Talmud? Tell me, Ammi, if 90 percent of Jews denied God, perish the thought, would Reform shift in that direction? If 90 percent of Jews accepted Jesus, perish the thought, would you go there as well? I hope the answer is "No!" For you personally, I am certain that it is, but I cannot say the same for the rest of your movement. (If you recall, you rejected homosexual marriage, but a few days later the CCAR endorsed it.)

So we have finally found a point of agreement. We agree that *yesh gevul,* that there is a limit. Ah, but where is that limit, Ammi? I'm afraid yours is far out in left field, far, far from the Torah.

Let me conclude with a quote from Isaiah Berlin, one of your favorite philosophers: "The Orthodox synagogue is the synagogue I am not attending, except on the High Holy Days" (quoted by British journalist Michael Ignatieff in *Isaiah Berlin: A Life*). Berlin was thoroughly secular, but when he wanted a synagogue, he knew where to find an authentic one.

Warmest regards,

Yosef

February 25, 2001

Dear Ammi,

In your last two postings, you leveled a very serious accusation against the Orthodox community. You claim that we have "marginalized" our secular Jewish brothers and sisters and abandoned them to assimilation. Nothing could be further from the truth.

There is a lot of hurt among secular Jews at the Orthodox ideological rejection of the other streams. As a Reform rabbi, you must share some of this hurt, although you say you take it in stride. Ammi, I consider you my friend, and I believe you consider me yours; we both know that the occasional sharp tone of our exchanges is not to be taken personally. It is important to me that you see exactly where we stand, and then you can decide for yourself if we have indeed marginalized you.

First, however, I want to say that the context of your accusation disappointed me. "The Classical Reformers also de-emphasized Jewish peoplehood: 'We consider ourselves no longer a nation, but a religious community.' (Pittsburgh Platform) This belief, foreign to Judaism, had the same disastrous consequences for our movement that it will have for Orthodoxy." Ammi, my friend, how can you compare the Orthodox to your Reform antecedents who declared themselves "Germans of the Mosaic faith" (or Americans in the case of the Pittsburgh Platform)? They were always running to catch up with the latest trend, and then

discovering that the times had left them behind. They yearned to assimilate into the oh-so-cultured German society, so they discarded Jewish
peoplehood and the dream of Zion. But that didn't work out so well.
Then they jumped onto the bandwagon of secular Zionism—just as the
wheels started coming off. Their numbers shrank through intermarriage and assimilation, so they became inclusive to gentile spouses and
accepted patrilineal descent, and suddenly, there are almost as many
gentiles as Jews on the membership rolls of some Reform temples.

ORTHODOX OUTREACH

I understand you resent our refusal to recognize Reform as a legitimate
expression of Judaism, but how can you even mention us and the
Reform rejecters of Jewish peoplehood in the same breath? How can
you say we have "given up on the Jewish people"?

You must be aware of the intense Orthodox outreach movement to
secular Jews. You must be aware of the thousands of talented Orthodox
men and women who have forgone lucrative careers in order to devote
their lives to outreach. You must be aware of the innumerable Orthodox rabbis and laypeople who donate their time to teach classes on
every conceivable Jewish subject, from basic Hebrew to advanced Talmud, on campus, in community centers, and even in private living
rooms. You must be aware of the many fine, tuition-free *yeshivot* that
serve young secular Jews who wish to explore the Torah seriously.

Today there are more Reform Jews studying with the Orthodox than
ever before. In fact, more than a thousand secular Jews are partici-
pating in the Partners in Torah program (646-227-1000), which pairs
them with one-on-one study partners at their convenience. There is
no preaching or sermonizing, just some good old-fashioned learning.
Knowledge is a good thing. People should have the skills to access the
classical texts on their own. They should have the opportunity to think
for themselves.

Anyone interested in classes, seminars, information, or accommoda-
tions for Shabbat—all free of charge—can contact any number of orga-

nizations or visit their Web sites. To list just a few that come easily to mind, there are Aish HaTorah-Discovery, Ohr Somayach, National Jewish Outreach Program, Torah Links, and Arachim Jerusalem. Not to mention all the Chabad Houses run by the ubiquitous Lubavitchers.

You wonder why we don't "invest in non-Orthodox Jewish day schools" that "can play a critical role in stemming the assimilatory trends you decry." Let me tell you a story. Not far from where I live, a Reform temple hired a young Orthodox woman for its educational program. One day, while the young woman was teaching the little children about the Exodus, the rabbi came in to observe. He stopped her in the middle and announced to the children: "Repeat after me, children. The stories in the Torah are not true! The stories in the Torah are not true!" This is just one little anecdote, but it reflects a pervasive attitude.

So tell me, should we invest in schools that teach blasphemous lies, that deny the truth of the Torah? Do you expect to ensure Jewish continuity by discrediting the Torah to the children? Quaint songs and matzah balls will not prevent young people from intermarrying and assimilating. Only the Torah, in all its awesome majesty, in all its overwhelming truth, has the power to inspire lasting commitment in the hearts of the Jewish people. We want to bring Jews back to the Torah.

Some people say we are only interested in secular Jews if we can make them Orthodox. That is not true. We have organizations such as Chai Lifeline, which provides support services gratis for children afflicted with cancer and their families, most of whom are non-Orthodox. We also give enormous sums—no strings attached—to Russian immigrants, most of whom are too indoctrinated against religion to have any interest in a commitment to Judaism. We fought for Soviet Jewry. We sent people behind the Iron Curtain before it was riddled with rust, when it was unfashionable and dangerous to go there. We facilitated the escape of the Iranian Jews when the Ayatollah came to power. We mounted the most heroic rescue efforts during the Holocaust. Even now, one of the main goals of our outreach efforts is to keep alive the tenuous thread of Judaism in as many people as possible. Certainly, we want all Jews to embrace Torah observance, but not all who attend classes make the commitment. Still, even those that stay uncommitted gain a deeper appreciation of the Torah once they have studied a little. They are less likely to intermarry and assimilate. All in all, I think we have shown a strong and abiding dedication to Jewish peoplehood.

THE HOLINESS OF THE JEWISH PEOPLE

You brought many beautiful quotations attesting to the holiness of the Jewish people as a whole and every single Jew as an individual, to the eternal durability of the covenant, to the reciprocal love between God and the Jewish people. You quote from the Midrash that the four species represent all Jewish people, and that God wants them to be bound together.

How true.

But you also convey the idea that the holiness of the Jewish people is the supreme value and that the practices and observances, the fulfillment of God's expressed will, are not really important, that being Jewish entails no special obligations, that God is content to let us have autonomy. This is an appalling misrepresentation. You quoted from Leviticus (19:18) that our role is "always to love one's fellow Jew as oneself." True. But why don't you also look a bit further in Leviticus (26:14)? "But if you do not obey Me, if you do not perform all these commandments, if you reject My decrees and scorn My laws, to neglect the performance of all My commandments, to break My covenant, then I shall also do this to you. . . ." Strong words, but you pretend they don't exist.

You accuse the Orthodox of "emphasizing the inviolability of beliefs over the sanctity of the Jewish people." It is incredible that you separate the two in your mind. What sanctifies the Jewish people? Sanctity comes only from beliefs.

We are profoundly aware of the sanctity of the Jewish people, and therefore we are mortified and disheartened that so many of our beloved brothers and sisters have been steered away from Jewish beliefs and are in danger of vanishing into the gentile world. Unlike the Reform, we have not come to terms with this "reality." We cannot accept it with equanimity, consoling ourselves that some of the intermarried bring their gentile spouses to the temples for services or specious conversions.

You and your colleagues should seek out the classes the Orthodox offer and encourage your people to take advantage of them. What's the worst that can happen? They might become Orthodox? The risk is not high. But even if they do, would that be so terrible? You keep saying you need a strong Orthodox stream. Well, here is your opportunity to contribute. Isn't it better that they become Orthodox than assimilate?

When your young people set out for India and points east to seek spiritual fulfillment, why don't you send them to us? To paraphrase Emma Lazarus, "Send us your uninspired, your youth, your befuddled masses yearning to be fulfilled, send us these, the restless, the confused," and we will teach them Torah. But you won't do it. In fact, many Reform rabbis warn young people visiting Israel to beware of Orthodox outreach people they may encounter at the Wall. Why is this so? What do you fear?

A bareheaded man once introduced himself to me at an Orthodox wedding as a "nonpracticing Orthodox Jew."

"I'm happy to hear that," I replied.

He looked at me strangely. "What do you mean?"

"Well, at least you acknowledge the truth of the Torah," I said. "That's the first level of observance. Right now, there seem to be some obstacles to your doing more. Hopefully, you'll overcome the obstacles and rise to higher levels. In that sense, you're like the practicing Orthodox. All of us lapse in some way from time to time; I don't believe there is anyone who has nothing for which to repent on Yom Kippur. And even if someone fulfills every commandment to the letter of the law, there are always deeper levels of observance. There's always room for improvement."

In Judaism, the place where you are is not as important as the direction in which you are headed. A minimally observant person who is learning and growing steadily at his own pace is considered very worthy. In Judaism, there is never a point when a person can sit back, pat his belly, and say, "Whew! I've done it. Now, I can relax." The main thing is to recognize that growth is the work of a lifetime.

In a number of Orthodox congregations across the United States, there are some people who drive to *shul* on Shabbat. Out of respect, they park their cars a block or two from the *shul* and walk the rest of the way. Although these "nonpracticing Orthodox" transgress the Shabbat laws, they have at least acknowledged them. At least they recognize that Judaism is a ladder that reaches very high and that their climb begins on a lower rung. At least they recognize that the higher rungs of observance are a worthy ideal, even if they are not there yet. As long as they are engaged in the process of climbing, there is no limit to how high they, or perhaps their children and grandchildren, will reach. Many great rabbis are descended from parents whose practical observance was minimal.

REFORM AUTONOMY

Reform, however, came along and legitimized nonobservance as a final destination. They told people that there is no ladder, that joining a Reform temple would free them from any obligation or guilt. Reform came to emancipate the Jews from the Torah, to assuage their guilty consciences, to give them autonomy. In the words of your own Alexander Schindler (quoted in the *New York Times*), "Reform Judaism has by its very nature accorded a good deal of authority to the individual. The tragedy is that too many Reform Jews at every level have seized on this right to opt to do nothing." That is where autonomy leads.

What exactly is autonomy? It is freedom from obligation. One does whatever *mitzvah* one wants to do if and when one feels like doing it. There is nothing that one is obligated to do. Autonomy is the exact opposite of a covenant, which creates obligations. It is like the difference between a casual affair and a marriage. Reform has tried to wriggle out of the sacred covenant of the Torah. They don't want the burdens and strictures of a marriage, but they are not against an occasional rendezvous when the mood is right. They want an amiable divorce. They want to remain friends.

Listen to what Isaiah Berlin, whose opinion you respect so much, has to say about autonomy. "It is as if I were to say: 'I have a wound in my leg. There are two methods of freeing myself from pain. One is to heal the wound. But if the cure is too difficult or uncertain, there is another method. I can get rid of the wound by cutting off my leg. If I train myself to want nothing to which the possession of my leg is indispensable, I shall not feel the lack of it.' . . . Every form of autonomy has in it some element of this attitude." *(Four Essays on Liberty)*

Here is a powerful description of Reform autonomy. They discerned "a wound in your leg," a conflict between the covenanted obligations of the Torah and the attractions of secular culture. So what did they do? Did they find a method of healing this wound, of finding a genuine accommodation? No, they convinced themselves that they didn't need the "wounded leg" of Torah observance, and they cut it off. Then they fed their constituency nice platitudes to drug them into spiritual senselessness, so that they wouldn't feel the pain of their slow death as a people.

In your postings, you express an obviously genuine love for God and the Torah. Why then don't you, and others like you, do something to heal the "wounded leg"? At the very least, encourage some level of Torah observance your constituency can accept as obligatory. You can at least find simple observances they can embrace not only as nice things to do once in a while but as daily obligations. It will give them a taste of the covenant.

THE LOST JEWISH ORPHANS

Let me digress with a little story. During the Holocaust, as the cattle cars carted off their human cargo to the camps, some parents entrusted their little children to the local convents. They knew the children stood no chance of survival in the camps, but they hoped against hope that maybe they themselves would somehow survive and come back to claim their precious little sons and daughters. And even if they did not come back, at least their children would survive to carry on the heritage of their family and the Jewish people, to keep the memories of their martyred parents alive.

Years passed. The crematoria belched their putrid black smoke day and night, and the forced laborers died like flies. And in convents, little Jewish children were growing up Catholic, and the images of their parents and the memories of their past faded slowly away. The War finally came to an end. A few hollow-eyed survivors did manage to return for their children, who barely recognized or remembered them, if at all. But all too many parents never returned, and the little orphans remained in the convents unclaimed.

At that time, a number of Orthodox men and women took it upon themselves to seek out these lost little Jewish orphans and restore them to their people—for their own sake, for the sake of their murdered parents, and for the sake of all of Klal Yisrael. Among these activists was the late Rabbi Yosef Kahaneman, dean of the Ponevezh Yeshivah.

One day, he appeared at a convent in which he had reason to believe there were Jewish children. He asked for permission to enter the orphanage to determine if any of the children might be Jewish, but he was turned away. "There are no Jewish children here," he was told.

He begged for a fifteen-minute audience with the children. To no avail.

Five minutes. Still to no avail.

Finally, he made a desperate plea for thirty seconds. What could he do already in thirty seconds? So he was given permission.

He came into the room and looked at the innocent faces of the assembled little children. Then he called out in a loud voice in Hebrew, "Hear O Israel, God is our Lord. . . ." He paused.

Suddenly, here and there, a child completed the verse: "God is One!" Jewish children!

The Shema, the Jewish confession of faith, was so deeply imbedded in the consciousness of these Jewish children that it flowed out when given the opportunity, even after all other memories had faded away.

The daily saying of the Shema is one of the great commandments of the Torah. And even someone with the busiest schedule can spare the few seconds to recite the words, in English if need be, in Hebrew if possible. It would infuse every day with a Jewish spirit, and go a long way toward reinforcing Jewish identity and promoting Jewish continuity. It would create and nurture a bond and a personal relationship with God. If nothing else, let the Shema become as deeply embedded in the hearts of Reform Jews as it was in the hearts of those Jewish orphans in the convent.

SAGES AND SECULAR JEWS

You try to give the impression that the Orthodox look down at secular Jews. Perhaps some of the unsophisticated ones do. But do you think for a moment that this is Orthodox ideology? Tell me, Ammi, do you think I look down at you? Why, even if a Jew sins deliberately, the Talmud demands (Berachot 10a) that we "embrace the sinner even as we decry the sin." Certainly today, when most secular Jews are brought up in ignorance and indifference, there are practically no sinners and no sins, just millions of Jews who have lost contact with God and His Torah and are in danger of disappearing.

You quote from the responsa of Rabbi Moshe Feinstein that "people buried in Reform cemeteries are evildoers who have denied our holy Torah." Based on this citation, you prove that the Orthodox "emphasize the inviolability of beliefs over the sanctity of the Jewish people."

I can't fault your scholarship on this citation, because you never saw the original source, just a mention in *Must a Jew Believe in Anything?* I don't need this book to tell me what Rabbi Feinstein said; I can look it up myself. But before I tell you what I found, let me give you a few other quotations that shed light on the Orthodox perception of secular Jews.

Listen to Rabbi Shlomo Hakohein (*Tifereth Shlomo*, Pirke Avot 1:6). "It is unseemly to speak about any fault or sin with regard to any of the Jewish people. . . . Rather, one must always defend them and speak to God of their good deeds, because all of them are holy, all of them are pure."

Listen to Rabbi Meir Simchah of Dvinsk (*Meshech Chachmah*, Deuteronomy 22:4). "If you observe another Jew transgressing the Torah, you may not hold it against him. If you knew what lay behind his actions, you would undoubtedly find all sorts of difficulties and uncertainties that led him to it, each according to his own situation."

Listen to Rabbi Shamshon Raphael Hirsch, the archenemy of Reform in Germany, in a letter dated March 27, 1877 (*Collected Writings*, vol. vi, p. 207). "Nowadays, thank God, we no longer have heretics as defined in our legal code, individuals with whom the law would have us avoid even personal association. . . . These individuals are already two and three generations removed from those who first set out to devise and propagate this defection. What Maimonides says regarding the Karaites in his day is fully applicable in our case as well (Yad, Mamrim, 3:3): 'But their children and grandchildren are considered to have been coerced . . . because they were raised in the ways of their errant Karaite parents. Therefore, we should attempt to bring them back, to draw them with words of peace until they return to the stronghold of the Torah.' We must maintain peaceful and friendly contacts with those of our contemporaries who have been raised in the ideas and lifestyles of [Reform]. We must translate into reality in our own lives the views and ways of true Judaism in a manner that will command the respect of others, hoping that such contact will be able to win their hearts and minds for all that is genuinely Jewish."

Listen to the Chafetz Chaim (*Marganita Tava* 17). "Try to help your fellow Jews, to pursue peace and to heed the Torah's commandment not to despise your brother, regardless of the extent of his transgressions. You must not cast epithets at him, nor use epithets that others have coined. All that is allowed is to rebuke him, but who in our generation knows how to rebuke properly? Perhaps if he had been taught differently he would have a different outlook. Do not judge another person until you stand in his place."

Listen to the Chazon Ish (Yoreh De'ah 2:16). "It is our obligation to embrace [our secular brethren], to the furthest extent of our abilities, with bonds of love."

So now that we have a better understanding of the Orthodox high regard for all Jews, irrespective of their level of observance, let us talk about Rabbi Feinstein. Ammi, you have completely misread this great Jewish sage. Rabbi Feinstein was the kindest, humblest, yet greatest person I have ever known. When I got your posting, I called one of his daughters for some vignettes of his life.

She remembers that the family used to patronize a coat store on Division Street on the Lower East Side of Manhattan. The owners were a Jewish couple who knew virtually nothing about Judaism. They could not even read Hebrew. They were also childless. Every year, Rabbi and Rebbetzin Feinstein would invite them to join the family at the Passover

Seder. They gave the secular couple a place of honor at the table and waited on them hand and foot. Never did these people experience anything but love and respect from the Feinsteins. Never did they hear even one word of rebuke or recrimination for their utter lack of observance. He must have sensed they would not be receptive, and he remained silent.

She also remembers when Rabbi Feinstein's relatives emigrated to Israel from the Soviet Union. These people, brought up under communism, were very distant from religion, but Rabbi Feinstein embraced them with unreserved warmth. He wrote to them regularly, inquiring about their health and welfare, their children, their financial circumstances. Never, not even once, did he preach to them or confront them about their lack of observance; he filled the pages with an outpouring of love and kindness. Those letters are today the treasured heirlooms of her secular relatives living in Israel.

Rabbi Feinstein is, in fact, the perfect example of the Orthodox attitude. Staunch and unswerving in his fealty to the Torah, both the Written Law and the Oral Law, yet warm and embracing to those who stray from it either deliberately or out of ignorance.

Let us now consider the statement of this wise and loving sage that "people buried in Reform cemeteries are evildoers who have denied our holy Torah." First of all, I take issue with the translation as "evildoers." In this case, "transgressors" would be more accurate; people who transgress the Torah are not necessarily evil, certainly not people who were never taught otherwise. Do you think Rabbi Feinstein would have called his secular relatives in Israel "evildoers"? Do you think he perceived the secular couple sitting at his Seder table as evil people? Granted, they were uninformed transgressors, but he did not condemn them for it. Had he considered them evil, he would never have invited them to sit at his table.

So let us go on. In what context did Rabbi Feinstein state that "people buried in Reform cemeteries are transgressors who have denied our holy Torah"? This was a halakhic responsum. What was at issue here?

Rabbi Feinstein was asked if a husband could have his wife's body disinterred from a Reform cemetery for reburial in an Orthodox cemetery. The guiding principle in this case is the statement of the Talmud (Sanhedrin 49a) that there are separate sections in the cemetery for transgressors of different degrees (see also Maimonides, Yad, Sanhedrin

14:9). Based on this, the Halakhah calls for grouping in the cemetery according to the level of observance. Orthodox Jews who were not Sabbath observers are grouped in their own section. Reform Jews, should they want to be buried in an Orthodox cemetery, would be grouped in yet another section, as Rabbi Feinstein explains in an earlier responsum (Yoreh De'ah 3:147). This is because their denial of the obligatory nature of the Torah places them on an even lower level of observance; there is no point in pretending they lived a Torah life.

Disturbing the dead, a very serious matter in Jewish law, is permitted only if absolutely necessary. Rabbi Feinstein had to decide if there was sufficient cause to disinter the body of a Reform woman only to have her reburied as a Reform woman in an Orthodox cemetery. And he ruled that there was not. Since she is buried where she belongs, why would we want to move her? He then extended his ruling further. Even if the woman had been fully observant, he points out, it would not be permitted to move her body, since a Reform cemetery is also a bona fide Jewish cemetery. Had she been buried in a gentile cemetery, however, she would most certainly have to be disinterred. As Rabbi Feinstein writes (ibid., 146), "It is forbidden to bury non-observant Jews among gentiles, since they have *kedushat Yisrael,* the holiness of the covenant."

If we go back to the original source and read the responsum, instead of accepting a mistranslated phrase taken out of context, there is actually nothing negative in what Rabbi Feinstein wrote. We find nothing that contradicts the warm feelings toward all Jews expressed in the Orthodox sources and shared by Rabbi Feinstein in abundant measure.

Ammi, I do agree with you that it is insufficient to absolve Reform Jews of blame due to ignorance, "recognizing the Jewishness of the sinner because of his birth to a Jewish mother but denying his religious authenticity." We most definitely acknowledge the religious authenticity of Reform Jews, but we deny that it flows from their Reform ideology. On the contrary, the Reform teachings tarnish it, because they reject the truth of the Torah and the Talmud, as we have discussed many times. Fortunately, Reform Jews do not need Reform ideology to give them authenticity.

A person born to a Jewish mother comes into the world as a member of an ancient royal family. But it is not enough to be a prince by birth.

You have to live your life as a prince. You have obligations, a legacy to carry on. What is this legacy? What does it mean to be Jewish?

To be Jewish is to bear witness, as did our forefather Abraham, to the existence of God even when the entire world denies Him. To be Jewish is to be a seeker of truth, as was our forefather Abraham, ready to give his life for his convictions. To be Jewish is to be kind, considerate, charitable, hospitable, as was our forefather Abraham. To be Jewish is to have a sense of duty to the world, to feel deeply that "all Jews are responsible for each other," to care about injustice, as did Moses in Egypt. To be Jewish is to sanctify God's Name by making a positive impact on the values of the world. As a nation, to be Jewish is to build communities admired by the world as models of justice and compassion, and ultimately a country that is a model of Jewish values and virtue.

Finally, to be Jewish is to have a covenant with God, a contract by which we undertake to sanctify His Name, and He in turn guarantees the success and eternity of the Jewish people, a contract that binds Him and us. Reform Jews express themselves in a Jewish manner at every step of the way, but they stumble at the last. That is where we part ways. We know the terms of the contract, and we recognize our obligation to abide by them. Reform, which intuits the covenant, makes of it whatever it wishes without consulting the Party of the First Part.

Every Jew is embraced and obligated by the covenant between God and His people, even if he fails to discern its terms; "all of them are holy, all of them are pure." Every Jew feels driven to discover the truth of existence and the meaning of life. That is why Jews are so success-oriented, so disproportionately represented among Nobel Prize winners, so prominent on the frontiers of medicine, science, philosophy, literature, so determined to achieve, to discover, to contribute. That is why Jews were in the vanguard of the socialist struggle against czarist oppression, and why they were also in the vanguard of the dissidents who brought down the corrupt Soviet Union. The Jew cannot rest. He must excel. He must fight evil and injustice. He must seek truth. What motivates him? It is the covenant engraved in his soul. It is his insatiable thirst for God and the transcendental. It is the inextinguishable spark of incandescent Jewishness in every Jewish soul that bursts into flame when it comes into contact with the Torah.

You are now contending with this Jewish spark, but you don't know how to deal with it. There is a tectonic shift in our affluent society, a suspicion that life needs a certain measure of spirituality in order to have meaning. Many Reform Jews are now turning their attention to cosmic questions. Is there more to life than crass materialism and gratification? Why are we here? What is the purpose of life? Is the bottom line of life the sum total of pleasure buttons we have pushed? What is so precious about being Jewish? What is so precious about the covenant? How do we get close to God? What happens to the soul after death?

Once again, the Reform movement finds itself scrambling to keep up with trends it does not control, this time in a better direction. You are reintroducing the role of *mitzvah* observance—optional, of course—in the hope that you can take the edge off the spiritual yearning of your constituency and keep them in the fold. But it is a futile effort. You cannot expect to inspire commitment without Jewish obligation, with the most strongly held belief being that no belief should be strongly held.

It is the Orthodox who recognize the innate authentic Jewishness of all Jews, regardless of what they practice. Reform doesn't even recognize the existence of authentic Jewishness. According to Reform, there are many truths, and therefore, there are none.

Orthodoxy will never recognize Reform as a legitimate stream of Judaism, because it is not. But we will never turn our backs on a single Reform or even totally assimilated Jew. Such a person is no less Jewish than Rabbi Moshe Feinstein himself.

Decades ago, the Orthodox rabbinate disallowed official contact with the non-Orthodox leadership so as not to legitimize them. I am not surprised that you find this policy irritating. On a number of occasions, you have actually expressed doubt that I would be allowed to go through with this project. As I told you, I asked the advice of several Orthodox sages before I agreed to do this. They encouraged me to proceed, since I am a talmudist and a writer rather than a practicing member of the rabbinate.

I want to conclude with a story. Back in the early fifties, three Shomer Hatzair boys in trademark shorts and sandals walked into Bnei Brak, an Orthodox stronghold in Israel, and asked to be taught Torah. Now the Shomer Hatzair, a Zionist youth organization that advocated socialist

materialism, was notorious for its antagonism to Judaism and its bois-
terous Yom Kippur parties while other Jews were fasting and praying.

The people in Bnei Brak were suspicious. There was no *baal teshuvah*
movement at the time, no Ohr Somayach, no Aish Hatorah, no Arachim
seminars. Why would Shomer Hatzair boys want to study Torah? What
did they have up their sleeves? On the other hand, if they really were sincere, how could they be turned away? So they asked the advice of the
world's greatest Torah scholar—the Chazon Ish, who lived in Bnei Brak.

"Teach them," said the Chazon Ish. And he explained. "Generations
ago, when virtually all Jewish people were observant, the grandparents
of these boys succumbed to the seductive allure of the secular world
and abandoned Judaism. What do you think their fathers and mothers
did? They ran to the synagogue, threw open the holy ark and poured
out their hearts to the Almighty. With tears streaming down their faces,
they pleaded, 'Please, Almighty God, give us back our children! Make
them come back!' Prayers never go to waste, especially not the prayers
of brokenhearted parents pleading for the salvation of their children.
But even such prayers could not bring back these children who had
deliberately turned their backs on the Torah. The grandchildren and
great-grandchildren, however, are a different story. Brought up in ignorance, they never turned their backs on the Torah. The prayers of their
ancestors, held in abeyance for so many years, have brought back the
boys who have come here today."

And then the Chazon Ish added with the clarity of vision that comes
from vast Torah knowledge, "Today there are only three of them. Soon,
they will begin coming in the thousands."

And he was right.

Today, we are witnessing a powerful renaissance of classical Judaism.
There are many thousands of *baalei teshuvah* (returnees to a Torah life),
with more coming all the time. Many other secular Jews are becoming restless and dissatisfied with the fashionable liberal creed they have
been fed in place of a solid spiritual diet. They want passion. Fervor. Inspiration. Meaning. Spirituality. Truth. Above all, they want truth. Why?
Because they are authentic Jews.

Warmest regards,

Yosef

April 11, 2001

Dear Yosef:

Well . . . at least I was impressed by your commitment.

I am grateful that you wrote in an unrestrained manner because you provided a good opportunity to assess your worldview. I do not feel that I have to respond to each and every point. I have responded where I believe a central point should be made. As for all the other thoughts people might have, I am content to let the record speak for itself and leave room for our readers to draw their own conclusions.

TRUTH AND CHANGE

For some time now, I have been intrigued by your propensity to misunderstand, exaggerate, simplify, and draw conclusions not stated or warranted. After all, you are a talmudist and have spent a lifetime engaged in critical analysis of the smallest details. The study of Talmud places a premium on the ability to appreciate the subtleties of language and to distinguish between even minor differences of thought. In your analysis of various talmudic passages you demonstrate that you have this ability.

So why, I keep asking myself, have you not applied the same discipline to our dialogue?

I am not sure. I do, however, have a theory.

If I had to choose a theme for everything you have written so far I would use your words "WE JUST NEED THE TRUTH." You probably mean exactly what you write. You need—really need—the truth. There are people who psychologically and emotionally need certainty in life. They need to have all the answers or they feel lost. The fact that life is full of uncertainties only increases this need.

Hence some folks have a propensity to construct a worldview that sets very clear parameters. They try to create a hermetically sealed environment that will prevent the penetration of alien stimulus. Everything that is outside the box is threatening. The easier it is outside to access and transmit information, the greater is the need to create fire walls to prevent invasion of foreign and "untrue" ideas. The greater are the challenges to the environment, the more dissonance they create and greater is the need to resist. Orthodoxy, like the rest of us, is informed by, and responds to, the general environment. Orthodoxy, like the rest of us, develops a philosophy to deal with modernity.

I am not suggesting that you fit this description entirely. You are an intriguing blend. You have agreed to engage in this public dialogue and to have your views challenged. Still, I think that you share many of the traits described above. Thus your writing is replete with terms like "distortion," "scandalous distortion," "appalling distortion," "lies," "big lie," "obvious lie," "fabrication," "false," "hoax," "duped," "drugged," "spiritual senselessness," "platitudes," "misrepresentation," "appalling misrepresentation," "incredible," "license to reject absolute truth," "aversion to truth," "ridiculous God you have invented," "only interested in distorting," "splattering the Talmud with mud," "do not respect the texts," "how gleeful you become."

The tone of your writing betrays a certain defensiveness. "Words spoken softly by wise men are heeded sooner than those shouted by a lord in folly." (Ecclesiastes 9:17) Your efforts to project certainty reveal uncertainty. Your so-called "proofs" hide a fear of being unmasked. If you really believe what you wrote, that "if even the smallest part of the Torah . . . [does] not come from God [then you are left with] a worthless roll of parchment," the stakes become unbearably high. Everything rides on your ability to "prove" that interpretations with which you disagree are "appalling misrepresentations," "scandalous distortions," "lies," "big lies," "obvious lies," "fabrications." It is either truth—as you see it— or fabrication. There can be nothing in between. Every word is divine or it is all a worthless roll of parchment.

Your need for truth—certainty—is not unique. We all want certainty. However, as in everything else in life, it is a question of degree. Where we draw the boundaries will differ, based upon our intellectual, environmental, and emotional experiences and proclivities.

Since I do not consider myself a relativist, and since I think that we must be able to search for, find, and speak the truth, I agree with you that we must be able to characterize the will of God. I have done this myself in my writing. It is not the case, as you contend, that "according

234 | AMMIEL HIRSCH

to Reform there are many truths, and therefore, there are none." I too believe that there is truth beyond human reality. But pronouncing God's truth should be done with trepidation and humility. To say that "God wants" something, or that a certain expectation constitutes the "will of God" is an awesome responsibility.

I have previously expanded upon this and will not add a great deal here. It is not, as you say, "a policy of anything goes . . . with the prevailing relativist winds of contemporary society." You are right to raise warning bells. Your caution against relativism is properly noted.

However, as I have stated before, my view is that we have accumulated millennia of wisdom, where we are entitled to conclude that history, experience, reason, discernment, moral judgment, insight, and intuition make a belief true or self-evident (not intuition alone as you repeatedly mischaracterize my views). At all times, I consider these truths to be filtered through human understanding ("the Torah spoke in the language of human beings")—and thus limited in principle and application to human understanding. It does not mean that we cannot speak of truth and divine origin, but we cannot place ourselves in the mind of God—or worse—replace the mind of God.

We do not disagree that there is a human dimension to the religious endeavor. In your description of the Oral Law, you concede that in explicating the Law transmitted from Moses the Sages "used their own words." We disagree on the proper role and balance of human discretion, particularly as expressed and applied in this contemporary generation. I appreciate your vote of confidence that "the feelings that resonate in [my] heart are unquestionably Jewish." Thank you. But I hope you will understand if I remind you that even beyond your vote of confidence, there is enough in Jewish tradition to give support to your view and mine. It is not a question of my "misreading of the Torah" or even— heaven help us—your misreading of the Torah.

Let me respond to a number of additional points that you raised bearing on the issues of truth and change.

AUTONOMY

You ask an excellent question: "What exactly is autonomy?" You answer that autonomy is "freedom from obligation"; "autonomy is the exact opposite of a covenant which creates obligations. It is like the difference between a casual affair and a marriage."

I find it interesting that you use the analogy of marriage. Our tradition uses that precise analogy to describe the covenant between God and the Jewish people. Autonomy is considered to be a central component of the covenant. An indispensable element in this marriage is the autonomy of the people—their freedom to accept or reject what God was offering them. The covenant would not have been valid had the people not had free will. It is by virtue of the exercise of the people's autonomy that the covenant is given everlasting value.

"Why were the ten commandments not said at the beginning of the Torah? To what may this be compared? A king who entered a province said to the people: May I be your king? But the people said to him: Have you done anything good for us that you should rule over us? What did he do then? He built the city wall for them, he brought in the water supply for them and he fought their battles. Then when he said to them, May I be your king? They said to him, Yes, yes. Likewise God. He brought the Israelites out of Egypt, divided the sea for them, sent down the manna for them, brought up the well for them. . . . Then he said to them: I am to be your king. And they said to Him: Yes, yes. Rabbi says: this proclaims the excellence of Israel. For when they all stood before Mount Sinai to receive the Torah they all made up their minds alike to accept the reign of God joyfully. Furthermore they pledged themselves to one another." (Mekhilta Bakhodesh)

It is the very exercise of free will that gives validity to the covenant between God and the Jewish people and our pledge to each other. Even when the Talmud relates a seemingly opposite conclusion, the rabbis are quick to point out the exercise of free will: "R. Avdimi b. Hama b. Hasa said: The Holy One, blessed be He, overturned the mountain upon them like an [inverted] cask, and said to them: 'If you accept the

Torah, fine; if not, there shall be your burial.' R. Aha b. Jacob said: This furnishes a strong protest against the Torah. Said Raba, yet even so, they reaccepted it in the days of Ahasuerus. . . . they confirmed what they had accepted long before." (Shabbat 88a)

When R. Avdimi's interpretation appeared to remove the element of free will from the people's acceptance of the Torah, there is an immediate objection and an attempt to reconcile any competing claims. If anyone were to argue that there was an element of coercion in the acceptance of the Torah, thus furnishing a strong protest against it, the Talmud clarifies that the people reaccepted it later on during the days of Ahasuerus.

Our tradition insists upon the exercise of free will. "Everything is in the hands of heaven except for the fear of heaven." (e.g., Niddah 16b) Akiva said: "Everything is foreseen but freedom of choice is given." (Avot 3:19). Maimonides affirmed that Man has the freedom to choose what he wants to do.

Belief in God cannot be coerced. Once, however, the belief is entered into, the sense of obligation flows therefrom. This sense of obligation is not inconsistent with autonomy. Autonomy encompasses freedom from coercion, but not necessarily, as you assert, freedom from obligation. It is not, as you write, that I imply that "God is content to let us have autonomy. . . . and that being Jewish entails no special obligations." Quite the contrary, the sense of obligation is enhanced by virtue of the autonomous exercise of free will.

You misunderstand the application of the concept of autonomy in the non-Orthodox religious world. It is not "legitimized nonobservance as a final destination," as you describe. Rather, it is an effort to encourage people to become more observant with greater and longer-lasting commitment, through their free and voluntary acceptance of the yoke of commandments. This is what freedom means in the Jewish sense. It is not the ability to do, or the desirability of doing, as we please, but the exercise of free will so we can better serve God.

The statement you quoted from Rabbi Schindler actually makes this point and is the opposite of what you intended. When he said that "the tragedy is that too many Reform Jews at every level have seized on this right to opt to do nothing," he was encouraging people to become more observant, not less. He was making the same point you were: He was saying do not confuse autonomy with lack of observance.

The concept of autonomy, like everything else, has a price. If you afford the individual the right to choose, he might choose to do nothing, as the Israelites might have chosen to reject the Torah at Sinai. Our tradition records that God offered the Torah to many other nations before He offered it to Israel, but that they all rejected it. Once the choice has been made through the exercise of autonomy, it is much more powerful than one that has been coerced, or embraced impulsively without thought.

The idea of autonomy is not foreign to Judaism. It is one of our great contributions to the heritage of mankind. Already thousands of years ago, millennia before modern thinkers began developing the concept of autonomy, we recognized the centrality of free will and autonomy in religious life. If we take seriously the biblical idea that human beings were created in the image of God, it follows that we are all worthy of dignity, respect, and freedom. "Did not He who made me in my mother's belly make him [the servant]? Did not One form us both in the womb?" (Job 31:15).

You characterize (Reform) autonomy as "a conflict between the covenanted obligations of the Torah and the attractions of secular culture." What are you talking about? I have been writing to you about the great Jewish ideas and the obligations flowing therefrom, and you insist on characterizing them as "secular culture." Is freedom a secular value? Is conscience a secular value? Is justice a secular value? What about equality, the existence of God, "in God's image," the sanctity of life, *tikkun olam*—the improvement of society—the creation of a better world and the perfectibility of life, optimism, the application of reason, the holiness of the Jewish people. These are core Jewish values. Do you consider these "platitudes to drug [people] into spiritual senselessness?"

Judaism so respects the individual person that even as early as the Bible we find human beings challenging God Himself. You write: "Who gave you the right to judge the ethics of the Torah? . . . Did Abraham question God's ethics when He told him to bind Isaac for a sacrifice?"

Challenging God is one of the great Jewish habits. Yes, Abraham challenged God—not during the binding of Isaac, but before: "Abraham came forward and said, 'Will you sweep away the innocent [of Sodom and Gomorrah] along with the guilty? What if there should be fifty innocent within the city; will you then wipe out the place and not forgive it for the sake of the innocent fifty who are in it? Far be it from You to do such a thing, to bring death upon the innocent as well as the guilty, so that innocent and guilty fare alike. Far be it from You! Shall not the Judge of all the earth deal justly?'" (Genesis 18:23ff.)

The implication of this passage is that God can even be persuaded by human beings. "And the Lord answered, 'If I find within the city of Sodom fifty innocent ones, I will forgive the whole place for their sake.' Abraham spoke up, saying, 'Here I venture to speak to my Lord, I who am but dust and ashes: What if the fifty innocent should lack five? Will you destroy the whole city for want of the five? . . . let not my Lord be angry if I speak but this last time: What if ten should be found there?' And He answered 'I will not destroy, for the sake of the ten.'"

It was Abraham's demonstrated willingness to challenge God, and God's openness to persuasion, that made his refusal to challenge God when it came to sacrificing his own son much more interesting and complicated.

There are instances in the Bible where God was persuaded by human beings: "The Lord further said to Moses, 'I see that this is a stiff-necked people. Now let Me be, that My anger may blaze forth against them and that I may destroy them.' . . . But Moses implored the Lord his God, saying 'Let not Your anger, O Lord, blaze forth against Your people. . . . Let not the Egyptians say, "It was with evil intent that He delivered them, only to kill them off in the mountains." . . . Turn from your blazing anger, and renounce the plan to punish Your people.' . . . And the Lord renounced the punishment He had planned to bring upon His people." (Exodus 32:9–14)

"And the Lord said to Moses, 'How long will this people spurn Me, and how long will they have no faith in Me despite all the signs that I have performed in their midst? I will strike them with pestilence and disown them.' . . . But Moses said to the Lord . . . , 'Pardon I pray the iniquity of this people according to Your greatness.' . . . And the Lord said, 'I pardon as you have asked.'" (Numbers 14:11–20)

The fact that as early as the Bible human beings could argue with God and God was open to persuasion presupposes a wide realm of human autonomy, reason, and free will.

The Talmud itself is a grand affirmation of the role of human beings in the religious endeavor and thus an assertion of human autonomy. That the rabbis could summarize—in "their own words," as you say— the main principles of Judaism, implies their autonomy to do so and thus alter Judaism's priorities. "The world is based upon three principles: Torah, worship and acts of loving kindness." (Pirke Avot 1:2) "What is hateful to you do not do unto your fellow, this is the whole Torah. All the rest is commentary." (Shabbat 31) "Love your neighbor as yourself, this is a (or "the") major principle of the Torah. . . . These are the generations of Man is an even greater principle." (Kedoshim)

Throughout Jewish life, individual communities had wide discretion to interpret Jewish tradition. The community rabbi had wide autonomy, and we find numerous differing and contradicting rulings by community rabbis. The synagogue is a great democratizing institution. One need not even be a rabbi to lead prayers or chant from the Torah.

You write that "a liberal-minded person might say that a merit-based priesthood would be superior to a hereditary one, but the Torah explicitly disagrees." Yet talmudic rabbis did exactly what you decry. Effective ritual authority was transferred from the hereditary priests, who were born into their positions, to communal rabbis, who earned their positions by merit.

AUTHORSHIP OF THE TALMUD

I still do not fully understand your view of the divine authorship of the Talmud. You write: "Is it evenly remotely possible that humans could create such a vast body of incredibly consistent material and deliver it to the people full-blown?" But you also write, "They (the Sages) used their own words" to write the Talmud. Well, if the Sages used their own words, does it not follow that the Talmud is at least partially human? Furthermore, if you believe that the Sages used their own words to articulate Jewish principles, why should you deny this right to future generations?

You write, "Talmudic rulings are not decided by the prevailing political or social fashions." But you also write, [A talmudic ruling] "must be consistent with established practice among the observant."

(By the way, the correct translation is not "among the observant," but "among the *people*." The phrase is best translated as "Go and see how the people are behaving.")

Is it not the case that if we are to observe what the people are doing, does that not imply that a ruling is at least in part dependent upon or informed by the prevailing political or social conditions (or as you more provocatively write, "fashions")? For example, the Talmud abrogates the practice of *eglah arufah*—public expiation of unsolved murder by the breaking of a calf's neck—because "when the murders increased the rite was given up." In the Bible, women who were suspected of infidelity had to drink bitter waters. This practice was abrogated because "when adulterers increased the bitter waters ceased to be employed." (Mishnah Sotah 9:9) In the Bible, debts were canceled on the sabbatical year. This was changed by Hillel because he saw that the people refrained from giving loans to each other before the sabbatical year (Mishnah Shevi'it 10:3). Aren't these reactions to the prevailing social fashions?

You write, "The historical context of the Talmud, from which it was such a radical departure, is a strong proof that it is indeed divine and timeless." What does this mean? Are you employing the prevailing political and social fashions to prove the divinity of the Talmud? Are you suggesting that the talmudic statement that a man can do as he pleases with his wife, like eating meat bought from a butcher, is such a radical departure from the era when "the Talmud was written when . . . pagan society considered women mere chattels" that it "proves" that the Talmud "is indeed divine and timeless"?

You write, "The Sages assigned the roles of cantor, reader, and the like to men . . . for reasons of modesty as well." Is not modesty, in part, a reflection of the prevailing social conditions? Is this from God, or might it be influenced even a little bit by the prevailing fashions?

You write, "The price of equality, according to you, is to become Reform." You know what? I might have more faith in Orthodoxy and the flexibility of Halakhah than you do. I am convinced that if there is an Orthodox will, there can be a halakhic way.

SLAVERY

You have a long passage on slavery in reaction to a rather brief reference by me to the issue. You go on and on as if I touched some Pavlovian nerve. You entirely missed my point in citing *Huckleberry Finn*. (Which adds poignancy to Mark Twain's statement that few things are harder to put up with than the annoyance of a good argument.)

I wasn't suggesting that Huck's view of slavery was consistent with the Jewish view, or that Mark Twain was interested in Maimonides' views on slavery. I was not trying to analyze the Jewish view of slavery by citing Mark Twain. I was making the point that Twain described a conflict between the religious obligation of Huck, *as defined by him and his community,* and Huck's sense of morality, which was making conflicting claims on him. I cited the passage because it is a particularly fine illustration of the point, and demonstrates that even non-Jews have some interesting things to say from time to time. That is all.

THE TORAH HAS NEVER CHANGED

I suggested that the Judaism we practice today is not the Judaism practiced in biblical times. You disagreed and wrote: "We keep the same Shabbat and festivals with all their observances and laws. We follow the same dietary laws. We live the same commandments. . . . All that has changed is that rabbinic courts added precautionary laws as a fence around the Torah."

I do not understand the root of our disagreement. If rabbinic courts added laws, this means that we have additional practices that were not present during the biblical era. You are, in effect, agreeing with me. The rabbis added volumes about Shabbat observance that render today's observance dramatically different than that of biblical times. Some festivals, like Chanukah, were not even mentioned in the Torah. You are not observing the same dietary laws as observed by the Israelites. There are today many, many more. Biblical husbands practiced polygamy. We do not. Biblical punishment required stoning rebellious sons. We do not. In general, the Bible advocated capital punishment. We do not. (Rabbi Akiva and Rabbi Tarfon said, "Had we been on the Sanhedrin no death sentence would have ever been passed.")

I am sympathetic to your concerns about change. You raise an important point. How to change, who is authorized to pronounce and implement change, when should change be considered—these are all very relevant questions. But to deal with the issue of change by stating "we live by the same commandments, values, and principles," to suggest that you can "prove" that "the people observed both the Written Law and the Oral Law during biblical times"—well . . .

Biblical life was followed by over two thousand years of Jewish history and amazing creativity. If you think that biblical Judaism closely resembled life in twenty-first-century Lakewood, New Jersey, New York City, or modern Israel, okay. As an autonomous Jew you are entitled to these thoughts.

I do believe, however, that we have maintained a consistency of thought and behavior on fundamental Jewish values and beliefs that entitles us to speak of an unbroken chain of tradition. It is not necessary to insist that our life is identical to, or closely resembles biblical life.

My only problem with the Baal Shem Tov story you cite is that you use it as an analogy to the transmission of the Torah. You suggest that as it is possible to transmit the story in an identical way, so too it is possible to transmit the Torah in an identical manner. I answered that even the transmission of a fairly simple story in an identical way over time is not possible, nor is the example a very good analogy. Otherwise, contrary to your accusation, I do not dismiss this story. I actually like it. It demonstrates your commitment to memory, tradition, and family.

One more point: I caution you again to be mindful of comparing differing views on the origins of the Torah to the Holocaust, and equating all those who do not agree with your perspective to Holocaust deniers.

JEWISH PEOPLEHOOD

You write: "There is a lot of hurt among secular Jews at the Orthodox ideological rejection of the other streams . . . you can decide for yourself whether we have indeed marginalized you. . . . I understand you resent our refusal to recognize Reform as a legitimate expression of Judaism. . . ."

I think I should clarify before you get too carried away. First, you have a tendency to use the words "secular" and "Reform" interchangeably. They are not the same.

Second, my argument was not that you are marginalizing us but that you are marginalizing yourselves. By refusing to meet, engage in dialogue with, and become involved in the community at large, you are unilaterally writing yourselves out of the life of the mainstream of our people.

Third, since I love the Jewish people and since I believe that we need one another, I am pained that groups within our people anger each other. Since I believe that the covenant of the Jewish people is at the heart of Judaism, for one group to refuse even to recognize the authenticity of others seems to me particularly egregious—especially when the "unrecognized groups" constitute the overwhelming majority of our people.

You write, "Orthodoxy will never recognize Reform as a legitimate stream of Judaism, because it is not." Please understand that the Reform and the other non-Orthodox movements do not need your recognition to be legitimate. It would be welcome if Orthodoxy put more emphasis on embracing them rather than trying to define the differences, but recognize or not, non-Orthodoxy is legitimate based upon other factors. You make it appear that your recognition is some kind of prize that we seek and that as long as you withhold it, ipso facto, Reform (Conservative, Reconstructionist?) is not authentic. It is like the Englishman who did not recognize Napoleon as the emperor, which did not, of course, deprive Napoleon of his throne.

If you are correct that ultra-Orthodox Jews give enormous sums of charity to non-Orthodox Jews, I am pleased. We do not see it in the (recognized) umbrella charitable entities.

My advice to certain parts of the Orthodox world is that they should spend less time concentrating on how different all other Jews are and how little they understand. Of course, I agree with you that "knowledge is a good thing," but less emphasis should be placed upon searching for ways to disqualify people. Even if Orthodoxy finds the interpretations of others difficult, it should focus more on admiring the commitment of those, who, propelled by powerful Jewish motivations, do Jewish deeds that perpetuate Jewish life and bring benefit to humanity.

You brought some quotes from various rabbis to demonstrate that, in fact, there is a Jewish obligation to do just that:

Do not hold transgressions against another Jew.
Always defend a fellow Jew before others and God.
Try to help your fellow Jews to pursue peace and not to despise your brother.
There is an obligation to embrace our brethren with bonds of love.

It is a shame that all too many in the Orthodox world do not follow this excellent advice. Perhaps more time should be spent emphasizing these ideas relative to non-Orthodox groups, rather than "proving" those groups' inauthenticity.

A brief point concerning Rabbi Feinstein: I am struggling to understand how the statement "people buried in Reform cemeteries are transgressors (evildoers) who have denied our holy Torah" expresses what you have told me were his warm feelings toward all Jews. Further, I am not convinced that the notion of evaluating a person's beliefs and observances during his or her lifetime in order to determine in what part of a cemetery they may forever rest furthers Jewish unity or our warm feelings for each other.

BIBLICAL CRITICISM

You devote about six pages to biblical criticism. I mentioned to you previously that I really do not feel that it is useful for us to delve deeply into this endeavor because it is hugely complicated and I do not consider myself to have sufficient expertise on the matter. Your response demonstrates you do not possess such expertise, either.

You felt it necessary to spend at least some time on this anyway. As you wish. We agreed that each of us could write whatever he wanted. If your attempt at criticism of biblical criticism encourages people to look more closely at the issue, this is for the good.

For those who will continue the search, I will briefly make a few cautionary comments arising from your description, so that in case they missed it, they will appreciate your predispositions and lack of training.

You call the endeavor "pseudoscience" and assert that "every child in Hebrew school knows more about the Torah than these self-appointed Bible critics."

You imply that Bible scholars are gentiles who have an anti-Jewish agenda. You write about the "nonsense of the enemies of Judaism and the Jewish people." You then go and quote W. F. Albright, the son of a Methodist missionary, to justify—erroneously—your position, which I guess could be characterized as "It's all nonsense" and that "the preponderance of the evidence supports the unity of the Torah's authorship."

You write that you have "checked out some of those volumes of yours [mine?!]. I could bring numerous additional sources if you wish."

I claim no ownership of those volumes. They are not mine. My advice to you and all others who seek to engage biblical criticism seriously is to study those volumes carefully, and read many, many more of them.

WOMEN (REDUX)

You write that in secular Western societies "people live primarily for themselves" and that the "overriding secular goal is individual achievement and gratification . . . people are by definition competing with each other. . . . Fairness is not the issue . . . the issue is not equality but success."

Your skepticism of modern life is apparent. I can only comment that most of the Jewish families I know are about more than "success" in the narrow way you defined it. They are also about love, respect, growth, self-improvement, happiness, procreation. Often the presence or absence of these elements determines "success."

In describing the traditional role of women in households, you write: "on an individual basis traditional roles are recommended, not mandatory. The Jewish woman must look into her own heart and decide. . . ."

I agree.

If you affirm that the lifestyle you have been describing is voluntary and not mandatory, this implies that alternative models are also in your view appropriate or at least tolerable. My suggestion then is for you to spend less time being so critical about alternatives that even you consider to be legitimately pursued. We both agree: Let women make up their own minds.

Finally, on the question of modesty, you write, "Modesty is apparently not one of your concerns. For us, however, modesty is a major concern."

Orthodox Jews are not the only people concerned with modesty. Modesty is one of my concerns as well. Modesty is a virtue. Like so many other matters, however, it is a question of degree, personal and societal standards, and subjective perspective. As I have written before on other issues, the fact that people have different views on the question of modesty should not preclude the establishment of certain standards. We should be able to reach some kind of common understanding of what is acceptable in society.

The question here is, Whatever an individual's personal standards might be, where should society restrict behavior through legislation (coercion), and where does the Jewish community draw the line on communal expectations?

With regard to legislation, my view is that the more freedom and the less coercion, the better. This does not mean that "anything goes," but it does assert that the maximum degree of freedom and tolerance should be afforded.

For the Jewish community, let each community decide for itself. Most Jews today live in free countries. If they do not like their community's standards, they have the option to join another (although the social pressure within the community to conform and the trepidation about leaving should not be underestimated). I am sure that some women appreciate your generous suggestion to play larger leadership roles in the community through the print media where they are not seen, but most modern women will not feel relieved by this generosity of spirit.

You write: "Should I accept the opinion of the Sages . . . or should I accept the opinion of your [my?!] contemporary thinkers whose values have led to . . . the ultimate debasement and denigration of women on an unprecedented scale?"

First, I claim no ownership over any contemporary thinkers. They are not mine. Second, I wonder whether it is, in fact, the case that women are now undergoing the *ultimate* debasement. Are women more debased today than, say, during talmudic times or during the Middle Ages? While there is still progress to be made, I actually think that, on an unprecedented scale, women are now less debased, more free, more respected, and better able to manifest their potential in twenty-first-century America than in any other place and time in history.

Third, I am not sure that the views of talmudic rabbis on the nature and role of women—rabbis who, you assert, lived during a period when society considered women mere chattel, and expressed thoughts by using "their own words,"—should be preferred over those of contemporary thinkers. We do not necessarily follow the medical advice of talmudic rabbis today. As you yourself write: "Would you presume to interpret X-rays or offer medical diagnoses without proper training?"

I have no problem with your standards of modesty insofar as you apply them to yourself. In fact, there is much to admire about the discipline involved in fulfilling these standards and the accompanying seriousness of purpose. But if such standards are invoked to prevent women from aspiring toward communal leadership and the myriad of opportunities for self-advancement, then my only advice would be to invite women to explore different standards that exist in other communities. If they choose to decline the invitation, or upon reflection prefer their own community's standards, that is their own business.

You write, "Modesty is a difficult concept for people raised in jaded America, where a casual hug and kiss between near strangers are as meaningless as a handshake."

I must be jaded. I see nothing wrong in a casual hug and kiss between men and women. I have often been hugged and kissed casually by women (and men) and have responded in kind, often in public in front of hundreds of people. It really is as meaningless as a handshake.

THE WESTERN WALL

You write: "I asked a friend at Agudath Israel to enlighten me. He explained that absolutely no one wants any woman to sit in jail for even one minute for donning a *tallit* at the Wall, but that the prohibition is to be temporarily included in a broader law, which carries a penalty of imprisonment, until a better law can be written."

There are two issues that I would like to highlight. The first is the question of the proper standards in democracies. I would be the first to express joy if Agudath Israel could, as you write, "enlighten" us on tolerance, democracy, and pluralism in the Jewish state. My experience, however, creates considerable doubt in my mind. A member of Knesset Ofir Pines articulated the principle well when he stated, "[Those who proposed the law] have forgotten that they live in a democratic society where people are not imprisoned for their gender." (*Jerusalem Post,* May 31, 2000)

Those who would propose in Parliament that women be imprisoned for praying at the Western Wall in a manner that does not suit ultra-Orthodox authorities simply do not appreciate what it means to live in a democracy. You should refer them to all those political philosophers whose writings you have recently begun studying.

Remember, we are talking about a public space. If an Orthodox synagogue wishes to establish certain standards of prayer, it is free to do so. Those who agree with these standards can attend such synagogues if they choose. Others who disagree are free to go elsewhere.

The Western Wall is not an Orthodox synagogue. The Wall is first and foremost a national shrine symbolizing not only religion, but also the undying spirit of the Jewish people to live in freedom in the Land of Israel. For years, the Israel Defense Forces have sworn in soldiers (including women) at the Wall. It is the heritage of the entire Jewish people. The Western Wall is no more an Orthodox synagogue than are all other parts of the Land of Israel.

Ultra-Orthodox authorities, however, essentially say my way or prison: "The Kotel is for all Jews. Everyone can come and pray. But they must behave as Orthodox people do in an Orthodox synagogue." (Rabbi Rabinovich, Chief Rabbi of the Holy Places, New York *Jewish Week*, August 15, 1997)

In democracies, competing groups expect to work out their differences by compromising a bit for the sake of the greater good. We should try to encourage the maximum degree of social harmony. There are solutions to the problems at the Western Wall that respect Orthodox sensibilities and at the same time take into account other needs. The Wall is big enough for all those who seek to pray there or simply stand in its presence. There could be hours during the week set aside for groups that have differing standards of prayer. Or a portion of the Wall could be dedicated for non-Orthodox use. One would think that Orthodox people, especially, would be happy that Jews would want to pray at the Western Wall, and would do everything they could to encourage prayer at the site.

But some ultra-Orthodox Jews simply want it all. They can get away with it because of the distorted political power that ultra-Orthodox parties possess.

Here then is the second issue. Most of these struggles we have in Israel, from the Western Wall to conversion, marriage, and "Who is a Jew?" are driven by the implacable opposition of ultra-Orthodox authorities to all forms of alternative Jewish religious expression. Let me cite just a few of many examples:

"The very fact that the Conservative Jews, who symbolize the destruction of the Jewish people, came to the place that is holiest to the Jewish people is a provocation. They have no reason to be in this place." (Chaim Miller, deputy mayor of Jerusalem, *Moment*, August 1997)

"Now the Supreme Court is trying to convert the holy place to a dance floor under the auspices of the Reform movement." (Member of Knesset Meir Porush, *Yated Neeman*, May 23, 2000)

"From the perspective of observant Jews . . . the fundamental question is saving the Jewish people from the terrible spiritual dangers of the Reform and Conservative movements." (*HaModia*, June 7, 1998)

"In every matter of importance to Eretz Yisrael these movements (Reform and Conservative) have constantly caused damage. . . ." (Rabbi Moshe Feinstein, as reported in *Yated Neeman*, February 13, 1998)

"Reform Jews have no place within Israel. They are a nation apart. We should vomit out these people. They should not live in Israel. . . . They are essentially dead." (Rabbi Ovadia Yosef, as reported in *Ma'ariv*, November 16, 1997)

"It is prohibited to pray in a non-Orthodox Temple at anytime. If one does not have an Orthodox synagogue within walking distance, one should pray at home. This is so even on Rosh Hashanah. . . . This ruling is affirmed by the prior ruling of such Torah luminaries as R. Moshe Feinstein." (Union of Orthodox Rabbis of the United States and Canada, the New York *Jewish Week*, September 26, 1997)

As I have stated before, people should be free to hold whatever opinions they want. However, it is important to understand the motivations of those who would advocate ultra-Orthodoxy at the Wall, exclusive Orthodox conversions in the State of Israel, and exclusive Orthodox control over religious life in Israel. Many of them are not friends of democracy. Many of them do not practice the kind of tolerance and love of fellow Jews you say you want to see.

In the late 1990s I was at the Wall praying with about twenty Reform rabbis. The police built a barricade around us to protect us from the unruly Orthodox mob that tried to do us physical harm. I did not see love in their eyes. I did not see tolerance. I saw, frankly, only hatred.

"Is this the city that was called Perfect in Beauty, Joy of all the Earth?" (Lamentations 2:15)

Ammi

April 18, 2001

Dear Ammi,

Well, it appears the debate has gotten down to the tone of my remarks rather that the substance. You cannot refute my arguments, so instead you point to my occasional use of rather strong language as proof that I am covering up undetected flaws. "Efforts to project certainty," you argue, "reveal uncertainty." How clever.

But really, it is all a matter of style. When *you* emphasize a point, you *italicize* it or <u>underline</u> it or put it into **boldface** type (remember when you wrote about my "need for **power**"?). As a writer, I don't use typography for emphasis, and exclamation points only rarely, and so I occasionally resort to emphatic language. When I see you twisting a talmudic passage out of shape, I observe a "distortion." When you are way, way out of line, I might comment on the "appalling distortion." Obviously, this sort of language rankles you, but believe me, there is absolutely no offense intended. As for my proofs and arguments, they stand on their own merits.

I have a few comments regarding some points you made. I will try to keep the language soft.

CERTAINTY AND UNCERTAINTY

You claim that I, and Orthodox people in general, "psychologically and emotionally need certainty in life." Therefore, our arguments and beliefs are not inspired by reason but by emotional need, and they can be dismissed without refutation.

First of all, it is quite amazing (Wait a minute, is "amazing" an emphatic word? Phew! It's not on your list.) that an entire community should suffer from the same personality disorder, a malady that induces us to cower behind "fire walls built against the invasion of foreign and untrue ideas." Perhaps it is something in the water, or could it be the kosher food? But even so, does that make our rational arguments less valid? If you love your child because you need to love her, does that make your love less genuine?

Ammi, my good friend, the Orthodox do not shield mature minds from alien ideas. I know full well that many thousands of Orthodox people will read your postings as well as mine. Nonetheless, I feel confident that they won't chuck their yarmulkes and long-sleeved dresses and head for the Reform temples.

Life is certainly full of uncertainties, as you point out. We never know what will happen the next day or if we will even live through the night. But when it comes to knowledge, we cannot be content with uncertainty. Truth and knowledge are good things. Accepting uncertainty is a defeat.

LIFE HAS CHANGED

You deny that "biblical Judaism closely resembled life in twenty-first-century Lakewood, New Jersey, New York City, or modern Israel." Well, it's true that they didn't have electricity, jet travel, computers, or e-mail in those days, but the religious aspects of life were not different. They learned Torah, ate only kosher food, avoided the thirty-nine labors forbidden on the Sabbath, and so forth.

The specific application of the principles of the Torah are all that have changed to keep up with technology, but the principles themselves apply to all times and places. That is their beauty. The Talmud discusses (Baba Kama 29a) a man walking with a jug of olive oil on his shoulder followed by another man with a beam on his shoulder. The man carrying the jug stops, and the one behind runs into him, smashing the jug with his beam. What is his liability? Now, in our times, we are not likely to see a man walking down Park Avenue with a jug of olive oil on his shoulder followed by another with a beam. But what if one of those shiny black limousines makes a short stop and the limo behind him smashes into his rear? The situations are worlds apart, but the same principles apply to both.

You mentioned quite a few instances where it seems to you that the Sages adapted basic Torah law to the times. For the sake of brevity, I will address just one of your citations. If you want clarification on the others, I will be glad to provide it. You quote from the Mishnah (Sotah 9:9): "When the murderers increased, the rite [of *eglah arufah*] was given up. . . . When adulterers increased, the bitter waters ceased to be employed." The Talmud explains these changes on the spot (Sotah 47b). The *eglah arufah* was used in cases of murder by person or persons unknown. Therefore, when murderers became brazen about their crimes, the rite was discontinued. The bitter waters could only determine if a woman was guilty of infidelity when her husband was faithful to her. Therefore, when adultery became rampant, the procedure was discontinued.

Once again, these are not changes but sanctioned adjustments. Do you think for one moment that the talmudic sages would have sanctioned your brand of "consistency of thought and behavior on fundamental Jewish values and beliefs that entitles us to speak of an unbroken chain of Jewish tradition"? Do you think even one single sage would have agreed that you have not broken the chain of Jewish tradition? You are free to do as you see fit, but do not seek validation in the Talmud. It is not there.

CHECK WITH THE PEOPLE

I am pleased to see that you are becoming more rigorous in your translations of the Talmud. I wrote that talmudic rulings "must be consistent with established practice among the observant *(puk chazi ma ama devar)*." You correctly point out that the exact translation is "go out and see how the people are behaving." From this, however, you incorrectly infer that "rulings are at least in part dependent upon or informed by prevailing political or social conditions."

The *puk chazi* rule appears three times in the Talmud. The first (Berachot 45a) applies to the proper blessing to make on certain drinks. The second (Eruvin 14b) applies to the proper construction of a Sabbath *eruv.* The third (Menachot 35b) applies to whether torn *tefillin* straps may be fixed or if they must be replaced. None of these issues involves "prevailing political and social conditions." In all these cases, an obscure point of law is being checked against widespread established practice.

The behavior of nonobservant people is, of course, irrelevant in this respect.

AUTONOMY

It comes as a surprise to me that you have reinterpreted autonomy and now equate it with free will. I, too, believe in free will. To your list of citations supporting the concept of free will, I would add a biblical citation (Deuteronomy 30:19): "I have set before you life and death, blessings and curses, choose life!" Our ancestors most certainly entered into the covenant of their own free will, but are you saying that every Jew today can choose to accept or reject the covenant of his or her own free will? Doesn't the ancient covenant obligate all Jewish people for all time?

Let me quote from one of your earlier postings. "The covenant was made for all time, not only with those standing at Sinai but also 'with those who are not with us here this day.' (Deuteronomy 29:15) It is an everlasting covenant that cannot be abrogated. As bleak as things might look for the Jews, God cannot abandon His covenant with the Jewish people, 'for the word of God is always fulfilled.' (Isaiah 40:8)"

Covenants are two-way streets. If God cannot abandon His covenant, neither can the Jewish people abandon theirs. And if all Jews are bound by the covenant, where does autonomy come into play? Of course, everyone has free will. A person has the free will to choose whether or not to commit murder, whether or not to steal, whether or not to observe the Sabbath, but does he have autonomy in these matters? Does he have the right to do as he pleases?

If you claim autonomy for yourself, do you grant God the same autonomy? Is it all right with you if God rethinks his commitment to the Jewish people?

Some covenant.

CHALLENGING GOD

You contend that God can be challenged and persuaded by human beings. I beg to differ.

In the pagan world, gods were perceived as immortal beings with supernatural powers ready to zap insubordinate mortals at will. The gods were no better than overgrown humans with tempers and drives. They fought, deceived, and plotted against each other. Abraham's monotheism did not just reduce the number of gods from many to one. It introduced a new and transcendent understanding of God as the Supreme Being, the Creator and Controller of all existence, perfect in knowledge, unaffected by emotion, incorporeal, insubstantial, unbound by space and time, completely beyond the grasp of the human intellect. God has no temper; when He gets angry in the Bible, it is just a metaphor. God's knowledge is limitless. As Maimonides explains in his *Shemoneh Perakim,* God does not absorb knowledge from without. He is all knowledge.

Can a human win an argument against such a God? Can a human challenge Him in debate? Can such a God be persuaded to see the error of His ways? And yet you write about "Abraham's willingness to challenge God and God's openness to persuasion." It is when you make statements like these that I am moved to respond with emphatic language such as "What kind of ridiculous God have you invented?" You can challenge and outwit pagan gods, but not the Master of the Universe. You can question God in the sense of requesting illumination, but you cannot question Him in the sense of challenging His thinking.

The citations you bring are all instances of prophets pleading for enlightenment, yearning to understand the incomprehensible, inscrutable ways of God, but always with humble acceptance, never with disagreement.

Warmest regards,
Yosef

April 25, 2001

Dear Ammi,

In several postings, you addressed some points of contention between Orthodox and Reform in Israel. You have raised such issues repeatedly, and I agree that they need to be aired. On other occasions, however, you have pressed me on my views about Israel and Zionism in general. I believe this is a better starting point for our discussion, since it will bring into focus the core issues that affect the future of the State of Israel. Let us first address the more crucial questions about what Israel represents and where it is going; then we can talk about our differences.

I want to pose a number of questions to you.

Why do you feel that Israel has the right to exist? Were we justified in returning after two thousand years and wresting the land from its current native inhabitants?

In an earlier posting, you wrote, "I am less concerned about whether the conquest of the Land of Israel occurred as described in the Book of Joshua than that for the Jews Eretz Yisrael is the Promised Land, that we have claimed this land for as long as there were Jews, that we have cultivated and loved this land, that we have treated it as a divine gift and as the centerpiece of the covenant with God—this to me is the essential point." Clearly, you do not believe, as I do, that God gave us this land as an everlasting inheritance and that He specifically told this to Abraham, Isaac, Jacob, and Moses. You are not even willing to concede that these people existed. So what actually is your authority for this "divine gift"?

Are we back to your vaunted intuition once again? Because we "claimed the land," does that make it ours? Because we "treated is as a divine gift," does that allow us to take it by force after an absence of two thousand years? Are the Arabs supposed to step aside because you intuit that God gave you the land? Is this fair and just? Is this even rational?

And what about the Law of Return, which allows only Jews unrestricted immigration to Israel? Is it fair? Why don't you consider this a racist law, as do the Arabs and many Israeli leftists?

What is your conception of a Jewish state that restricts the immigration of other peoples? Is this democratic? Is it really a state? Should it act as the guardian and advocate for Jewish people all over the world as Theodor Herzl envisioned? In what way should Israel be specifically

Jewish as opposed to a nondenominational secular democracy? And if you are not interested in a Jewish state, merely a democratic, multiethnic Israel/Palestine, what makes you a Zionist? You wrote, "The Zionist idea is the philosophical underpinning of the State of Israel." You are the director of a Zionist organization. What does Zionism mean to you, and how does it dovetail with your democratic, egalitarian, and pluralistic ideas?

Ehud Barak, the former prime minister of Israel, and his colleagues are totally secular people, the exemplars of the post-Zionist generation intent on severing Israeli society from any connection to Judaism or Jewishness in any form whatsoever. This is the basis of the "secular revolution" in which you have invested your hopes. Did it ever occur to you that you are a pawn in their unscrupulous game, that they are using you as a dupe to undermine the role of Judaism in public life? They want to create a state detached from its Jewish roots and its Jewish identity. Is this what you want? Is this your brand of Zionism?

How do you feel about the hundreds of thousands of Russian gentiles being allowed into Israel? Former Minister of Absorption Yuli Tamir stated that Israel has brought in many gentiles as part of the process of the secularization of the state. Do you agree with this policy? Or are you prepared to pronounce a blessing over their heads and declare them Jews? Yasser Arafat wonders why Israel objects to the return of a million Arabs yet opens its doors to a million Russian gentiles. A very good question, don't you think?

Many knowledgeable observers of the Israeli scene consider the internal demographics of Israel the greatest threat to its continued existence in the long term. Today there are close to 1.5 million Israeli Arabs living in Israel. If they organized properly, they could elect at least fifteen Members of the Knesset even today. And what about tomorrow? While secular Israelis have a low birth rate, a high abortion rate, and a high emigration rate, Israeli Arabs have a very high birth rate, and they are staying put. Within forty years or so, they could conceivably constitute a majority of the population of Israel. Even if not, they would most likely form the largest single party in the Knesset. In a coalition with some of the more extreme leftist parties, they could control the government and force a union with the Palestinian state.

How do you feel about such a prospect? Does it concern or frighten you? Do you think anything could or should be done about it?

What is your vision of Israel, its past, its present, its future? I await your response with great interest.

Yosef

May 1, 2001

Dear Yosef:

You have asked me to begin the final major discussion of our dialogue about Israel and Zionism. I think that it is good and proper to conclude our discourse with a discussion about Israel. So much of what we have discussed is translated into reality through our engagement with the State of Israel and its underlying Zionist idea. By exercising collective Jewish power, Israel is the testing ground for many of the values that we have articulated throughout our exchanges.

As you know, much of my professional life relates to religious and political events in Israel. I have so much to say that I hardly know where to begin. You have asked some specific questions that I will address shortly. But first I would like to begin at the beginning. When discoursing on Israel people often speak in shorthand and assume, erroneously, that they share the same assumptions.

So with your indulgence I will first lay out the theological foundation for my approach to Israel and Zionism. In our discussions we have touched on many of these themes, because the Zionist idea is integral to Judaism. The idea of the national existence of the Jewish people in the Land of Israel is not a twentieth-century innovation; it is as old as Judaism itself. The idea of the national restoration of the Jewish people in the Land of Israel is not a modern reform; it began the day after the Romans destroyed the Jewish kingdom in 70 C.E. The contemporary political movement called Zionism is the latest, most eloquent expression of these sentiments.

EXPRESSING THE COVENANT IDEA
OF PEOPLE AND LAND

The nourishing source of Judaism that sustained us through the ages was the belief in the covenant between God and the Jewish people. All of Jewish history, all of our monumental accomplishments in thought and deed, are really about the implementation of the covenant—our struggle to understand its content and live up to its obligations.

The foundation of Judaism is already clear in the Bible: The establishment of a covenant between God and the Jewish people that is permanent and cannot be severed by either party; and the granting of the Land of Israel to the people of Israel. This arrangement was not for purposes of self-aggrandizement, conquest, ego, or pride. Rather, the covenant had one central aim: to bring blessing to humanity (Genesis 12:3)—to do "what is just and right." (Genesis 18:19) "This is My servant, whom I uphold, My chosen one, in whom I delight. . . . He shall teach the true way to the nations . . . and the coastlands shall await his teaching. . . . And I have grasped you by the hand. I created you and appointed you a covenant people, a light to the nations, opening eyes deprived of light." (Isaiah 42)

While each of our lives is precious, our existence within the peoplehood of Israel is what connects us to the ultimate. Judaism is the faith of the Jewish people. There can be no Judaism without the Jewish people.

The cornerstone of the covenant between God and the Jewish people is the Land of Israel. Nations require national territory within which they may grow, prosper, and attain national prominence. "On that day the Lord made a covenant with Abram saying, 'To your offspring I give this land. . . .'" (Genesis 15:18) "The Lord had appeared to [Isaac] and said, 'Reside in this land and I will be with you and bless you; I will give all these lands to you and to your offspring.'" (Genesis 26) "God said to [Jacob], 'You whose name is Jacob, you shall be called Jacob no more, but Israel shall be your name.' Thus He named him Israel. And God said to him . . . 'The land that I gave to Abraham and Isaac I give to you; and to your offspring to come will I give the land.'" (Genesis 35)

While the Jewish people existed for two thousand years outside the

Land of Israel, this was not our natural state of existence. It was the reality. We made the best of it. Rather than grow old and die, which was what happened to other conquered nations that were separated from their land, Judaism stayed forever young. Laws and practices were developed to deal with life as it had become. At all costs, the urgency was to keep the people alive. We made our peace with the Diaspora, but separation from the land was considered temporary, not permanent. Dispersion was an interruption of, not a replacement for, our national existence in the Land of Israel.

It is not so much a question of where individual Jews decided to live. Rather, the theological and emotional connection between the Jewish people and the Land of Israel was never severed. While both could exist without the other, they were both incomplete while apart. Just as the people need the land to achieve fullness and wholeness, so the land needs the people. The land fits the Jewish people. "It sometimes happens that a man is himself comely but his clothes are unbecoming, or he himself is ungainly while his clothes are becoming. In the case of Israel, however, they are suited for the Land and the Land is suited to them." (Midrash Rabbah, Masse)

How we loved this land. Throughout our history, we took delight in its stones and cherished its dust. (Psalms 102:15) It is a land "flowing with milk and honey," (Deuteronomy 11:9) a bountiful land where the mountains drip wine and the hills wave with grain. (Amos 9) It is a land where heaven and earth meet, where the partnership between God and humanity can be realized most vividly. It is a land that God "looks after, on which He always keeps his eye." (Deuteronomy 11:9–13) Ultimately, the land would be the harbinger of the redemption of the world. Upon the deliverance, none who live in Zion shall say, "I am sick." (Isaiah 33:24)

Exile never broke this love affair between the people of Israel and the Land of Israel. In fact, the longer was the exile, the greater was the romance and affection we felt. "By the rivers of Babylon there we sat, sat and wept, as we thought of Zion. (Psalms 137:1) Better the deserts of Israel than palaces abroad. (Midrash Rabbah, Lech Lecha)

"My heart is in the East, and I in the depths of the West. My food has no taste. How can it be sweet? It will be nothing to me to leave all the goodness of Spain. So rich will it be to see the dust of the ruined sanctuary."

"Would that I were on the wings of an eagle, so that I could water your dust with my mingling tears. How I shall kiss and cherish your stones. Your earth will be sweeter than honey to my taste." (Yehudah Halevi)

Every day in our prayers, we yearned for restoration: "Sound the great shofar for our freedom; lift up the banner to bring our exiles together and assemble us from the four corners of the earth." "Return in mercy to your city Jerusalem and dwell in it as you have promised. Rebuild it soon in our days as an everlasting structure. . . . Blessed art thou, Builder of Jerusalem." "May our eyes behold your return in mercy to Zion." Every year we concluded the Passover Seder, the great redemptive festival of freedom, with the words "next year in Jerusalem."

Zionism understands this unquenchable Jewish yearning to return to the land most profoundly, and is the most eloquent expression of the love affair between the People of Israel and the Land of Israel. It could not be just any land. The Jewish people had to return to *this* land. *This* is the Promised Land. When in the early twentieth century Theodor Herzl proposed the establishment of a national home in Uganda, the people ultimately rejected the proposal, even though they were enduring the most ruthless and merciless anti-Semitism. Better to suffer persecution, hardship, and even death than to sell our birthright for a mess of temporary political porridge. Zionism meant the return to Zion. Any other land would betray the history, legacy, and destiny of the people. If the reconstitution of the Jewish people was to have future significance, it required our reconnection with the ancient past in the land of our ancestors. This is the land where our character was formed. This is the land where our destiny was forged.

Have you ever walked through this land, Yosef? Have you ever been moved by the romance of it all? Have you ever strolled the streets of Jerusalem tracing the footsteps of King David, wondering what it must have been like to live in the first Jewish kingdom? Have you ever sat at an outdoor café in Tel Aviv and been overwhelmed with the thought that a mere eighty years ago this world-class city was all sand? Have you ever stood on the hills of Galilee and allowed your mind to wander and wonder how these rolling hills waving with grain and these valleys heavy with fruit were swamplands a century ago? Have you ever simply marveled at the fortitude of this people that braved disease, destitution, desolation, and deprivation to restore this land to its vitality, as predicted in the ancient prophecies: "I will restore My people Israel. They shall rebuild ruined cities and inhabit them; They shall plant vineyards and drink their wine; They shall till gardens and eat their fruits. And I will plant them upon their soil, nevermore to be uprooted from the soil I have given them." (Amos 9:14–15)

Have you ever felt that in some way all this is pleasing to God?

PEOPLE MAKE HISTORY:
WE DO NOT SIT AND WAIT FOR GOD

We see in Judaism an emphasis on life as it is. God loves the world. The world is essentially good: "and God saw all that He had made, and found it very good." (Genesis 1:31). God loves human beings. Made in the image of God, they are perfectible. Even more, human beings are aware that they are created in God's image and thus must strive to imitate God. "Beloved is man for he was created in the image of God; it is by special divine love that he is informed that he was created in the image of God." (Pirke Avot 3:18)) Society can be improved through law: "You shall appoint magistrates and officials . . . and they shall govern the people with due justice. Justice, justice shall you pursue." (Deuteronomy 16) Human beings can be taught to overcome their evil impulses: "He has told you what is good and what the Lord requires of you: Only to do justice and to love goodness, and to walk modestly with your God." (Micah 6:8)

Judaism offers a spectacular vision for mankind—unity, wholeness, perfectibility in this world. Judaism is the ultimate expression of optimism in humanity. Unlike some other faiths that are essentially pessimistic about life and that encourage the faithful to discard all that is worldly and rush to a higher existence, Judaism takes history seriously. The instrument of improvement and perfection is humanity itself working in partnership with the God of History. Judaism is not only spiritual. We can no more spend our days meditating alone on a mountaintop than a fish could live out of water. Judaism is first and foremost physical. Even the sign of the covenant is physical, a circumcision of the flesh.

By selecting Abraham, God affirms that the way to redemption is through history. Human beings must act in order to bring about a more perfect world: "The Lord said to Abram, 'Go forth from your native land.'" (Genesis 12:1) Only after Abraham acts, only after the old man leaves his father's house and all that he knew, can the destiny of Abraham's progeny be realized. "Abram went forth as the Lord had commanded him." (Genesis 12:4)

As Moses stood at the shores of the sea with the Egyptian army fast closing in, he prayed to God to deliver the people. God answered, "My children are in distress, and you stand there reciting long prayers. Why are you praying to Me?" (Mekhilta) Do something yourself. Cast your rod over the waters of freedom. Jewish freedom was earned not by God alone and not by the Israelites alone. It was born of a partnership between God and the Jewish people.

Jews, a tiny percentage of the human race, have made such wondrous contributions to humanity because we believe in humanity. We are active in society because we believe in society. We have accomplished great things because we believe in accomplishing great things. We make history because we believe in making history.

Zionism thrust the Jewish people back into history. If Judaism expects human beings to seize control of their destiny in order to redeem humanity, then the primary actors of history are nations, not individuals. "The Lord said to Abram . . . I will make of you a great nation . . . and all the nations of the world shall bless themselves through you." (Genesis 12)

For two thousand years, the Jews wandered, accomplishing great things and enduring great tragedies, but always yearning for restoration and self-determination. At no time did the Jewish people abandon its conviction that we would return as actors in the grand drama of history: "I will put My breath in you and you shall live again, and I will set you upon your own soil." (Ezekiel 37:14). The Diaspora experience was never considered the end of history, only the prelude to a more perfect existence, which would be ushered in by human beings harnessing the forces of history.

The unprecedented success of the Zionist movement in taking a scattered people that had lost its land, language, and national center, and restoring it to a central role in history, is a triumph of the human spirit and an accomplishment of universal significance: "We are engaged in a creative endeavor the like of which is not to be found in the whole history of mankind: the rebirth and rehabilitation of a people that has been uprooted and scattered to the winds. It is a people half dead. . . . What we seek to establish in Palestine is a new, re-created Jewish people. . . . We seek the rebirth of our national self, the manifestation of our loftiest spirit." (A. D. Gordon, in *The Zionist Idea,* ed. Hertzberg, pp. 382–83)

Zionism takes history and the Jewish people's role seriously. It inspired an entire people to awaken from its slumber and take back control of its own destiny. It admonished a weary and persecuted nation: "You are in distress and all you do is bemoan your circumstances and pray for your deliverance. Do something! Lift up the banner of freedom and restore yourself."

THE STATE OF ISRAEL HELPS KEEP
THE JEWISH PEOPLE ALIVE

A Place of Refuge
Zionism rescued Jews from persecution and death. If all that Israel did was to save Jews—*dayenu*—that, in and of itself, would have been enough. For there is no greater sanctity nor more urgent task than to ensure the survival of the Jewish people. There can be no compromise on Jewish survival, nor does our insistence on living need any explanation or rationalization.

All too few Jews escaped the Holocaust. At the date of her birth in 1948, 600,000 Jews lived in Israel. Had it not been for the Zionist movement, most of them too would have perished. Within eighteen months following the declaration of the state, an additional 340,000 Jews arrived. Many of them were survivors of death camps, languishing as displaced persons whom no country wanted. Between 1948 and 1953, the Jewish population of Israel doubled.

Hundreds of thousands of Jews from Morocco, Tunisia, Yemen, Iran, Syria, Lebanon, Algeria, Egypt, Iraq, and Libya poured into Israel in the years after independence. One can imagine what would have happened to most of them had they remained in those countries.

In the last ten years, approximately 1 million Jews have emigrated from the former Soviet Union. Fascism and communism ravaged their bodies, savaged their spirit, and depleted their numbers. That there was a Jewish state that advocated for their freedom and offered them a place of refuge that no other country would, allowed for the survival and dignity of whole communities.

A Place of Hope

For a people to survive, it is not enough to exist physically. A nation needs a focal point. A nation needs a culture. A nation needs a land and a language. A nation needs vibrancy and vitality. A nation needs hope.

Israel is a testament of hope over despair. Its very existence says to the world that if the Jews can do it, after all they endured, other peoples can also dare to hope.

Even during the darkest hours, Jews expressed hope. I once visited Theresienstadt with a group of rabbis. It was winter. I could not imagine how anyone could have lived through even one winter without adequate food and warmth. After spending the morning revisiting the sufferings of our people, we were eager to leave. Our guide replied that there was one more place we should see. We stopped in front of a peasant's home. Czech families now live in the barracks of the prisoners. A man opened the door to his backyard and unlocked the door to his potato storage cellar. The potatoes had long been removed because, as he told us, the officials in the museum pay him to keep it empty.

He told us that as he was clearing out his storage cellar one day, he discovered a strange-looking drawing that he thought might be important. He notified the authorities, who began scraping off the soot and dirt, and they uncovered many colorful Hebrew letters. As they continued cleaning up the cellar, it became clear that this place was a secret synagogue. Somehow hungry, bedraggled, and tortured prisoners found a way to construct a secret house of worship and to pray to the God of Redemption who would one day rescue His people from their suffering.

Israel is the antithesis of Theresienstadt. It represents hope, life, freedom. As such it has universal meaning: "We shall live at last as free men on our own soil, and in our own homes peacefully die. The world will be liberated by our freedom. . . . And whatever we attempt there for our own benefit will redound mightily and beneficially to the good of all mankind." (Theodor Herzl, *The Jewish State*, quoted in *The Zionist Idea*, ed. Hertzberg, pp. 225–26)

A Place of Identity

The Jewish state is not the object—the be-all and end-all—of Jewish existence. To worship a state is fascism, not Judaism. But the Jewish state is the most significant contemporary framework through which to express and develop Jewish values. In this role, it is of monumental importance. Nearly half of all the Jews of the world live in Israel. Demographers tell us that Israel's Jewish population will continue to increase in absolute numbers and relative to Jewish populations around the world. Within a generation, a majority of the world's Jews are projected to live in Israel. Already today the majority of Jewish children are born in the Jewish state. Israel is the only country where the Jewish population is increasing through natural growth.

Therefore, whatever Israel does, it does in the name of the Jewish people. Israel's actions, by definition, are the actions of the Jewish people. Its values are Jewish values. Its accomplishments are Jewish accomplishments. Its flaws are Jewish flaws. This is how most Jews see it. This is how most of the world sees it.

The State of Israel is the ultimate testing ground for the relevance of Jewish values. For the past two thousand years, when Judaism was developing its rabbinic tradition, we had no collective powers or responsibilities. It is one thing to sit in the various diasporas of the world and articulate standards of behavior for individuals and nations. It is quite another thing to test the relevance of such standards through the collective expression of Jewish sovereignty. We have learned a thing or two about the difficulties of implementing Jewish values in a complicated world. When you have no sovereignty, you can afford a certain luxury and purity of thought. We have discovered that exercising sovereignty in a manner compatible with Jewish values is much more difficult.

Israel enhances and expands Jewish identity. In America and throughout the Western world, religious identity tends to be personal. Religion to most people means a set of beliefs—a dogma or creed. Religion tends to be a private matter. In working with many candidates for conversion, I found that usually the most difficult concept for potential converts to grasp is the notion of Jewish peoplehood. It is so foreign to their religious experiences.

Alas, American Jews also increasingly see Judaism as exclusively a religious creed. There is diminishing understanding of the centrality of Jewish peoplehood. American Jews, like Americans generally, want to "feel the spirit." They forget that Jewish spirituality is not an exercise in individualism, but the collective efforts of the Jewish people to discover and do God's will. Even the greatest Jew, Moses, was nothing more than a human being, with considerable human strengths and weaknesses. His importance was measured not primarily by how close he was to God, but by how this relationship advanced the destiny of the Jewish people. Being part of the Jewish people is what gives the Jew religious status and significance: "You shall be My treasured possession among all the peoples. Indeed, all the earth is Mine, but you shall be to Me a kingdom of priests and a holy nation." (Exodus 19:5–6)

A Jew is defined not by his fealty to some Jewish dogma, but by his membership in the Jewish people. Jews do not even pray in isolation. Jewish prayer is communal. Even the most central prayer, the Shema, is addressed to the entire people: "Hear O Israel, the Lord is our God, the Lord is One." The entire people experienced revelation. The entire people entered into the covenant.

American Judaism—in all its various movements—leans toward the contraction of Jewish identity because emphasis is placed on the individual person or the individual community often at the expense of the klal—the entire people. Israel expands Jewish identity because it restores the centrality of Jewish peoplehood. Thus, Israel is critical in keeping alive the authentic spirit and beliefs of Judaism. As Israel's population grows, it will increasingly determine the tone and spirit of world Jewry. There is no more powerful influence on world Jewry than the exercise of sovereignty by the majority of the world's Jews. Nothing can compare in influence to the role of a sovereign Jewish state.

It is one thing to survive for two thousand years without a state. It is quite another thing for the Jewish people to prosper without a state now, under conditions of modernity. In premodern societies, Jewish identity was enforced by internal and external circumstances. The question "Why be Jewish?" was largely irrelevant. But today, when almost every Jew residing outside of Israel is, in effect, a Jew by choice, when to some degree Jews ask themselves regularly "Why be Jewish?" the people requires the attributes of peoplehood—land, language, culture, religion, sovereignty, self-determination, to expand Jewish identity and cultivate the deep roots of Judaism.

Have you ever thought, Yosef, what the world would be like if Israel did not exist today? Would the world be a better place? Would the Jews be better off? Can Judaism be permanently relevant to the world if in the global village of internationalism there is no Jewish nation alongside all the other nations of the world to advocate for Jewish values, and if there is not at least a minimal national presence of Jews to carry the message?

ARE THE ARABS SUPPOSED TO STEP ASIDE?

You write, "Because we 'claimed the land,' does that make it ours? Because we 'treated it as a divine gift,' does that allow us to take it by force after an absence of two thousand years? Are the Arabs supposed to step aside . . . ?"

Are you engaging in sophistry here, or are you sincere? Do you of all people question the religious, moral, and legal right of the Jewish people to create a sovereign state in the Land of Israel, or are you simply being provocative in a talmudic sort of way?

You and I have written only about our beliefs. This book is about Judaism. Other people have other beliefs. Our faith alone cannot establish the international legality of a state or determine its borders. The right of the Jewish people to return to Zion and there to establish a sovereign Jewish state was embraced by a majority of the nations of the world and duly authorized in international law by the United Nations. That is what gives it international standing. The Jewish state was to exist not to the exclusion of any others, but alongside the Arab states.

In the immediate aftermath of the Holocaust, whose purpose was to obliterate entirely the Jewish people, it was a rare moment of morality and conscience for a world that was otherwise largely indifferent to the plight of the Jews. Perhaps some countries were inspired by this most resilient of peoples. Maybe they also felt a bit guilty. Whatever their motivations, for one shining moment they did the right thing. At the same time, the aspirations and conflicting claims of others were taken into account. Their yearning to live in freedom was generously addressed. The borders set aside for the Jewish state were considerably smaller than those described in the Bible, or even those originally promised by the British or the League of Nations.

To be a Jew is to yearn for peace. The very first statement of the modern Jewish state included, "We offer peace and unity to all the neighboring states and their peoples, and invite them to cooperate with the independent Jewish nation for the common good of all." (Declaration of Independence)

The yearning for peace is so ingrained in Jewish consciousness that it is picked up, almost through osmosis, by Jews not even particularly knowledgeable in Judaism. When I served as a tank commander in the Israel Defense Forces, I was stationed in the Sinai Desert. After the peace accords with Egypt were signed, we spent weeks hoisting all of the machinery of a modern army onto trucks and trailers, returning them to Israel proper. Finally, the soldiers departed. We stepped onto our bus. This was the last day, we prayed, that the army would ever set foot in Sinai. We would never return as soldiers. Before we crossed the border, the bus stopped in front of a makeshift sign that probably had been placed there by a particularly proud, romantic, and emotional soldier. On it, he wrote the words, *Lo nasognu, vitarnu lema'an hashalom*— "we have not retreated, we have compromised for the sake of peace."

That sign has stayed with me all these years. I still have a picture of it in my house. It symbolized for me what this exercise in Jewish self-determination is all about. Amid all these instruments of awesome military power—tanks, artillery, guns, and soldiers—there was one lonely sign stuck in the middle of the desert that said it all. Despite our military might—the Egyptian army would never have kicked us out of there by force—it is not about power, but about peace. "Not by might nor by power, but by My spirit, said the Lord of Hosts." (Zechariah 4:6)

The Arabs are not supposed to just step aside. But how we yearn that they would step up and extend the hand of friendship and peace. They can always win over the Jews with words and acts of peace. Some of them already have.

JEWISH AND DEMOCRATIC STATE

You ask, "In what way should Israel be specifically Jewish as opposed to a nondenominational secular democracy?"

First, this notion peddled by some Jews that Judaism and democracy are incompatible is really a canard. It reveals a misunderstanding of both Judaism and democracy. I have expanded upon this at length throughout this book. While it is obviously true that democracy in the form practiced today was not practiced in antiquity, many of the values underpinning democratic government formed the basis of the Jewish approach to social life. Judaism is entirely compatible with democracy. In fact, it is plausible to argue that Jewish values contributed to the development of democratic government. Many of the early political theorists were deeply religious men who gleaned their convictions about democracy from the Bible. Israel's democracy openly proclaims that "the precepts of liberty, justice and peace *taught by the Hebrew Prophets*" will characterize the Jewish state. (From the Declaration of Independence)

Second, even if I were an Orthodox Jew, and even if I did not accept the above understanding of Judaism (many Orthodox Jews do), I would still think that the case for democracy is overwhelming. The evidence of its superiority is all around us. You yourself, as do most of the world's Jews, live in a democracy. If it is good for you living in America, and it does not compromise your Judaism, why would it not be equally valid in the Jewish state? Is it not particularly ironic that some non- and even anti-Zionist Orthodox Jews fight to impose halakhic law on the Zionist state they have chosen to reject?

Third, even if I were an Orthodox Jew, and even if I were not persuaded by any of the above points, I would still think that Orthodox Jews would insist upon Israel being a democracy. For it is a matter of life and death. Only by being a democracy can Israel attract the loyalty of most of the world's Jews and its own citizens. This support means life itself for the Jewish state and the more than 5 million Jews residing within it. A nondemocratic Israel would begin to look very much like all of its nondemocratic Middle Eastern neighbors, and would quickly lose the support of the United States and other Western allies and admirers. Therefore, even from the perspective of a strictly ultra-Orthodox Jew who might believe that all of the answers are mandated by a Halakhah that precludes democratic government, surely when life is at stake, even you would concede that certain laws can be suspended. This is in the finest of halakhic traditions, no?

So even if I thought that Judaism was incompatible with democracy—which I don't—and even if I thought that religious law would be superior to secular law for the Jewish state and its citizens, a fifth of whom are not Jewish—which I don't—there are still plenty of reasons to prefer democracy over theocracy for Israel.

Those who would advocate replacing Israeli democracy with something else advocate disaster for the Jewish people. They have a premodern worldview. They must be opposed. No theocracy can be part of the modern Western world. A theocratic Jewish state would be quickly abandoned by the enlightened world and would collapse under its own intolerance and narrow-mindedness in short order.

At the same time, I firmly believe that Israel is, and should remain, a Jewish state. This is not incompatible with democracy. Many democracies define themselves in religious terms. The American model of separation of church and state is not the only democratic model. For example, the Queen of England is the head of the established church of that nation.

At all times, Israel should offer the full panoply of democratic rights to all of its citizens, Jews and non-Jews. In that assumption, Israel's non-Jewish citizens will live as a minority with all of the rights and obligations of every other citizen. "The State of Israel will promote the development of the country for the benefit of all its inhabitants; . . . will uphold the full social and political equality of all its citizens, without distinction of race, creed or sex; will guarantee full freedom of conscience, worship, education and culture. . . . We . . . call upon the Arab inhabitants of the State of Israel to . . . play their part in the develop-

ment of the State, with full and equal citizenship and due representa-
tion in its bodies and institutions." (Declaration of Independence)

If Israel is a Jewish state, it should have an interest in promoting
Jewish values. I have two brief comments: First, the state has an interest
in promoting those values that are consistent with its founding principles. Ultra-Orthodox politicians have exploited democracy for their
own narrow purposes and have managed to extract state funds to support institutions that are often antidemocratic and intolerant.

It is an inversion of logic that so much money from mostly non-
Orthodox taxpayers funds ultra-Orthodox institutions that do not believe in the concept of a Jewish state, do not believe in upholding equality
without distinction of race, creed, or sex, do not believe in the guarantee
of full freedom of conscience, worship, education, and culture—and, in
short, are opponents of democracy and not loyal to the state's founding
democratic or Zionist principles. The state is funding those very institutions that use this support to educate the next generation of citizens in
antidemocratic and intolerant ways. By funding these institutions, the
state is undermining its own prosperity, stability, and security.

Second, the state, in promoting Jewish religious values, must do so in
a manner consistent with democracy—that is, equally and in a non-
discriminatory manner. The state must treat all of its citizens equally.
Repeatedly, Orthodox-controlled government agencies violate democratic norms and standards. Time and again, the Israeli Supreme Court
strikes down discriminatory practices.

I distinguish between Israel being a Jewish state and one that would
be ruled as a theocracy by Jewish law. Israel's character should be Jewish. Its national holidays should be determined by the Jewish calendar.
Its symbols should be Jewish. Its language should be Hebrew, the language of the Jewish people. Bible, Talmud, Jewish thought, and Jewish
history should be taught in schools. The overwhelming majority of
Israelis agree with this proposition.

But Israel's system of government should be democratic, not theocratic.

This is the best way to accomplish what Orthodox Jews say they
want—to encourage more Jews to take Judaism seriously. It is the very
intrusion of an aggressive, coercive Orthodoxy in the national life of

Israel that repels so many Israelis who might otherwise be attracted to Judaism. Religious feeling cannot be imposed against the will of the majority. Permanent and enduring religious identity cannot be coerced. Religion is at its best in the modern world not when it is imposed by force of law against the will of the majority, but when it persuades the majority by force of arguments. Judaism is most effective when it is respected by the people, not rejected as primitive or resented as coercive. Most Israeli Jews are not, as you implied, enemies of religion. Most of them, in their own ways, are passionate about their Jewish identity. Most of them, however, are lovers of liberty and freedom, and look to synthesize these values with religion in determining the character of a modern Jewish state. This actually reflects a profound understanding of Jewish values, no? Since when is liberty contrary to Jewish values? ("And you shall proclaim liberty throughout the land for all its inhabitants," Leviticus 25:10)

Religious coercion causes great and unnecessary friction between observant and nonobservant citizens of Israel. The live-and-let-live spirit of democratic life that often facilitates resolution of social conflicts is largely absent from the all-or-nothing, scorched-earth approach of many ultra-Orthodox Jews, who openly proclaim that they do not know about, care about, or favor democracy. There is only God's law—as interpreted by them—and, as they constantly remind us, divine law takes precedence over human law.

Somehow, Yosef, I find it difficult to believe that God is so narrow-minded. Why does God always have to be portrayed as a fundamentalist? Maybe God also appreciates non-Orthodox Jews. Do you think that might be possible?

THE LAW OF RETURN

While the Law of Return is somewhat complicated, it is not as flawed as you imply. You write: "Why don't you consider [the Law of Return] a racist law? . . . Yasser Arafat wonders why Israel objects to the return of a million Arabs yet opens its doors to a million Russian gentiles. A very good question, don't you think?"

Not really. I think it is a question that reveals a lack of sensitivity to, and understanding of, the notion of a Jewish democratic state and the needs of the Jewish people. Then again, it is not surprising that Yasser Arafat misunderstands both the Jewish experience and democracy. All democracies have immigration laws that give preference to certain categories of people. For years, America gave preference to Jewish immigration from the Soviet Union. Was this racist? The assumption was that if you were Jewish you were, by definition, subject to political persecution and therefore qualified for political asylum.

If America gave preference to the immigration of Jews, is it unreasonable to suggest that the Jewish state itself should also give Jews preference? Remember, we are talking about expedited procedures. Any person who seeks to become a citizen of Israel can do so if he fulfills the criteria of naturalization. These criteria are similar to those of many countries.

The rationale for the Law of Return, which guarantees citizenship to all Jews, is inspiring and historically just. In effect, the newly born Jewish state said to the remnant of our people who were locked out of almost every country during World War II, and to the masses who were locked into Arab countries, there is one place in the world that will always be home to you. We will never lock you out. If for no other reason, consider Israel a permanent place of refuge for you if you ever need it. This is the essence of self-determination. It is precisely what many Jews sought when they concluded that anti-Semitism could not be eradicated: the establishment of a Jewish national home where we would have the ability to determine our own destiny. No longer would Jews be abandoned to the bigots and anti-Semites of the world. If they wanted to contribute to the upbuilding of the Jewish state, or they simply wanted to be left alone and live in peace and dignity, they had an open invitation for the first time in two thousand years to return to Zion.

Any Jew and every Jew could come. No one would ask what your views were on any particular issue, or even whether you actually supported the concept of a Jewish state. Even non-Zionists, even ultra-Orthodox Jews who would become ideological opponents of the very state that offered them citizenship, could, if they wanted, come and live in Israel.

Should Israel have told all of those hundreds of thousands of survivors and displaced Jews of Europe whom nobody else wanted after

World War II, "If you seek refuge you will have to find another country"? Should Israel have told all of those hundreds of thousands of impoverished and despised Jews it rescued from Muslim countries in the late 1940s and early 1950s, "We do not want you"? Should Israel have told the tens of thousands of starving and destitute Ethiopian Jews it rescued in the late twentieth century, "Stay on the planes until we make up our minds"? Should Israel have told the million Soviet Jews who immigrated to Israel in the 1990s and who were oppressed by the Soviets for being Jewish and "Zionist sympathizers" "Sorry, we weren't really serious. Stay in the lands of the Soviets"?

I do not know where you got the number of a million Russian gentiles. Are you using it as a figure of speech—i.e., a lot of non-Jews—or do you literally mean a million gentiles? Of the roughly million new immigrants from Russia since the beginning of the 1990s, the best estimate is that some 25 to 30 percent of them are not Jewish according to Halakhah. Most of these people have at least one Jewish parent, consider themselves Jewish, identify themselves as Jews, and were often persecuted by the Soviets for being Jewish. The remaining 70 percent of immigrants are Jewish according to the strictest Orthodox standards.

The criterion of Jewishness for the purposes of the Law of Return is what Hitler used in the Nuremberg Laws—in reverse. Any person who would have been sent to the gas chambers by Hitler—a person with a Jewish grandparent—has an open invitation to breathe the free air of the Jewish state. This is the ultimate victory over Hitler.

Whether Yasser Arafat understands all this is not the central question. Since when do we look to him for moral guidance or for sensitivity to the Jewish condition?

Ammi

June 2, 2001

Dear Ammi,

I am addressing the following issue in a separate posting, because I don't want to obfuscate the broad issues relating to the Jewish state with petty arguments.

I take issue with your statement that "it is an inversion of logic that so much money from mostly non-Orthodox taxpayers funds ultra-Orthodox institutions." You, who are so sensitive to "canards" about the Reform, should be extra careful about issuing canards of your own.

The Orthodox in Israel, counting both *dati* and *charedi*, form a substantial percentage of the Jewish population. But let us talk statistics regarding the *charedi*, or ultra-Orthodox, as you call them. It is difficult to determine the exact figures, but since 18 percent of the members of the Knesset are *charedi*, we can conservatively assume that at least 10 to 15 percent of the population is essentially *charedi*. The question is, Are these people receiving a disproportionate share of government funding?

You contend, in all innocence I hope, that the ultra-Orthodox are getting much more than their fair share. It is not the first time you have repeated this odious canard of the Israeli antireligious. However, I find it hard to believe that the majority would allow such a thing to happen, that they would take no corrective action other than insistent whining. So I contacted a friend in Israel who put me in touch with an organization called Manof. What follows is based on information I received from them.

The total budget of the Israeli government in 1999 was approximately 215 billion Israeli shekels. I will not belabor you with the long list of government sources of income, but income tax brought in only 58 billion shekels, about 25 percent of the total. At most, you can say that the non-*charedi* Israelis contribute proportionately more to this 25 percent than do the *charedim*, some of whom study in *yeshivot* for years before entering the workforce. In all other sources of government income, such as sales and value-added taxes, import duties and rental income from government properties, there is no difference. The shortfall is, therefore, the share of the 25 percent of government revenue that comes from income taxes that the underemployed portion of the *charedi* sector would pay were they fully employed. So let us say they should be paying 2.5 percent to 3.5 percent, and let us say they are only paying 1.3 percent to 1.8 percent. We're not talking about big numbers.

Now let us consider what the government spends on the *charedi* sector. The Bituach Leumi stipend per child cannot be considered, because it relates to the child rather than the parents; no one, I hope, is against the birth of *charedi* children. The issue then is education. Does the *charedi* sector get too large a share of the education pie?

In total, the government spends about 16 billion shekels on non-*charedi* schools and 750 million shekels on *charedi* schools. This means that *charedi* schools receive only 4.5 percent of the education pie although they serve more than 10 percent of the population. In addition, none of the money the government spends on television programs for the schools is targeted for the *charedi* sector. The antidrug and anticrime budgets for the school system are also irrelevant to the *charedi* schools. (There are 140,000 *charedim* in Bnei Brak, and the only police are traffic cops!)

You know, it actually looks like the *charedi* sector is getting less than its fair share rather than more, but that's neither here nor there. The main thing is that you should stop repeating those anti-*charedi* canards so glibly. They are simply not true.

And they are certainly not constructive.

All the best,

Yosef

June 2, 2001

Dear Ammi,

This morning my son and daughter-in-law were blessed with the birth of a baby boy in Jerusalem, and it looks like I'll be headed there very shortly. It is frightening to have the kids so far from home in such a volatile situation, but I am also frightened for my uncles and aunts, my nephews and nieces, my numerous cousins and all my Jewish brothers and sisters who live in Israel and must endure constant danger and anxiety.

Undeclared war is raging in Israel even as we exchange our views and comments about the future of the Jewish state. Just about every day, bombs and bullets kill men, women, and children on both sides of the conflict. What is it all about? Why are we there? Why are we fighting? More poignantly, why are we dying? What are our ultimate goals and prospects in the Holy Land and how motivated are we to achieve them?

These difficult, complex questions gnaw at the consciousness of those living through the experience in Israel and those of us sitting on the sidelines and biting our knuckles in anxious frustration. What are the Jewish people doing on top of a powder keg in the broiling Middle Eastern sun? It is somewhat absurd to say we are there for safety. Israel is a not very safe place in a not very stable region, nor is it likely to become significantly safer in the foreseeable future. Even if we could make peace and sign treaties with all our Arab neighbors, a few radical Islamic upheavals here and there would render those treaties worthless scraps of paper.

You began your last posting with warm and beautiful sentiments of a general nature regarding the Land of Israel. I can't imagine that anyone would disagree with most of what you wrote. Nonetheless, I would like to get beyond your lofty thoughts to the specific areas of our disagreement.

It appears that you have misread the provocative questions I posed to you as statements of position. There is no point in my correcting your mistakes. I will simply state my position in no uncertain terms, and our differences will become clear.

It is impossible to love the Torah without loving the Land of Israel at the same time, and I love them both very deeply. I have been to Israel many times, and I still feel a breathtaking thrill of anticipation each time the plane begins to descend. I am always moved by the sheer holiness of this place, by its closeness to the Divine Presence, by its indelible association with the Torah and the Jewish experience. I get a spiritual high the moment I step off the plane, and it stays with me long after I leave.

You are, of course, more likely to find me at the Western Wall than sipping aperitifs on a Tel Aviv sidewalk, but I have traveled the length and breadth of the land and cherish every bit of it. I love all the people, with or without *kippot;* it is exhilarating to me that just about everyone I meet in this country is my brother or sister, that our common ancestors lived here for thousands of years, that the pebbles alongside the roads have witnessed the ebb and flow of our sacred history, the migrations of the patriarchs, the conquest of the land, the festive pilgrimages, the invasions of imperial armies, the streams of weeping exiles, the exultant returns. Wherever I go, I hear the echoes of the past, my past.

But Israel is more than a land with a past. It also has a present and a future. It has become a modern society, bustling with activity, productivity, creativity, and sheer exuberant vitality, rollicking, raucous, rambunctious, an utter delight. But there are also deep divisions and profound problems, all of which find expression in and around the current Palestinian *intifada;* it is like a serious illness that prompts a full examination.

There is a struggle going on in Israel today that will decide whether the Jewish state survives or collapses. I do not mean the struggle between Jew and Arab. I believe the Jewish state can survive that struggle. But I am not sure it can survive the internal struggle between secularism and religion.

History has shown us that, over the long term, sheer force cannot prevail over idealism. "Might makes right" may win you some battles, but it will not give you permanent victory. Look at what is happening in Northern Ireland; hundreds of years of occupation have not eradicated Irish nationalism. And how about all the captive peoples of the Soviet Union? It was inevitable that they would eventually break loose.

In Israel, we have a standoff between the Arabs and the Jews. The Arabs lay claim to the land because they were the majority prior to the twentieth century, and they lay claim to Jerusalem as one of the holiest sites of Islam. I know that some Jewish propagandists contend that Jerusalem is not important to the Muslims, but it is not for us to interpret other people's religions for them. So the Arabs come to the table with a strong ideological and nationalistic position. They reject the Zionists, whom they regard as European colonists, pawns of Western civilization. They reject the imposition of a Jewish state on the land by the imperialist powers. They reject the right of a people to reclaim a land from which they have been virtually absent for two thousand years.

What is our position? If we claim the right to be here because the United Nations gave it to us and because we have guns and tanks and jet fighters, not to mention nuclear weapons, we are doomed to failure. The Arabs will never accept us on the basis of our superior firepower. They will fight and resist for decades, even centuries, until they are ultimately victorious. But if we insist that God consecrated this land and gave it to us, that this divine gift is our inheritance everlasting, that our periodic exiles and returns are between God and us and no business of anyone else, then we have a position that the Arabs must respect. They will not view us as armed bandits but as a people with a claim based on the deepest, most sacred convictions. They may not agree with our ideology, but they will respect it. And perhaps we will find a way to compromise and reach a lasting peace.

The early Zionist leaders understood this. Most of the Zionists rejected the Jewish religion and dreamed of a state in which Jewish peoplehood would be defined by the secular norms of land, language, and culture rather than adherence to the Torah and the ancient covenant. Nonetheless, the thoroughly irreligious David Ben-Gurion quoted constantly from the Prophets. In 1899, Theodor Herzl reached out to the rabbinic leadership of Eastern Europe and praised them because "they have not yet forgotten the national traditions and have a strong religious sentiment" (quoted by Yoram Hazony in *The Jewish State: The Struggle for Israel's Soul*). Yet a few short years earlier, the same Herzl wrote that "one must baptize Jewish boys before they must account for themselves, before they are able to act against it and before conversion can be construed as weakness on their part; they must disappear into the crowd" (quoted by Paul Johnson in *A History of the Jews*). Obviously, this man cared nothing for the Jewish religion, and yet he understood that Zionism would have no legitimacy without at least a nominal connection to Judaism.

Therefore, it seems to me that the impetus for a "secular revolution" in Israel threatens to undermine the claims to legitimacy of the Jewish state. When Shulamit Aloni, former education minister, denounces school trips to Auschwitz as too "nationalistic" because "what's important is that they come back better human beings, not better Jews," when she demands that all references to God be eliminated from military memorial services, then what is the justification for a Jewish state? When the history books in the government elementary schools begin with the Greeks and do not mention the Jewish people until Alexander invades the Middle East, what is the justification for a Jewish state? (For Heaven's sake, even French textbooks begin with "Our ancestors the Gauls . . .") When the chief justice of the Israeli Supreme Court insists that "the values of the state of Israel as a Jewish state are those universal values common to members of democratic society" (Hazony, *The Jewish State*), what is the justification for a Jewish state? If this is what we profess to believe, then we are indeed intruders who wrested the land with no justification but force. If we wanted a secular, dejudaized, democratic state, we didn't have to locate it in Israel. Is there any chance that the Arabs will ever come to terms with such a state? I think not.

An article that appeared in the Israeli newspapers about two years ago, well before the current troubles, told about a notorious Palestinian terrorist named Salah Tamari who had lost heart in the struggle. While languishing in an Israeli prison, he came to the realization that the Jewish state would never be dislodged and that the Palestinians should therefore cut the best deal they could get and be done with it. He shared his views with those of his fellow inmates who were also of the Palestinian terrorist persuasion, about thirty men in all.

On the first night of Passover, he saw one of the guards eating a pita bread sandwich.

"Are you Jewish?" he asked the guard.

"Yes, I am," the guard replied.

"Then why are you eating that pita?" asked Salah. "Don't you know that Jews are forbidden to eat bread on Passover?"

The guard was taken aback for a moment by the Arab's question. "I am not obligated to commemorate," he finally said, "events that happened to my people over three thousand years ago. They do not relate to me."

Salah was stunned. He stayed up all night to digest what he had just heard. The next morning, he summoned his comrades and told them what had happened. "If these people feel no connection to their past," he said, "if they are willing to disregard their national traditions, then their roots are no longer in this land. We can be victorious over them. Disregard what I have told you before. We must never make peace with them. We must fight and fight until we achieve complete victory. They cannot stop us."

I shuddered when I read this article, because I knew that he spoke the truth. If we sever our connection to the past, if we no longer believe that God gave us this land, we will never be able to hold on to it. The Arabs will never relent. The more we move in the secular direction, the more we concede the moral high ground to the Arabs.

Moreover, without these convictions our own side will crumble of itself. Anyone who thinks we can turn Israel into California is sadly mistaken. The ceaseless pressure from the Arabs will erode the Israeli populace's will to resist. Most modern Israeli literature already takes a dim view of the Jewish state. Why live there? Why die for it? It is a theme that resonates with all too many Israelis who are only interested in enjoying a comfortable bourgeois life. What would be the point of fighting and struggling to create California in Israel when you can just as easily move to the real California? And hundreds of thousands of Israelis have indeed already emigrated for greener pastures; more will undoubtedly follow. Of course, many claim they are ready to jump onto a plane and return at the first hint of hostilities, but we all know they aren't coming back. In a few generations, most of them will be intermarried, and then they'll be gone for good.

I truly believe that the only hope for the Jewish state is the continuation and reinforcement of its strong identification with the Torah. There is a tremendous outreach movement under way in Israel. Thousands of Orthodox men and women are teaching Torah to secular Jews with extraordinary results. According to my sources in Israel, the *ba'alei teshuvah* number in the many, many thousands. Furthermore, many secular Israelis who are not yet prepared to commit to a Torah life are at least enrolling their children in Torah schools, if simply to keep them out of the government schools, which rank first in the world in school violence according to a recent article in *Ha'aretz* (March 23, 2001, "Israel Tops the Hit Parade"). The number of secular Israeli parents sending their children to *dati* and *charedi* elementary schools is growing by leaps and bounds.

It is a desperate struggle for the soul of the Jewish people, and the tide seems to be turning in the direction of the Torah. But the secularists are not giving up without a fight. They are doing everything in their power to undercut the role of Judaism in public life, including the manipulation of the demographic makeup of Israel. As I mentioned earlier, former Minister of Absorption Yuli Tamir has stated that Israel has brought in many Russian gentiles in order to secularize the state. It is definitely having an effect. Israel is swamped by people with little or no Jewish identity.

I know you are rather liberal when it comes to Jewish identity, but there is a limit. If Hitler sent someone with one Jewish great-grandparent to the gas chambers, does that make that person a Jew? Since when does Hitler determine who is Jewish and who is not? As far as I'm concerned, if that great-grandparent had been the person's mother's mother's mother, he would be Jewish, otherwise not. But even you, who recognize both matrilineal and patrilineal descent, must draw the line somewhere. Otherwise, anyone with the smallest drop of Jewish blood would be Jewish, which would include most of the people in Europe and the Middle East as well.

Most of these Russians with one remote Jewish ancestor are not Jewish, nor do they consider themselves Jewish. A friend who hosts a weekly radio program in Israel told me that now, for the first time, Israeli kids are being called "dirty Jew" in their own schoolyards by Russian immigrant children. Hardly a sign of a strong Jewish identity.

If the Orthodox prevail, the Israeli people will regain the moral high ground and the deep attachment to the land that will arouse them to defend it tenaciously and with idealistic conviction. If the secularists prevail, the future of Israel will depend on the quixotic hope that the Arabs will suddenly be inspired to make peace and forgo their ambitions of victory. The religious struggle, it appears to me, is also the struggle for the political survival of the Jewish state and the physical survival of its people.

So where do you fit into this picture, Ammi? I know you insist that you too are proposing a religious underpinning to the Jewish state, but with a Reform flavor. But I think it is unconvincing. Language, flag, culture, calendar observances, these are all good things, but they are too superficial to carry real weight in these circumstances. We need a strong conviction that we are here by divine right, that God spoke explicitly to the patriarchs and gave them and their offspring this land for all time.

You write, "The cornerstone of the covenant between God and the Jewish people is the Land of Israel. . . . On that day the Lord made a covenant with Abraham saying, 'To your offspring I give this land. . . .' (Genesis 15)."

Strong words. The land belongs to us, because God specifically told Abraham that He was giving him the land. Excellent.

And yet you write in an earlier posting, in response to my asking if you believed Abraham existed, "I concede that I would be fascinated if archaeological evidence were to emerge 'proving' the existence of Abraham. However, theologically, I am less concerned about whether Abraham really existed. That the Torah asserts the uniqueness of the Jewish people, and that through the Jews humanity will be blessed, is for me the fundamental point of the passage about Abraham's selection."

So you are not convinced that Abraham ever existed, and if he didn't exist, God could not have spoken to him and gifted the Land of Israel to him and his progeny. So this covenant, this divine gift that gives our people a right to the land is really a myth, a cherished legend, an intuition perhaps.

You cannot bring yourself to say in so many words that God gave us the land. Instead, you wrote in that same posting: "I am less concerned about whether the conquest of the Land of Israel occurred as described in the Book of Joshua than that for the Jews Eretz Yisrael is the Promised Land, that we have claimed this land for as long as there were Jews, that we have cultivated and loved this land, that we have treated it as a divine gift and as the centerpiece of the covenant with God—this to me is the essential point."

Pretty words, but what do they mean? We "claimed this land," we "treated it as a divine gift," but you cannot bring yourself to come right out and say that God said so, because you don't really believe He did. You sense it, you feel the breeze on your face as you look upon the land from the mountaintop and you sense . . . something, an impression, an intuition that God wants us to have the land.

Ammi, I do not doubt you. I believe you really do feel this intuition. I believe you really do believe that God wants us to have the land. But I'm afraid your intuition is too insubstantial a foundation for a Jewish state upon which millions of Jewish lives depend. Your intuition will not convince the Arabs that they must compromise, nor will your intuition inspire the Jews to risk their lives and the lives of their families to defend the Jewish state. If Reform cannot inspire its adherents with enough Jewish dedication to eschew intermarriage, will your intuition inspire them to shed their blood for Jewish ideals?

I think your interposition into the religious struggle in Israel will only roil and muddy the waters. It does not offer real solutions.

Israel needs the opposite of a secular revolution. The state needs to advocate Orthodox ideology, as Herzl did, as Ben-Gurion did, even though they were far from Orthodox. The state needs to declare more loudly than ever the truth of the Torah as its most crucial organizing principle. As for observance, let everyone progress at his or her own pace; let them be "nonpracticing Orthodox" for a while if that is all they can do, but let them avow the truth of the Torah and the divine gift of the land. Do I expect this to happen? Not really. But one never knows. I think it is more likely to happen than your yearning "that [the Arabs will] extend the hand of friendship and peace."

What I propose does not conflict with democracy, which I ardently endorse. (I don't know where you got the idea that Orthodoxy is antithetical to democracy.) I emphatically do not believe that people should be coerced to be observant in their private lives, but I believe that the Torah should play a prominent role in public life. The national airline should not fly on Shabbat. The army should serve only kosher food. Government offices should close on Jewish holidays. Jewish identity should be determined by immutable Torah law, not by political expediency. And the like. As for the business of government, Parliament should be elected by a democratic process, and it should govern by democratic principles. I do not think we disagree greatly here, except on the issue of Jewish identity, which we have discussed a number of times. If there is personal religious coercion in Israel today, I do not favor it, nor do I feel compelled to defend it.

I also beg to differ with your statement that "ultra-Orthodox institutions do not believe in the concept of a Jewish state." That is an inaccurate generalization.

Most of us are very much in favor of a Jewish state but not particularly enamored of the present one, which is ideologically antagonistic to Judaism but tolerates it for political convenience. Most of us are not excited by a state conceived by Herzl, who was prepared to lead the Jewish people to the baptismal font, and founded by irreligious people like Ben-Gurion. This state is certainly not the fulfillment of the prophecy of Isaiah; there are more plowshares being beaten into swords in Israel than the other way around. The secular Zionists set out to create a modern Western state on the eastern shores of the Mediterranean, and we are paying the price for it now, as I have explained at length.

What would I have preferred in the interim before the fulfillment of the prophecies of Isaiah? Believe it or not, I find myself inclined to agree with some of your forebears in the Reform movement in the early twentieth century. As you know, the Reform movement in the late nineteenth century rejected the idea of Jewish peoplehood and, consequently, the idea of a return to Zion. After they decided again that we are indeed a people, they still persisted in their rejection of Zionism. In the Columbus Platform of 1937, they finally accepted the idea of a Jewish homeland but not a Jewish state. They didn't officially come around to the idea of a Jewish state until 1976, when it was already falling apart.

"I believe in the rebuilding of the ancient homeland from the philanthropic and cultural points of view," Morris Lazaron, a leading Reform rabbi, wrote in 1937. "But nationalism . . . is a *hukat hagoyim* [i.e., an illicit custom of the gentiles]. Behind the mask of Jewish sentiment, one can see the specter of the foul thing which moves Germany and Italy. . . . This is not for the Jews." (quoted by Hazony).

I kind of agree with that idea. Perhaps it would have been better to establish a Jewish homeland with the Right of Return in a binational state with full democratic rights for all its citizens, even if that would have left us in the minority. I am uncomfortable with the idea of a Jewish state that is not founded on Torah principles and Torah law. You unwittingly touched on this yourself when you wrote: "It is one thing to sit in the various diasporas of the world and articulate standards of behavior for individuals and nations. It is quite another thing to test the relevance of such standards through the collective expression of Jewish sovereignty. We have learned a thing or two about the difficulties of implementing Jewish values in a complicated world. When you have no sovereignty you can afford a certain luxury and purity of thought. We have discovered that exercising sovereignty in a manner compatible with Jewish values is much more difficult." I agree with you, but I am not as ready as you are to forgo that "purity of thought."

Would a Jewish homeland in a binational state have worked out any better than what we have now? Could we have avoided five wars, incessant fighting and terrorism, occupation of territories and the radicalization of the Palestinian people if we had gone the other route? Would a Jewish homeland alone have served as a safe haven for Holocaust survivors? I suspect that it might have worked out fairly well, but I really cannot say so with any degree of certainty or conviction. No one can possibly know. Today the issues are pragmatic. Are we safer because of the state? Perhaps; perhaps not. One thing is certain. We cannot undo the historical events of the past century. The best we have is the present state. It cannot be transformed safely in the foreseeable future.

So that is the bottom line of our differences. You idolize the state. I accept it. You are full of starry-eyed hope. I, unfortunately, am not.

Warmest regards,

Yosef

June 14, 2001

Dear Yosef:

There you go again. . . .

You are too ready to jump to preconceived conclusions and do not spend enough time really trying to comprehend what I write.

Let me respond briefly to a number of points you raise.

TAX MONEY AND DEMOCRACY

You quote my statement that "it is an inversion of logic that so much money from mostly non-Orthodox taxpayers funds ultra-Orthodox institutions." You then write: "You who are so sensitive to 'canards' about the Reform, should be extra careful about issuing canards of your own."

Yosef—reread what I wrote and your answer. I expressed a perfectly valid opinion—for the Zionist state to supply so much money to non- or anti-Zionist institutions is an inversion of logic. This is not a "canard." At most, it is an opinion with which you do not agree. There is nothing untrue here. Even in your (tortured and inaccurate) response to me, you do not challenge the notion that ultra-Orthodox institutions receive a lot of money. Your position is that they do receive a lot of money but that it is proportional. We agree on the underlying fact, that ultra-Orthodox institutions receive considerable state support. So where is the "canard" here?

My point was not to get into a tax argument with you. Rather, it was to assert, as I wrote: "The state is funding those very institutions that use this support to educate the next generation of citizens in antidemocratic and intolerant ways. By funding these institutions the state is undermining its own prosperity and security."

YOU DID NOT ADDRESS THIS POINT

You write that you "ardently endorse" democracy. Well, why then do you think it is wise to fund institutions that openly proclaim that they are antidemocratic? This is what I would have wanted to read from you—not some tax argument. You write, "The state needs to advocate Orthodox ideology," at the same time as you write that you ardently support democracy and that Orthodoxy does not conflict with democracy. You even write, "I don't know where you got the idea that Orthodoxy is antithetical to democracy."(!)

Believe me, I did not come up with that idea on my own. I got that idea of Orthodoxy—or rather ultra-Orthodoxy—from ultra-Orthodox spokesmen themselves. "What binds us is God's law, not man's law" is a favorite refrain of theirs.

So, Yosef, why should the state be promoting ultra-Orthodox ideology if, by the definition of many of its spokesmen and the practice of many of its institutions, ultra-Orthodoxy conflicts with democracy?

Is it your position that you reject those interpretations of Halakhah that assert that Halakhah and democracy are incompatible? If so, say it. Coming from you, a Halakhist, that would be an important contribution. Do you reject such assertions of Judaism in favor of my own understanding that Judaism and democracy are compatible? How would you answer those who assert that "immutable Torah law" (your words) requires that the Jewish state be a theocracy? You write, "I am uncomfortable with the idea of a Jewish state that is not founded on Torah principles and Torah law." Is it then fair to impute that since you also believe in democracy and "do not favor" coercion that you are in agreement with me as to my understanding of the compatibility of Judaism and democracy? Would you then also agree that the state should not be funding institutions that are ultra-Orthodox, anti-Zionist, and oppose democracy?

You use the phrase "odious canard of the Israeli anti-religious." Be careful, Yosef. Give people the benefit of the doubt. There are some antireligious Israelis but not all that many. Poll after poll, survey after survey, demonstrates that large majorities of Israelis believe in God. The data suggest that most Israelis have respect for Jewish tradition—despite close exposure to a politicized religious establishment that drives many of them crazy. Most Israelis conduct Seders on Passover, light Chanukah menorahs and Shabbat candles. They are hardly antireligious.

However, while most Israelis are not antireligious, they are very much against religious coercion. I count myself among their ranks. There is a huge difference. Even many Orthodox Jews in Israel agree. Many acknowledge that the worst thing for Orthodoxy and Judaism has been the behavior of the religious establishment and its association with the powers of the state. Do you agree?

Do not be so quick to jump on the propaganda bandwagon describing political opponents as "antireligious." You mention that you do not normally sip aperitifs in Tel Aviv cafés—but perhaps you might be referring to some such people when you use the term "antireligious." Since I do, from time to time, sit in cafés, I can tell you that most of those people you think are antireligious are not so at all. They might not be Orthodox. They might not even be observant. But most of them are certainly not antireligious. I have repeatedly tried to emphasize in this book that if you are not Orthodox it does not follow that you are not religious. Moreover, if you are secular, it does not follow that you are antireligious. Again and again you use and misuse these characterizations.

Yosef, when you go to Israel, spend some time talking to the people. Seek out those who do not dress or think like you. You might learn a thing or two that might surprise you. You might come away with a whole new understanding. I can recommend a number of Tel Aviv cafés where you can meet a good cross-section of people you might have previously assumed are antireligious. Talk with them. Listen to them and try to understand them. They will be eager to talk with you—precisely because most of them are not antireligious. Even Orthodox Jews can take a few moments out of their day, at least once in a while, to relax in the Tel Aviv sun and get to know—really know—your Israeli brethren.

In my view, you mischaracterize the struggle raging in Israel. I do not think it is one of "secularism and religion," as you write. As indicated above, most Israeli Jews are not secularists in the manner commonly understood in the West, and most of them, even if they are not observant of Jewish tradition, certainly do not seek to destroy it.

I believe that a more accurate definition of the struggle is "What is the proper role of religion and state in the Jewish state?" On one side stands the majority that feels that Israeli society should be based upon the values of democracy, tolerance, and pluralism, melding Jewish tradition with the requirements of democracy. On the other side stand the antipluralists who openly proclaim that Israel should be a theocracy governed by their understanding of Jewish law. I agree with you that the outcome of this struggle will determine the character of the Jewish state for many years to come.

By the way, Yosef, from everything I can gather from your writing, you are actually on my side of this debate. You write that you believe in democracy and reject religious coercion. That's good enough for me. Whether El Al should fly on Shabbat and which government offices should be closed, as you write, are issues that we could resolve quickly, because apparently we share the same assumptions on the governance of society.

ARE YOU A ZIONIST?

Yosef, you did not address this question. You write, "We are very much in favor of a Jewish state, but we are not particularly enamored of the present one."

Come on, you can do better than that. Are you in favor of this Jewish state, now? Many fervently Orthodox Jews openly proclaim that they are anti-Zionists because their understanding of Judaism forbids the creation of a state until the arrival of the messiah. Is that your position? Are you in favor of this Jewish state? It is the only one we have. It is the only one we will have. So will you work to develop and strengthen this state, so that at the end of your labors you will be "enamored" with it? When you write that "the army should serve only kosher food"—a position with which I agree—are you implying that *charedi* Jews too should serve in the army alongside their modern Orthodox and non-Orthodox brethren?

You write that the state is "ideologically antagonistic to Judaism." (I suspect that what you really meant is "ideologically antagonistic to ultra-Orthodox Judaism," which is also not accurate.) In its founding document Israel openly proclaimed its connection to the Jewish heritage. The Declaration of Independence states proudly that Israel is to be a Jewish state. Most of its Jewish citizens are not antagonistic at all to this notion. Quite the contrary, they are prepared to fight to defend it.

You write, "The secular Zionists set out to create a modern Western state . . . and we are paying the price for it now." First, are you suggesting that you are against the creation of a modern Western state? Would you be more in favor of a state that is premodern and non-Western—say, something like Iran, Saudi Arabia, or Afghanistan?

Second, let me remind you that there were many Orthodox Jews who were and are today Zionists. Some of the greatest Zionist leaders were Orthodox. Others, like Rabbis Abba Hillel Silver and Stephen Wise, were also not secular, but deeply religious people. Even pioneers like Ben-Gurion, as you rightly point out, were knowledgeable about Judaism and attached to Jewish tradition. They loved the land and found profound meaning in the rehabilitation of Jewish life on its soil.

Third, as to the price that we are paying, Yosef, again, I ask you to be more penetrating. The question is not whether life in the Middle East is difficult. The question is whether, in your view, it would have been preferable had Israel not been created at all. Do you give credence to my description that Israel saved and continues to save Jews—physically, spiritually, and emotionally? If so, does it not fulfill an important—vital—function? If not, do you think it would have been preferable for, say, the millions of descendants of Jews from Arab countries currently living in Israel to have stayed in those countries? Would it have been preferable for the roughly 600,000 Jews living in Israel in 1948 to have been trapped in Europe during the War? Are the million Jews from the former Soviet Union better off now or under the Communists? Are they and their descendants better off in Israel or in Kiev, Moscow, or Minsk?

You write that I "idolize the state." Again, try not to exaggerate, mischaracterize, or overstate. Judaism is against idolatry. Nowhere did I write that I idolize Israel. In fact, I was careful to point out that to worship a state is fascism, not Judaism. I do, however, admire this plucky, intense, courageous, vital, vibrant, strong, and self-confident Jewish state. Israel testifies to the indomitable will of the Jewish people to live, prosper, and contribute to society. I do not believe myself to be "starry-eyed," as you write. I am fully aware of Israel's many flaws and challenges. I am active in the debate on how to correct our mistakes and rectify our flaws. I am also aware of, and full of respect for, Israel's many wonderful qualities.

One of the most fascinating passages of our entire exchange was your statement that you find yourself "inclined to agree with some of [the] forebears in the Reform movement in the early twentieth century." So, maybe Reform has something to teach you after all.

You should always keep this openness to Reform thinking. It is good for you and for our people. However, unfortunately, on the question of Zionism you have come to this understanding too late. We abandoned it long ago.

Do you not find something delightfully pleasurable in the notion that you, a *charedi* rabbi, are advocating positions that nineteenth- and twentieth-century Reform rabbis advocated, while I, a twenty-first-century Reform rabbi, am only too happy to leave such positions on the ash heap of history? For this delicious irony alone, our efforts have all been worthwhile!

RUSSIAN IMMIGRANTS

Your response to me contained a certain inconsistency. You write "as far as I'm concerned, if that great-grandparent had been his mother's mother's mother, he would be Jewish, otherwise not." You then state "most of these Russians with one remote Jewish ancestor are not Jewish."

Are you saying that most of these Russian immigrants have mothers who are not Jewish? After all, if their mothers were Jewish, you would consider them Jews, no? In fact, Yosef, you would consider them Jews even if they themselves did not consider themselves Jews, right—as long as the maternal line was Jewish?

How do you know the lineage of "most of these Russians"? Have you investigated the maternal and paternal line of most of the Russian immigrants to determine who, in your opinion, is Jewish (according to your definition, not mine)? And, if, say, you were able to determine who had a maternally Jewish line, would you agree that they are entitled to immigration rights?

I agree with you that the Jewish identity of many Russian immigrants might be different from immigrants coming from the West. But the Russian immigration is blessed, talented, and contributes so much to Israeli society. In time, with proper attention and absorption, like immigrants before them, they will become fully integrated into Israeli society.

RELIGIOUS APPROACH

After I detailed my beliefs and to support them cited at length biblical and postbiblical passages of God's election of the Jews and His granting to them of the Land of Israel, you wrote, "You cannot really bring yourself to come right out and say that God [gave the land to the Jews] because you don't really believe He did."

You have raised these objections at every stage of our discussion. How much clearer could I be? I wrote, "The foundation of Judaism is . . . the establishment of a covenant between God and the Jewish people that is permanent and cannot be severed by either party, and the granting of the Land of Israel to the people of Israel."

Now, at the end of this book, we have come full circle. Yosef, you simply cannot understand, or at least feel that you are unable to acknowledge that you understand what I have been describing throughout these many months. I guess that's okay. It is out there for the record. Perhaps in the unfolding years, you will gain a deeper appreciation and perhaps even a greater respect for, or at least sensitivity to, the efforts made by others. And if not, well, one cannot expect to get everything in life.

For the last time, I want to reiterate that my approach to the sacred texts is not literal. I do not read the Bible as a history book. That is too limiting. The sacred texts transcend history. This is what makes them sacred.

BACK TO THE BEGINNING

And so, to end where we began: Since the days of Moses, we have been yearning for leaders who speak with the Almighty face-to-face. What would we do without those few superior souls who, sheltered under the heavenly wings, are, like the celestial angels, privileged to inhabit the place where only absolute truth is uttered?

Were it not for the guidance of these few superior souls, how would the rest of us know what to do? To marvel at those who have been allowed to know with perfect accuracy the divine will; to admire those who possess the truth and zealously protect its secrets from those who seek to destroy all that is good and noble—Yosef, I know it is a hard task for you and your colleagues.

When you write "nor will your intuition inspire the Jews to . . . defend the Jewish state," are we to understand that your knowledge of absolute truth is the inspiration we all need? As you know, people like me have been defending the state, successfully, for over fifty years. Unlike Modern Orthodox Jews, ultra-Orthodox Jews have, by and large, avoided serving in the army. Are you now calling on *charedi* Jews to go out and help us defend the Jewish state by, as you write, "shedding their blood," if necessary? Or is it also the mark of an absolute-truth–possessing man that God wants him only to articulate the principles that others "shed their blood" to defend? After all, were these superior persons also to shed their blood and leave us all alone, how would the rest of us know what is true? This, essentially, is the argument of the ultra-Orthodox draft dodgers and their political sponsors in Israel. They argue that their study of Torah and absorption of absolute truth is more important to the security of the state than those who serve in the army. Only they know— really know—the truth. The rest of us only sense or feel or intuit, or doubt or search or reason or experience, or whatever. Hence we are expendable in "shedding blood" but they are not.

Yosef, with all the awareness of one who you feel has been kidnapped by false ideas, I nonetheless insist that you too are my brother. You are bound up with me in the bonds of everlasting Jewish life. It is this greatest of dramas that sustains and connects us. You think that you possess absolute truth? I suppose I have to accept you for who you are. I will also keep a brotherly eye out for you so that you do not go overboard with your convictions. I will try to bail you out of trouble when you go to extremes and prevent you from getting into trouble in the first place. Know always that it is out of deep love for the Jewish people that we, so distanced from the warmth of the Eternal and so ignorant of absolute truth, nonetheless feel obligated to rein in some of the excesses of an ideology that presumes to know all the answers. What are brothers for?

This above all: We are members of the Jewish people—princely, proud heirs of a great treasure. Let the debate rage.

The Jewish people lives forever and ever!

June 22, 2001

Dear Ammi,

It's good to be back, although I already miss Israel, especially my children and my new grandson. I had the pleasure of spending an enjoyable evening with your parents at the Ramada Renaissance. They are really wonderful. You'd be surprised at how much I know about you now. Don't worry. It's all good.

The first thing I did when I came home, of course, was check my e-mail. I found your posting waiting for me.

THE DIVINE GIFT OF THE LAND

I was somewhat surprised at your language in defense of your views. You seem to impugn my intellectual capacity to grasp the profundity of your statements. "Yosef, you are reading but not absorbing what

296 OF ME REINMAN

I am writing. . . . You simply cannot understand . . . what I have been describing throughout these many months."

Ammi, my good friend, I refuse to take offense, because I do not believe you intended to be offensive. It was simply your frustrations getting the better of you. You know perfectly well that I have not misunderstood your positions. I have held them up to the bright light of reason, and they have not fared well.

We have been around this block often in our correspondence. Now you are upset that I have pinned down your inconsistency on the divine gift of the land. You quote God's words to Abraham as your authority, but you are not convinced that Abraham ever existed. In your opinion, he is more likely a parable, a fable, a legend, a myth. According to you, God never articulated this "divine gift" to anyone. You have simply discerned His thoughts and wishes through intuition, inspiration, deduction, and whatever other oblique methods you use to probe the Divine Mind. According to you, the covenant is not a genuine pact between God and the Jewish people but an endlessly malleable and reinterpretable construct of human beings expressing their intuitive sense of chosenness.

You have found a way to claim all the privileges of chosenness without accepting the obligations that come along with it. You have fashioned a one-way contract that allows you to pursue a life informed by secular liberal values, free of the encumbrances of religious observance and commitment, and define it as Judaism.

You write, "My approach to the sacred texts is not literal. I do not read the Bible as a history book. That is too limiting. The sacred texts transcend history. This is what makes them sacred." But the narratives of the Bible are clearly factual. The sacred texts make a point of repeatedly impressing the people with the importance of remembering everything that happened. "Only take heed to yourself, and watch yourself exceedingly, lest you forget the things your eyes have seen and lest they depart from your heart all the days of your lives, but make them known to your children and your children's children, the day you stood before God your Lord at Horeb, when God said to me, 'Assemble the people for Me and I will let them hear My words.'" (Deuteronomy 4:9–10)

The sacred texts you cherish so much are not compatible with the vague ambiguities you would have us swallow. There is a saying in Yiddish that *"men ken nisht tantzen oif aleh chasiness;* you can't dance at every wedding." That is solid, traditional Jewish wisdom.

I realize that your kind of nebulous approach may appeal to certain American Jews with only a casual interest in their Jewishness and an aversion to interference in their assimilation and possible intermarriages. But ambiguity will not provide a moral high ground for the State of Israel. You once mentioned to me that you wish "our neighbors had been Swedes." But that is not reality. Our neighbors are Arabs, and vague abstractions will not wash with them. If we cannot claim with conviction that God communicated through prophecy with Abraham or Isaac or Jacob or all of them and specifically gifted the Promised Land to them, we will have no credibility with the Arabs; they will view us as interlopers with no legitimate moral claim to the land, and they will never make peace with us.

As for the Israelis themselves, the idealism of secular Zionism has run its course. Whether you like it or not, we now live in the post-Zionist age, when new generations of secular Israelis are not bound to the land by any powerful ideals. A young secular Israeli relative, the child of Russian immigrants (he is fully Jewish, a descendant of the Baal Shem Tov in fact; his mother is my first cousin), attends university in Florida on a soccer scholarship. He sees no reason, other than family ties, to endure the hardships and danger of living in Israel. I do not think these vague abstractions would inspire him to think otherwise.

ANTI-RELIGIOUS ISRAELIS

You may be correct that most Israelis believe in God and adhere to a few nominal religious practices. I certainly hope that this is the case. You have no right to offer the condescending advice that I should "spend more time talking to people who do not dress and think like you." How do you know that I do not? I would wager that I spend much more time talking to secular Jews than you do to *charedim,* present company excluded.

Be that as it may, you cannot deny that a number of highly influential antireligious Israelis in government, academia, literature, and the arts, people like Shulamit Aloni, Yossi Beilin, and others, are determined to sever the connection between Judaism and the state. You must also know that the demonization of the Orthodox is high on their agenda. You should steer clear of these people.

The fact is that the Orthodox contribute heavily to the state coffers, and they should not be denied the funds to educate their children as they see fit. Do you think Orthodox children should be coerced to attend state schools that will indoctrinate them against the classical Judaism of their parents?

The overwhelming majority of the Orthodox does not advocate the dissolution of the state, and the Orthodox schools certainly do not teach such things to the children. They teach them good things like Torah, Tanach, Talmud, Halakhah, Mussar, Jewish thought and history. Only a few minuscule sects, such as the Neturei Karta, are in favor of dismantling the state, and these groups do not take any money from the state.

MODERN-DAY LEVITES

As for your barbs about the Orthodox aversion to the army, you make it sound as if the Orthodox are cowards or worse when you know perfectly well that this is not true. It is more of the malicious propaganda of the antireligious Israelis.

As you know, most of the Orthodox do not choose the scholarly life. They serve in the military with honor and distinction and are acknowledged as among the finest and bravest defenders of the Jewish state. Others choose to devote their lives to serious Torah study, which requires many long years of intense, uninterrupted concentration and is incompatible with military service. But these too are defenders of the state in a very real sense.

According to the Torah, the Jewish people are always beleaguered on two fronts—the physical and the spiritual. What would be the good of the physical survival of the Jewish people if the cost were its spiritual demise? Torah is not transmitted through books alone. It needs to be learned in the context of personal relationships between revered sages and mentors and their disciples. Therefore, the Levites do not bear arms in Jewish wars. Their task is to keep the flame of Torah burning brightly, to learn, to study, to absorb, to teach, to illuminate, to keep the people close to God.

Maimonides writes (Yad, Shemittah v'Yoveil 13:13), "Not only the Levites but every individual who is moved by his spirit and intellect to stand before God to serve Him . . . also becomes exceedingly sanctified. . . ." The people studying in *yeshivot* are the Levites of our times. The survival of our people depends on them. They are the most powerful force in the world for the furtherance of Jewish identity. Wherever a community *kollel* (a small nucleus of Torah scholars) was established—be it in Chazor Elit, Dimona, and Sderot in Israel or in Vienna, Amsterdam, and Moscow, or in Manalapan, New Jersey—the inevitable result has been a rise in Jewish identity, awareness, and vitality. No matter how many Torah scholars we are producing, the Jewish people could use more.

The great *yeshivot* of Europe, the fountainheads of Torah for the Jewish people, were destroyed during the Holocaust. Torah was on the verge of extinction. But decades of struggle have re-created them. Once again, we have great *yeshivot* that produce our rabbis and teachers, our ambassadors of Torah, our learned laypeople who spread the light of Torah in all walks of life. These modern-day Levites forgo lucrative careers to study Torah, to receive it from the earlier generation and pass it on to future generations. They form a small percentage of the population of Israel, but they are indispensable to the Jewish state. If some people take advantage of the system to avoid military service unfairly, it is unfortunate. I do not condone it. But I call on you to respect and appreciate the vast majority of *yeshivah* students who are dedicated scholars. Walk into the Mirrer Yeshivah in Jerusalem, Ammi, or the Ponovezh Yeshivah in Bnei Brak. In spite of yourself, you will be impressed. I guarantee it.

DEMOCRACY AND COERCION

This business about the Orthodox being antidemocratic and in favor of religious coercion is also absolutely ridiculous. The ideal to which we aspire is a state in which virtually all Jews are observant, as was the case in most European communities of the pre-Reform era. Such societies could be governed by Torah law, as were those aforementioned communities. In that case, the law would be determined exclusively by Halakhah, and only the process and function of government would be democratic.

But no one would suggest that such a system is feasible in a society where a significant minority is nonobservant, let alone in Israel today, where a significant majority is nonobservant. Therefore, as long as we do not have a fully observant society, we should at least make sure that official functions of the state are consistent with Torah law, as we have discussed. Apparently, you have no problem with this. Good. Otherwise, there is no serious stream of Orthodox opinion that seeks to coerce people to be observant in their private lives.

I know you are having frustrating problems with some of the Orthodox politicians who play political hardball with you, but let us try to keep things in perspective. Our discussion should not deteriorate into petty finger-pointing across the Knesset aisles. I do not know much about what goes on in Israeli politics, nor do I care to find out. Spare me.

THE ASH HEAP OF HISTORY

Throughout our correspondence, you have been peppering me with the same question: "Are you a Zionist?" I believe I have made my position very clear, but you need familiar labels. I support the state, despite its numerous flaws, because I am a pragmatist. I agree with you that "it is the only one we have," but I do not agree that it is "the only one we will have." When it comes to Israel, you seem to lose your capacity for nuanced thinking. You see the choice as between two extremes, a decadent Western state and Afghanistan. I believe we can do better. I pray and hope that we can create a free and beautiful Jewish state with the very highest moral and ethical standards, not a mirror image of all the worst in American society. I pray and hope we can build the kind of state about which our ancestors dreamed in the ghettos of Europe. I do not think we have accomplished that yet.

Does that make me a Zionist? The answer is irrelevant to me, but for some reason, it is relevant to you.

Regarding the idea of a binational state, you found "something delightfully pleasurable in the notion that you, a *charedi* rabbi, are advocating positions that nineteenth- and twentieth-century Reform rabbis advocated, while I, a twenty-first-century Reform rabbi, am only too happy to leave such positions on the ash heap of history. For this delicious irony alone our efforts have all been worthwhile!"

First of all, you misunderstood what I wrote. I did not "advocate" a binational state in my capacity as "a *charedi* rabbi." I merely speculated, as an individual, that it might have achieved similar accomplishments while avoiding incessant war. It is impossible to know what might have been, and it is impossible to go back. Today it is no longer a viable option, and I do not advocate it in any way. I wrote this very clearly.

As for your ash heaps, let me remind you that your movement once dumped the notion of Jewish peoplehood on the ash heap of history, before you found the good sense to retrieve it. You dumped the idea of Jewish statehood on the ash heap of history, before you jumped onto the Zionist bandwagon in 1976. You dumped the *bar mitzvah* ceremony on the ash heap of history, before you retrieved that as well. And let us not forget that you dumped observance on the ash heap of history, although there seems to be a tentative movement under way to retrieve some of this as well. Don't be so quick to thumb your nose at the stuff you toss on the ash heap of history. You might come back to retrieve it someday.

RUSSIAN IMMIGRANTS AND JEWISH IDENTITY

You seem to have had some difficulty with my statement that "most of these Russians with one remote Jewish ancestor are not Jewish."

The math is simple. Every person has eight great-grandparents. Only one—his mother's mother's mother—determines his Jewishness. Among people with only one unspecified Jewish great-grandparent, the chances are seven to one against any individual being Jewish. Therefore, it is safe to say that most Russians with only one remote Jewish ancestor are not Jewish.

Come on, Ammi. You are being a little disingenuous about these Russians, aren't you? No one denies that huge numbers of non-Jews are coming into Israel from the former Soviet Union, mostly for economic and political reasons.

According to an article in the New York *Jewish Week* (December 3, 1999), "this year, more than half of such immigrants are non-Jews, and officials say the number could climb to seventy or eighty percent in the near future. These people . . . number in the hundreds of thousands." Eric Yoffie, a leading Reform rabbi, is quoted in *Ha'aretz* (February 28, 2000): "There are hundreds of thousands of non-Jewish Russian immigrants in Israel." Another article in *Ha'aretz* (January 31, 2000) reports that "in 1999, 53 percent of the immigrants were not Jewish according to Halachah . . . 38 percent of the 1999 immigrants do not even have a Jewish father." An article in the *New York Times* (December 6, 1999) warns, "Israel will soon be flooded not just with non-Jews but also with those infected with the anti-Semitism of their homeland."

It seems to me that you are slightly understating the case when you admit "that the Jewish identity of many Russian immigrants might be different from immigrants coming from the West." Nonetheless, you welcome this immigrant stream because it "is blessed, talented, and contributes so much to Israeli society. . . . In time, with proper attention and absorption, like immigrants before them, they will become fully integrated into Israeli society." They may become fully integrated into Israeli society. But they will not so easily become integrated into the Jewish people. Are we supposed to hand out Jewish membership cards as door prizes to new immigrants? This is not a blessing, Ammi. It is a disaster.

Amos Hermon, head of the education department at the Jewish Agency, is quoted in the *Ha'aretz* article (January 2000) as saying: "This situation is a social time bomb. On the face of things, there is no reason that my son will not start going out with a Russian girl in a few years, a girl who is perhaps not Jewish at all. Once he falls in love with her, go explain to him that she is in fact not a Jew and that it is inappropriate for him to marry her. And there could be tens of thousands of others like my son. The result is liable to be a mass of mixed marriages in Israel, the Jewish state. This in itself could lead to ruptures in many families, and to the deepening of the rupture between the secular and the religious in Israel."

So what is your solution, Ammi? To offer Reform conversion to these non-Jews with latent or overt anti-Semitism? Don't be naïve. They will take your offer cynically, garner all the benefits of nominal Jewishness, and laugh in your face.

Do you know that according to the latest projections the Israeli Arab population, citizens of the state, will reach 32 percent of the population by the year 2020? The Arabs, assuming they remain united, will have the most powerful party in Israel. Do you think for a moment that these ersatz Russian converts will struggle to maintain Jewish identity and a Jewish state in the face of the ascendant Arab power?

And what about the Chinese, Filipinos, Romanians, and Polish migrant workers in Israel? What if they come knocking at your door, asking to be transformed into Jews so that they can settle in Israel with full citizenship rights and benefits? Will you withhold Reform conversion from them? When they assure you with earnest faces that they have seen the light of Judaism, will you peek into their souls to see if they are sincere?

And yes, how about the Arab expatriates? One of these days, they may discover that Reform conversion is their ticket back to Israel. They don't have to negotiate for their own Right of Arab Return. They can return as Jews! All they need to do is agree to become Reform, and they're in! Boom. Once they're back, of course, they can do whatever they wish in democratic Israel. You don't need to respond on this, because I don't believe they would ever do it. I'm just making a point.

The secular forces inviting you into Israel and supporting your efforts are bent on destroying Jewish identity, not preserving it. According to *Ha'aretz* (February 2000), Yossi Beilin, a leading Israeli leftist, wants to reshape the "entrance gate" to the Jewish people by "secular conversion" and "self-definition." He foresees "a situation in which a person who is not Jewish, and does not view himself as a member of any other religion, turns to the Jewish community in his neighborhood and asks to be registered as a member. If the community is convinced, after talks and reviews, that the request to join is honest and sincere, it will register the new Jew without performing any religious ceremony." He is convinced that if this idea is accepted "we will be a bigger people and a more attractive people."

A. B. Yehoshua, one of the most celebrated Israeli novelists, goes even further. "[I realize] this looks crazy, unrealistic now, but perhaps in another one hundred, two hundred years it will be possible. . . . We have to turn this people into a people without a [distinctive] religion. . . . Let the members of the Jewish people be Christians, Muslims . . . religiously, there should be a number of different options so that our people can belong to various religions." (Quoted by Yoram Hazony in *The Jewish State*)

Heaven help us. What happened to Jewish identity? What happened to Judaism? What happened to the covenant? Where are we heading, Ammi? The Jewish state is dissolving before our very eyes.

There was a very disturbing article about intermarriage in *Commentary* (March 2001) by Jack Wertheimer, professor of American Jewish history at the Jewish Theological Seminary. It used to be that marrying Jewish was an important value, but not any longer. Today most American Jews see no reason not to marry out. In a 1995 survey of Conservative youth actively engaged in Jewish life who had recently celebrated a *bar mitzvah* or *bat mitzvah*, nearly two-thirds thought it was "okay for Jews to marry people of other religions." Two-thirds!

Are liberal Jewish streams contributing to this horrendous trend? We can argue endlessly. I believe Reform leads to intermarriage, and that by condoning and validating intermarriages you destigmatize, legitimize, and ultimately encourage them. You consider this a canard.

Let me quote from a letter to the editor by Marc Gellman, president of the New York Board of Rabbis, responding to the Wertheimer article in the June issue of *Commentary*. "The Reform movement has vaulted past Conservative Judaism in numbers of members and size of congregations, and all of this growth is from the obvious fact that intermarried couples feel more accepted in Reform temples than in any other branch of Judaism. Even Reform rabbis like myself, who do not perform intermarriages, have benefited from a huge influx of intermarried couples who have nowhere else to go. The pariah status of intermarriage is dead and gone in the Reform movement, and with it the shame and the guilt. Most rabbis are just no match for powerhouse intermarried couples who do not want to hear nuanced reservations based on Jewish law from someone who drives on the Sabbath and eats shrimp."

Ammi, I know that you would not perform an intermarriage ceremony and that you do not eat pork; I hope that extends to shrimp as well. But take a good look at the overall reality of your movement. Strong Jewish identity among your American constituency, whether it is because of Reform or in spite of it, hangs by a tenuous thread. We are witnessing the tragic erosion and assimilation of American Jewry, and it is painful. But move this scenario to Israel, and we will also see the collapse of the Jewish state and the physical endangerment of its Jewish population. It is beyond unthinkable.

Why don't you wait fifty or a hundred years before you pursue your ambitions in Israel? Give things a chance to work out. I don't know what the ultimate political solution will be, but I do know that to reach safe harbor the Jewish state needs to be founded on a powerful Jewish identity. Jews standing shoulder-to-shoulder in Israel need to feel secure and confident in each other's Jewishness; they should not have to wonder if the others are patrilineals, ersatz converts, gentile spouses, or self-defined seculars. Otherwise, Israel as a Jewish state is doomed.

As for us, Ammi, the vast and unbridgeable ideological chasm that separates us does not, and certainly should not, diminish the kinship and brotherly love we feel for each other. But if, by unilaterally changing the definition of Jewish identity, you prevent us from accepting each other as brothers, as fellow Jews, a dialogue of this sort would never take place. We would simply tip our hats, smile politely, and go our separate ways.

It would be a terrible loss.

You conclude, "The Jewish people lives forever and ever!"

Amen.

Yosef

AFTERWORDS

September 17, 2001

Dear Ammi,

There were many things I had wanted to say in this Afterword, but as I sit down to write, all I can think about are the piles of rubble that used to be the World Trade Center in New York City and the thousands of people buried underneath. There is so much hatred in the world, so much evil, so much suffering, so much senseless violence.

When people disagree, their first impulse is often toward anger and coercion, but these do not solve anything; they only make matters worse. It seems to me, therefore, that one of the great accomplishments of this book is to show that people who hold radically different views, who are struggling for the soul of a nation, can be friends and brothers even as they engage each other sharply in the arena of ideas.

In the course of the twenty months during which we have exchanged these postings, many other things were going on in my life, including the completion and publication of other works, the *bar mitzvah* of one child, the marriage of another, the birth of a grandchild, and the death of a dear family member. Nonetheless, I can honestly say that not one day passed that I did not think about this book. Not one day passed that I did not feel on my shoulders the terrible weight of responsibility to all those Jews who would be swayed by our critical debate. You must have felt the same.

Jewish people from all walks of life and all points of the ideological spectrum, as well as many gentiles, no doubt, will expect our book to be an honest portrayal of the ideas of Orthodoxy and Reform. It is a humbling thought. I believe we did our best to challenge each other's views and articulate our own, and hopefully, people will feel that what they are reading is not propaganda but the truth about who we are and what we represent. Hopefully, they will acknowledge our work as a job well done.

We have both put tremendous effort into composing these postings, and it would be unrealistic to expect the readers, whatever their affiliation, to grasp the full import of the arguments in one reading. I hope, therefore, that thoughtful readers will review the book a number of times, giving careful consideration to both sides of the argument. I also hope they will look further and explore the great wealth of classic and contemporary works of our three-thousand-year-old heritage and all the materials available through modern media and Web sites. We cannot give them knowledge. All we can do is point the way and let them acquire it on their own.

In our postings, we have both cited various sources in which our readers can find broader discussions of subjects we have merely touched. I would like to add just a few recommendations.

For classical texts: *The Talmud*, Schottenstein Edition, *The Chumash*, Stone Edition, and *The Artscroll Siddur* (Mesorah); Aryeh Kaplan's excellent *The Living Torah* (Moznaim).

For an introduction to classical Judaism: Herman Wouk's *This Is My God: The Jewish Way of Life* (Little, Brown); Emanuel Feldman's *On Judaism* (Shaar); Hayim Halevy Donin's *To Be a Jew* (Basic); Mordechai Katz's *Understanding Judaism* (Mesorah); Alfred J. Kolatch's *The Jewish Book of Why* (Jonathan David); Esther Jungreis's *The Committed Life* (HarperCollins); Maurice Lamm's *The Jewish Way in Love and Marriage* (Jonathan David); Lawrence Kelemen's beautiful *To Kindle a Soul: Ancient Wisdom for Modern Parents and Teachers* (Leviathan).

For Jewish thought: Samson Raphael Hirsch's *Horeb: A Philosophy of Jewish Laws and Observances* (Soncino) and *Collected Writings* (Feldheim); J. David Bleich's *With Perfect Faith: The Foundations of Jewish Belief* (Ktav); Lawrence Kelemen's *Permission to Believe* (Targum).

For a taste of mysticism: Dr. Judith Mishell & Dr. Shalom Srebrenik's outstanding *Beyond Your Ego* (C.I.S.); Aryeh Kaplan's *Meditation and the Bible* (Moznaim); Alexandre Safran's *Wisdom of the Kabbalah* (Feldheim).

Readers can find hundreds of additional titles in the catalogues of these publishers. It would be my pleasure to offer guidance to anyone who contacts me through my publisher or e-mail (*yosefreinman@yahoo.com*).

Ammi, you and I agree that there is a special covenant between God and the Jewish people. I think we also agree that it is important for our people to define their lives by this holy covenant, to feel passionate about it, to be inspired by it, to discover that a life defined by Torah is profoundly meaningful and fulfilling. Should our book stimulate a more passionate interest in the Torah among our people, secular and observant alike, I would consider it the greatest reward.

For myself, this has been an incredible intellectual and emotional journey. My expertise is mostly in the fields of talmudic civil and business law, and I had to work long and hard to analyze your talmudic and midrashic citations and view them in the broader context of the Oral Law. Doing so has expanded and deepened my knowledge and understanding of the Talmud and reinforced the foundations of my beliefs. It also helped me better crystallize and articulate some of the most basic principles of classical Judaism.

At the same time, I have gained a new sensitivity to my secular brothers and sisters. Now more than ever, I understand that so many of them yearn for some kind of religious expression of their Jewishness that will connect them with their ancestors and their illustrious history. From what I have read and heard over the past twenty months, and from the strong feelings expressed in your postings, Ammi, this yearning seems to reflect more than national pride but a true hunger for spiritual connection and fulfillment in a Jewish way. It was moving to discover a powerful Jewish heartbeat despite the widely reported apathy. It gave me a feeling of hope.

On a personal note, Ammi, I feel that in you I have gained a friend, even though we disagree on just about all the basic tenets of Judaism. In our early postings, I expressed a hope that we might one day be friends, but I do not think I really expected it to happen in more than a superficial way. But it has. I feel close to you, and to your family, although I have not yet met them in person. The two of us have enjoyed many pleasant conversations unrelated to our joint venture. I have found you kind, gracious, and reasonable; you're not such a tough guy after all, Ammi, but I won't tell anyone if you don't want me to.

Today is Erev Rosh Hashanah. In a few hours, the new Jewish year begins. May God grant us, our families, our people, and all the people of the world a year of peace and joy. May He give all humankind the wisdom to usher in a new era of enlightenment and good will so that the world can be the beautiful place He designed it to be.

My warmest regards and best wishes to your family.

Yosef

———————

October 1, 2001

Dear Yosef:

The belief that our existence makes sense and that we are part of something larger than ourselves is what we call faith. Articles of faith, by definition, cannot be proven. We must take a leap of faith. Our book is about what happens to you after you jump.

You and I agree on many things—more than you care to admit. One such agreement is that Jews answer the question of "how to make sense of this world" by looking to Torah. In this search, you and I are confronted with the opposite sides of the same problem. In looking to our sacred texts, wherein revelation lies, a literal understanding poses immense challenges in dealing with the world as it is. We must explain evidence of the world that contradicts what is written in the texts. We must also explain events that are beyond reason, like talking donkeys and people swallowed alive and spit out by big fishes.

On the other hand, a nonliteralist approach forces us to ask where is sanctity and truth. As you have rightly pointed out, if we are prepared to distinguish among biblical truths, then how do we decide what is true and what is not? Who decides? If we are free to interpret the sacred texts liberally, where do we draw the line? If the part about talking donkeys is not literally true, what about the crossing of the Red Sea, the revelation on Mount Sinai, or all of the ethical injunctions and prophetic values that so appeal to us?

These are the central questions of faith—any faith with a revealed textual tradition. All of this book and all of Judaism revolve around these central questions. The importance of our debates is not in winning the argument but in advancing the discussion. It is in the interplay between certainty and doubt, permanence and change, that Judaism develops. It is in raising the relevant questions and providing satisfactory answers that we keep our faith vibrant and moving forward. Our answers might not be identical. We should not be afraid of disagreement; rather, we should welcome it: "Any controversy that is for the sake of heaven is destined to endure." (Pirke Avot 5:17)

"There is nothing new under the sun." (Ecclesiastes 1:9) We have not produced original content. All the questions and all the responses we have raised have been raised before, both by ancient and modern thinkers. We have cited many of them. Nor does this book add significant philosophical contributions. We have touched upon Jewish philosophy, but only superficially. Rather, if there is any originality, it is in form. We have allowed interested lay readers to be exposed to argument and immediate counterargument from people representing dramatically different approaches to some of Judaism's central questions. This occurs all too infrequently in our polarized Jewish world. I suspect that most readers will find themselves agreeing with any one of us only part of the time, and sharply disagreeing with us on other occasions. It would not at all surprise me if some of our colleagues in the Orthodox community might find themselves nodding in agreement with my perspective more often than they thought they would. We have allowed our readers to observe rabbinic disputation, close up and personal, on a popular, not academic, level. Our contributions are modest. If we have stimulated and encouraged those who might be intrigued by any part of this book to continue to search, then our efforts were worthwhile.

Yosef, like you, I have enjoyed this effort. Since I spend so much of my public life speaking in thirty-second sound bites to the media or, at most, thirty-minute speeches to different audiences, it was a pleasure and a relief to spend time articulating the underlying principles motivating me. You have challenged me—at times a bit acerbically—to think more deeply about Judaism. I have welcomed and rejoiced in these challenges.

Yosef, you have granted me the last word. This fact alone might trouble some of your colleagues. While you can take care of yourself, and you hardly need (or desire) any defense from me, for the sake of the broader community, let me emphasize that you have done an important and courageous thing. The publication of this book conveys in symbolic and tangible ways that it is possible for Jews to reason together. It is utter nonsense to suggest that we have grown so far apart as to render each other nonpartners in the work of Judaism.

Like the biblical Joseph, you refuse to abandon your brothers no matter how far you think they may have strayed. You have reached out to your siblings in the Jewish community: "I am Yosef, your brother!" (Genesis 45:4)

Good for you. You have shown the way for others. It is far better to be part of the family than to be estranged.

In abiding friendship, and with my best wishes for good health and great satisfaction,

Ammi

INDEX

ABOUT THE AUTHORS

Ammiel Hirsch is Executive Director of the Association of Reform Zionists of America/World Union for Progressive Judaism, North America. His editorials, articles, and sermons appear in newspapers around the world. He lives in New York City.

Yosef Reinman's monographs and articles have appeared in many Jewish periodicals. His Biblical commentaries and studies of Talmudic law are standard texts in many yeshivas. He lives in Lakewood, New Jersey.

A NOTE ON THE TYPE

This book was set in Monotype Dante, a typeface designed by Giovanni Mardersteig (1892–1977). Conceived as a private type for the Officina Bodoni in Verona, Italy, Dante was originally cut only for hand composition by Charles Malin, the famous Parisian punch cutter, between 1946 and 1952. Its first use was in an edition of Boccaccio's *Trattatello in laude di Dante* that appeared in 1954. The Monotype Corporation's version of Dante followed in 1957. Although modeled on the Aldine type used for Pietro Cardinal Bembo's treatise *De Aetna* in 1495, Dante is a thoroughly modern interpretation of the venerable face.

Composed by NK Graphics, Keene, New Hampshire
Printed and bound by R. R. Donnelley, Harrisonburg, Virginia
Designed by M. Kristen Bearse